The Festival of Pīrs

The Festival of Pīrs

Popular Islam and Shared Devotion in South India

AFSAR MOHAMMAD

OXFORD
UNIVERSITY PRESS

OXFORD
UNIVERSITY PRESS

Oxford University Press is a department of the University of Oxford.
It furthers the University's objective of excellence in research, scholarship,
and education by publishing worldwide.

Oxford   New York
Auckland   Cape Town   Dar es Salaam   Hong Kong   Karachi
Kuala Lumpur   Madrid   Melbourne   Mexico City   Nairobi
New Delhi   Shanghai   Taipei   Toronto

With offices in
Argentina   Austria   Brazil   Chile   Czech Republic   France   Greece
Guatemala   Hungary   Italy   Japan   Poland   Portugal   Singapore
South Korea   Switzerland   Thailand   Turkey   Ukraine   Vietnam

Oxford is a registered trade mark of Oxford University Press
in the UK and certain other countries.

Published in the United States of America by
Oxford University Press
198 Madison Avenue, New York, NY 10016

CIP data is on file at the Library of Congress

9780199997589
9780199997596 (pbk.)

9   8   7   6   5   4   3   2   1

Printed in the United States of America on acid-free paper

For Kalpana and Anindu

CONTENTS

PREFACE

Writing this book is like going back to my childhood and reliving the beautiful moments of my childhood. As I finish this book, many innocent faces and exciting places endlessly flash through my mind clearly refusing to fade out from my memory. My nine-month stay in the village of Gugudu, and my whirlwind trips through several other neighboring villages reminded me that every village speaks almost the same language. Of course, Gugudu is not my home; when I started field work in this village, it was just a "field" for me. As the days went on, this field has begun to change its face and started becoming friendly. Now it's almost my second home.

Although it's a popular tourist spot, the village has still its naive ways. The people are still a closed group who know each other very well and easily recognize others as outsiders. It's not uncommon that hundreds of devotees and pilgrims visit the local pīr-house. However, they don't stay more than one day. I stayed in this village for nine months. During the first week of my field research in this village, everyone was skeptical about me and felt as if a stranger was intruding into their private space. But things changed as my face became familiar to them. As time went on, they started inviting me for breakfast, lunch, and dinner. Even now some of these villagers send me wedding invitations from their families. At this moment of finishing this book, I remember each acquaintance from this village just as I remember my family.

After I returned from my field research, when I was still struggling with the large quantity of data gathered from Gugudu, Professor Charles Hallisey raised key questions about the figure of a local saint called Kullayappa and his role in a public ritual tradition of Muharram. Numerous meetings with Hallisey made my path clear, and each conversation with Hallisey remains forever in my memory.

The city of Madison has brought a sea change in my life, both academic and personal. The academic and cultural life in Madison forced me to take huge leaps in my life. This all started with my long-time association with Professor Velcheru Narayana Rao, which actually started in Andhra. When I first met Narayana Rao in 1985, I didn't imagine that this association would make me cross borders. Now I feel very happy about this experience and remain thankful to Narayana Rao.

My graduate life in Madison would have been incomplete without the wonderful and generous professors that I studied with, such as Kirin Narayan, Joseph W. Elder, Vinay Dharwadker, and Tejumola Olaniyan. I only realized the importance of Kirin Narayan's courses on cultural anthropology and ethnography when I did my field research. Joseph Elder has always been friendly and supportive, and I am indebted to him for encouraging me to pursue this project on Muharram. Professor Mark Kenoyer, the director of the Center for South Asia in Madison-Wisconsin, has always been kind to me, and he has offered me several semesters of financial support. Toward the end of my graduate program, Professor Donald Davis made a big impact through his example as a kind person and a hardcore academician. Many conversations with Don Davis leave me unsettled even now and have provoked me to ask questions from a totally unexpected angle. It's my privilege to have had Charles Hallisey, Kirin Narayan, Velcheru Narayana Rao, Donald Davis, and Ann Hansen on my committee. When I was struggling with my writing, Professor Syed Akbar Hyder and Ali Asani were there to help me find a way.

Madison has given me caring friends in the real sense of the word: Chris Chekuri, Amara Keerthi Liyanage, Sangeeta Desai, Mukoma Ngugi, Shenghai Li, Damcho Dianne Finnegan, Jane Menon, Jessica Athens, Krista Coulson, Ashok Rajput, Amelia Liwe, Alex Miller, Austin Smith, and many others. I'm particularly grateful to the South Asian community in Madison and Chicago that made my life easier during the early days in a foreign land. During my stay in Madison, Chris Chekuri took every care to guide me through those unfamiliar paths of the Madisonian life.

Field research in India was a real learning experience by itself. Thanks to the funding provided by the American Institute of Indian Studies (AIIS), I stayed in Gugudu for nine months. It was a pleasant surprise to make good friends with some of the AIIS fellows. Most importantly, the two-day conference in Delhi was a professionally and personally enriching experience.

The presentations and conversations with a new group of South Asian scholars were unforgettable, and some of the participants, including Luke Whitmore, Venugopal Maddipati, and Holly Donahue, have now become my good friends.

After field research in India, I received a number of opportunities to present my work at many academic centers, such as the University of Heidelberg, the North Carolina Center for South Asia studies, Duke University, and Emory University. I benefitted from the helpful suggestions made by the participants, including Ann Gold, Joyce Flueckiger, Kirin Narayan, Leela Prasad, David Gilmartin, Jim Masselos, and Sandria Freitag. I have also presented work at the American Academy of Religions and the Annual South Asia Conference in Madison. I am thankful to my friends and participants at these conferences. Karen Ruffle has always been helpful and has spent hours and hours discussing my work. Christian Haskett and Robert Phillips always have been there to help me with good suggestions at coffee houses, restaurants, and conferences. Professor Frank Korom has kindly shared his thoughts and writings. Joyce Flueckiger, Tony K. Stewart, and Jack Hawley have been helpful in many ways and encouraged me to focus more on the key concepts—local Islam and localized Islam. Vasudha Narayanan, Torsten Tschacher, Tracy Pintchman, Neilesh Bose, and Corrine Dempsey have encouraged my work.

While working on my book, I'm fortunate that I got a position at the University of Texas at Austin, which has now become my second institutional home. I have had the great pleasure to have friendly colleagues and well-wishers such as Professor Patrick Olivelle, Joel Brereton, Martha Ann Selby, Kamran Ali, Oliver Freiberger, Kathryn Hansen, Carla Petievich, and Sankaran Radhakrishnan. I shall be always grateful to Syed Akbar Hyder for all his friendship and keen interest in my work. As my well-wisher and the chair of the department of Asian studies, Professor Selby gave me full support, and without her help it would have been impossible to finish this book. Special thanks go to Dana Johnson, who read and edited each chapter very carefully.

I am thankful to my friends Lisa Mitchel, Davesh Soneji, Carla Bellamy, Kavita Datla, Andrea Marion, Anandi Leela Devaki, Diana Hochner, Jamal Jones, Michael Collins, Jesse Knutson, Blake Wentworth, Keely Sutton, Harshita Mruthinti, Alladi Uma, M. Sridhar, K. Sreenivas, and Ashfaq Ahmed for their support during various phases of this work.

I have experimented with using some of the chapters from this book with my students in various courses such South Asian Saints and Yogis, Indian Religions and Poetry, Devotion in South India, Muslim Saints in

South Asia, and South Asian Islam: Ethnography. I've always had brilliant students who raised key questions and made me rethink my work.

At Oxford University Press, I especially would like to thank Theo Calderara and his team for their quick responses, particularly, Theo's patience and utmost care in seeing it through to publication. I am also enormously thankful to the anonymous reviewers who made me revisit my written pages and helped to improve the quality of the work, and Marcia Youngman's comments improved the quality of the book.

As a writer himself, my father Shamsuddin Kowmudi had big dreams to see my works published. Unfortunately, he is no longer here to share this exciting moment. My mother Munawar Begum was my first teacher, who taught me Urdu, Arabic, and the Quran. She told me many stories about Muharram, and she has been a guide not only in my personal life but has shown me a path to make my field research a fruitful exploration.

I dedicate this work to my wife Kalpana Rentala and my son Anindu for their constant patience during the years of this writing project and for the many things that we share in our lives.

The Festival of Pīrs

| Introduction

A Pilgrimage for the Pīr

"It's a long journey. I know, but this is my only pilgrimage, and it will make the rest of my life meaningful and purposeful. While making this journey, I will remember the story of the martyrdom and remember the sacrifices made by the *pīru swami* (pīr-god), and each memory will enliven my life," said Lakshmi, a sixty-five-year old pilgrim from a remote village in the South Indian state of Tamil Nadu. She had traveled more than five hundred miles by train and then taken a special pilgrims' bus to visit a local pīr (Sufi spiritual master and teacher) named Kullayappa in the small village of Gugudu in the neighboring state of Andhra Pradesh. When Lakshmi arrived in Gugudu, she walked straight to the local shrine, known locally as the *pīr-makānam*, or "pīr-house." The pīr-house is home to both the pīr Kullayappa, thought to have brought Islam to this village some eight centuries ago, and Hanuman, the monkey-god and most obedient devotee of the Hindu god Rama. Most devotees who visit the pīr-house, whether Hindu or Muslim, first perform the ritual of *fātehā*, or recitation of the first verse of the Quran, to the pīr, before breaking a dry coconut as an offering in front of Hanuman.

When Lakshmi arrived at the shrine, there were already thousands of devotees eagerly standing on their toes to catch a glimpse (*darśan*) of the pīr-god and offer him their gifts. As it was difficult for Lakshmi to get close to the entrance of the pīr-house, I gave her my hand and helped her finish the ritual. When she offered her gift—an embroidered red cloth, a packet of sugar, and a jasmine garland—the custodian of the pīr-house recited the *fātehā* on her behalf and returned the packet of sugar to her. Throughout the ritual, Lakshmi, with her hands folded, gazed with intense devotion at the metal battle standards installed inside the house. These standards, 'alam in Urdu and pīru in Telugu, represent the memory of the grandsons of the Prophet Muhammad. These pīr-houses can be found being visited by both Muslims and non-Muslims in many public devotional spaces in Andhra Pradesh. People visit as a display of their devotion to the family of the Prophet and its followers, and they pay their respects to the martyrs who sacrificed their lives for the well-being of their community.

At the pīr-house in Gugudu, the metal battle standard of the local pīr Kullayappa attracts almost all of the rituals and devotional practices. Decorated in red and green embroidered festive clothes and bedecked with flowers, the standards looked beautiful the day that Lakshmi arrived to the village. For Lakshmi, that moment of devotion before the pīr-house was very intense, and when I glanced at her, her eyes were full of tears. When I looked again, she immediately burst into tears, and said, "You know, my son! This could be the final moment of my life and I really wouldn't care if I died, after this great moment. I took ziyārat darśanam (sacred journey) of the pīru swami and I received his fātehā prasādam (sacred food). I offered him my humble gift of food and cloth. I saw him up close. This is enough!"

This book tells the story of the pīr Kullayappa—an alternative and local story of the martyrdom of the grandsons of the Prophet Muhammad—as understood in the village of Gugudu. It focuses on how the hagiography of this local pīr has shaped the shared devotion which occurs during the holiday of Muharram, or as it is locally called, "the festival of pīrs" (pīrla paṇḍaga). On a theoretical level, this book is about a popular manifestation of Islamic devotion, one that in a pluralistic context keeps itself in a dynamic dialogue with non-Muslim practices. Using evidence from various public devotional narratives and ritual practices, my argument is that our understanding of living Islam remains incomplete if we do not consider the local, pluralistic devotional settings in which it sometimes occurs. What makes the public celebration of Muharram in Gugudu so important to the local community, and what aspects of devotion contribute to the formation of this local Islam? This book seeks to address these two primary questions through an examination of Gugudu's local and popular transformations of normative Islam, giving particular focus to the various devotional rituals that blend Muslim and Hindu practices during the festivities around the holiday of Muharram.

Local devotees, both Muslim and Hindu, practice a shared set of rituals and other modes of devotion in memory of the martyrs of Karbala. While narrating a local version of this important story of battle and martyrdom, the devotees who gather at these public rituals recreate locally the actual battlefield located in modern-day Iraq. This local Karbala becomes a crucial public ritual site on the tenth day of Muharram. I use two key terms to explain the processes which are occurring in the devotional life of this village. These are *localized Islam* and *local Islam*, the former being a relatively fixed structure that upholds normative Islamic beliefs and practices, and the latter being a less-fixed, living form of Islam developed by and for the particular to this village and its inhabitants. To put it simply, *local Islam* is a repertoire of various inclusive religious practices that embraces diverse devotional traditions in one specific place. In contrast, *localized Islam* comprises a set of practices considered exclusively for Muslims. These are based on what adherents believe to be the normative, global, and only true form of Islam. As a public ritual, Muharram in Gugudu becomes a site of tensions between these two forms of Islam, the *local* and *localized*. Examining this tension, and the ideas and practices that constitute each, can offer us deeper insights into the local formation of Islam.

Scholars engaged in contemporary debates use four terms—*local, vernacular, localized* and *living*—to distinguish between the religion's various manifestations in South Asia today. As defined by Joyce Flueckiger, the term "vernacular Islam" suggests the need for wider study of local religious expressions of Islam, in South Asia and beyond. According to Flueckiger, "Muslims live in particular cultures, locales, and geographies that influence their practice and create local knowledge and variation. Knowledge and practice particular to a locality can be identified as vernacular Islam." In an effort to "remind us that 'universal' Islam is lived locally," her work brings us closer to the study of Islam in "a particular place."[1]

The term I prefer to use in this work—*local Islam*—has strong parallels with Flueckiger's "vernacular Islam." However, my intention here is to also emphasize another process at work locally, one that I like to call "localized Islam." This term highlights the efforts of some Muslims to combat local Islam by trying to *localize* a global form of the religion. In this work, I use both *local* and *localized* Islams to highlight the competing yet connected processes which go into in the making of contemporary lived Islam. As Dale Eickelman observed in an essay on local Islam, "The main challenge for the study of Islam in local contexts is to describe and analyze how the universalistic principles of Islam have been realized in various social and historical contexts without representing Islam as a seamless essence on the one hand, or as a plastic congeries of beliefs and practices on the other."[2] In the book *The Graves of Tarim,* Engseng Ho discusses "resolute localism" as a valued local status and as a concept that denotes the coexistence of the local and cosmopolitan in vital ways.[3] In a recent study on Pakistan and Bangladesh, Yasmin Saikia observed how the religiocultural site of lived Islam serves as an "emancipatory space" that "reintegrates the vocabulary as understood by the people."[4] These studies help us to see how various features of the local and cosmopolitan work together in the making of the local.

My argument in this book is founded on the premise that "universal" Islam becomes localized by a complex and multivocal process that may not be reducible to only one term like "vernacular" or "local." In my research I found that these terms could not be applied without alteration or modification in a local context, as one must take into account differences across caste groups, as well as the effort by some Muslim groups, particularly after the rise of religious nationalism in last two decades, to define and enforce a singular and global version of Islam against what is perceived as local innovation (*bid'a*).[5]

In thinking through this complex process of "localization," one must also consider the usefulness of terms like "syncretism," "creolization," and "hybridity." These terms have been well discussed in contemporary scholarship on South Asian religions, but not without their share of controversy. For instance, "syncretism" presupposes that the categories of Hindu and Muslim identities are separate, and scholars have debated whether or not this gives it serious conceptual limitations.[6] Similar problems arise in the usage of "creolization" and "hybridity." As scholars such as Robin Cohen and Charles Stewart have observed, the notion of creolization has its history in colonialism.[7] Likewise, one cannot separate the term "hybridity" from the history of post-colonialism.[8] I have made a conscious choice to distance my analysis here from these theoretical terms in favor of ones that are less value laden.

The Public Celebration of Muharram: Local Islam and Localized Islam

Since the rituals of Muharram are centered on the hagiography of local pīrs, the public celebration of Muharram is called "the Festival of Pīrs"—*pīrla paṇḍaga*—in Telugu. This book begins by emphasizing that the particular translation of the Muharram tradition in Gugudu is a clear instance of *local Islam*, as it adapts and appropriates local devotional practices very extensively. To portray this instance of local Islam, as it is practiced in Gugudu, and also to understand the various manifestations of what I call "localized Islam," I will depend largely on local devotional vocabulary and its multiple interpretations. Moreover, as will become clear, these two forms of Islam operate and engage with each other on both domestic and public levels.

For the first ten days of the month of Muharram, Shi'i Muslims throughout the world remember the Battle of Karbala, which took place in 680 C.E. in present-day Iraq. The battle, in which Imam Husain, the grandson of the Prophet Muhammad, was martyred along with his supporters, is significant in the historical memory of Islam. The battle especially marks the rise of Shi'ism as a distinctive Islamic sect that took the side of 'Ali, the son-in-law of the Prophet, in a dispute over the legacy of the Prophet.[9] Thus, Muharram has become a public religious event that recreates the Battle of Karbala through theatrical imagery and various rituals.[10] When devotees and pilgrims such as Lakshmi describe Karbala, they thus refer to this reenactment of the historical locale and events, not the original in Iraq. In other words, for thousands of pilgrims who visit the shrine every year, Gugudu is their Karbala.

According to the Gugudu story of Muharram, the pīr Kullayappa is the eldest grandson and heir of the Prophet Muhammad. Other family members of the Prophet, including Imam Husain, the protagonist in the historical events of Karbala, are described as the younger brothers of Kullayappa. The local story holds that Gugudu is the home of the martyrs of Karbala, with Kullayappa being predominant among them. Each year in the month of Muharram, hundreds of thousands of devotees visit Gugudu. They take immense pride in this local devotional culture and the memorialization of the pīr's life story that occurs through the public festivities of Muharram. Here we should recall the devotional terms that Lakshmi used—*pīru swāmi*, *ziyārat darśanam,* and *fāteha prasādam.* The term *pīru swāmi* means "pīr-lord," and in the village of Gugudu this refers to Kullayappa. *Ziyārat darśanam* is a blended term that means "sacred journey," a combination of the ideas of "visitation" or *ziyārat* in Islam, and "divine sight" or *darśanam* in Hinduism. *Fāteha prasādam* is another blended term, and one that combines fundamental elements of Islam and Hinduism—*fāteha* is the first verse of the Quran, and *prasādam* is the sacred food received by a devotee after ritual worship in a Hindu temple. The use of these terms is not unique to Lakshmi. Thousands of devotees and pilgrims who visit Gugudu every year use the same vocabulary to talk about their devotional practices centered on this shrine. This locally specific vocabulary effectively circumscribes their entire religious experience, at the center of which is the pīr (Figure 0.1).

FIGURE O.I   A blend of Islam and Hinduism: the *pīr-makānam*, with Hanuman on the top left.

In a way, these stories and practices from Gugudu help us to comprehend the ritual transformation of Islam in a local public space. These local manifestations of Islam in public spaces are a product of the multilayered and diverse regional devotional traditions that permeate South Indian religious life. Exploring these local dimensions of Islamic devotion can contribute to current scholarship on Islam by revealing an extended realm of Shi'ism and devotion to the family of the Prophet, specifically through the prominence of the narrative of Karbala in the local devotion in South India. During my fieldwork I witnessed that many of the public devotional spaces which scholars describe as embodying local Islam are in fact far more complicated than this, requiring a more nuanced and multilayered approach to understand them thoroughly.

In the wake of recent political, social, and religious developments in South Asia and elsewhere in the Islamic world, new understandings of public devotional spaces among Muslims are crucial to the study of Islam. Through such developments, local Muslims and non-Muslims alike have had to confront a wave of religious reformism, manifest as set of "localized" forms of Islam, including emphasis on the authority of "Islamic" texts, and enforced control of devotional spaces since the 1990s as a result of religious nationalism, globalization, and the increasing influence of middle-class sensibilities. Whereas different versions of localized Islam strive to distinguish and remove non-Islamic elements from Muslim practices, local Islam like that in Gugudu clearly privileges a pluralist form of devotional life.

Through examination of public rituals and personal narratives, my work suggests that this local Muslim devotion is a distinctively inclusive and multilayered tradition that remains open-ended in many circumstances. As I have pointed out, however, this inclusive tradition is now being challenged by another process, what I call *localized Islam*, which privileges a normative version of Islam. In the context of Muharram, and the various discourses that exist around it, it is important to highlight the increasing tensions between locally produced and localized versions of Islam. As I will argue, this distinction is central for understanding the multiple manifestations of contemporary lived Islam that exist in Andhra Pradesh in particular, but also the larger Islamic world generally. In the public celebration of Muharram in Gugudu, popularly known as "the Festival of Pīrs," (*pīrla paṇḍaga*), these two aspects of Islam compete for privilege of place through the legitimization of their particular forms of devotion.

Although Muharram is primarily an event on the Muslim calendar, its observance in many places in Andhra Pradesh, including in the village of Gugudu, combines aspects of many devotional traditions: local and localized manifestations of Islam, South Indian Hindu temple practices, devotion to Islamic holy persons, the idea of shared pilgrimage between Muslims and Hindus, and most interesting of all, a locally specific repertoire of blended Islamic and Hindu devotional practices. This diverse devotional life at the level of the village expands our understanding of devotion to the martyrs of Karbala, not only here but in the wider world. Similarly, this local Muslim devotion encourages us to see diverse devotional forms of Islam in their specific local social and historical contexts. However, what Eickelman calls *local Islam* is, according to my argument in this book, a manifestation of a localized Islam. These locally produced forms of Islam emphasize the embeddedness of local Islam in a pluralistic community of both Muslim and non-Muslim populations, as well as how Islam in a particular place is linked to processes at work in the larger Islamic world.[11]

In addition, the fact that thousands of pilgrims visit local pīr-houses and "Karbalas" not only during the month of Muharram but throughout the year means that the village of Gugudu extends beyond its borders as a sacred site. At another level, the Muharram tradition is not confined by spatial or geographical boundaries. In the practices of Muharram in

Gugudu, village and regional traditions mingle with unique local devotional practices. Though the formation of the village (*ūru*) is closely connected to certain rituals like *faqīri,* a vow of temporary asceticism practiced by devotees during Muharram in Gugudu, the local tradition of Muharram as described here extends far beyond the geographic boundaries of the village, thanks to the thousands of pilgrims who come from different parts of South India to participate in these public devotional practices that cross religious and regional boundaries.[12]

Devotees who visit Gugudu perform rituals like visiting the pīr-house, worshipping the local pīr, fire-walking, undertaking a temporary ascetic practice known as *faqīri,* and finally participating in the public processions on the seventh and tenth days of Muharram, which serve to recall the sacrifices made by the martyrs of Karbala.

Both Muslims and non-Muslims in Gugudu use unique local terms to distinguish their devotional practices not only from universal Islam but also from the Shi'i Islamic practices popular in nearby Hyderabad. Most Muslims in Gugudu now claim that their specific practices of Islam are true and proper, in a seemingly direct challenge to the growing notion of "true Islam" (*asli Islam*), as preached by reformist Muslim groups.

Religious nationalism since the 1990s has created a heightened effort to cultivate this authoritative "true Islam," even in remote villages in Andhra Pradesh.[13] Local devotees in villages such as Gugudu have resisted these efforts through their enthusiastic and persistent celebration of Muharram. Their efforts to counter this prescribed and authoritative Islam have become a major part in the regular remaking of a living local Islam. Popular forms of religious practice highlight the accommodation and appropriation of non-Muslim devotion. Yet during my research I observed that there was a consistent effort by some to differentiate these shared forms of devotion from an authoritative version of Islam. Whereas local Islam draws the entire community around the shrine of the pīr to participate in a fluid ritual life, this authoritative Islam tries to draw practitioners away from the shrine, and toward a more mosque-centered religion. Moreover, for at least two decades there has been a concerted effort to establish a textual mode of Islamic practice through promotion of the Quran and related interpretative materials in local translation. This new development appears to be a response to the rise of Hindu nationalist politics and, as I have already mentioned, the public events of Muharram in Gugudu have become a site of tension between two versions of Islam. The complex and diverse nature of Muharram in Gugudu allows us to see the unique contours of devotional life in a given place, and also the self-consciousness and even pride that a community may have about the distinctiveness of its practices, stories, sacred spaces, and religious history. The public events of Muharram have become a particularly visible site of contestation for these two forms of Islam, one blending Islamic and Sufi practices with non-Islamic local practices, and the other trying forcibly to remove these non-Islamic practices and bring local practices more into line with a normative Islam that is based on the Five Pillars.

Modes of Localized and Local Islam

In Gugudu, we can see two specific modes of localized Islam: first, the paradigm of Karbala, which provides a ritual and narrative framework for pīr-related devotional practices, and, second, the localization of a universal Islam based on the Five Pillars. Various caste groups that participate and perform in these rituals and storytelling traditions perceive and interpret these practices in their own way, depending on their caste and family histories. In a way, then, even these understandings of localized Islam are not singular in their meaning and essence. In the end, personal and family histories take the lead, and the framework of universal Islam undergoes deeper revisions.

One of the tasks in this book is to reveal the tensions even within the various versions of localized Islam. I will analyze three specific features that I observed in Gugudu as forming the framework of localized Islam: (1) Karbala at the center; (2) reformism under the concept of "true Islam" (*asli Islam*), and (3) the questioning of the validity of public rituals such as the pīr's processions and ritual vows.

1. Karbala and Muharram

Both Muslim and non-Muslim devotees in Gugudu identify primarily with the story of the Battle of Karbala. For many Muslims who adhere strictly to this version of Islam, Muharram is a commemorative event in honor of the martyrs of Karbala, especially Imam Husain, and most rituals in this context follow the pattern of Muharram rituals found also in Hyderabad. Several studies of Islam focus on these Shi'i-centered pattern of Muharram. Scholars of Islam in South Asia such as David Pinault, Vernon Schubel, Syed Akbar Hyder, and Karen Ruffle have analyzed various aspects of Muharram in Hyderabad in India and Karachi in Pakistan. Pinault's work shows how the family of the Prophet plays an intercessory role in various rituals practiced by Shi'a in Hyderabad. Schubel's study analyzes various domestic and public aspects of Muharram rituals in Pakistan. Hyder's work helps us to understand various modes in narrative retellings of the Battle of Karbala. And in her work among female Shi'a in Hyderabad, Ruffle sheds light on various sainthood practices. These studies have all focused on Muharram in an urban context.

As we will observe in this book, these urban-centered Muharram practices differ from villages such as Gugudu. For many Muslims and non-Muslims, the public rituals of Muharram become a stage for the display of tensions between Hyderabadi and non-Hyderabadi practices. Most Muslims and non-Muslims perceive the Muharram practices of Hyderabad as characteristic of normative Islam, a manifestation of localized Islam, as they are borrowed and adapted from Shi'ism.

2. Mosque as Center: The Reformist Mode of Islam

Mosques are central to many reformist Islamic activities in Gugudu and other places. Reformist groups have made an effort to diminish the importance of local shrines like the pīr-house in Gugudu at least for three decades. During my research in Gugudu, I observed that the local mosque functioned as a center for many reformist activities. The recent upsurge in mosque-centered activities has had a significant impact on devotional spaces in both urban and rural areas, and many of the younger generation of Muslims have begun to participate in these activities, which include prayer five times daily, Islamic sermons inside and outside the mosque, and the distribution of pamphlets and booklets that spread the message of "true Islam."

3. The Validity of Public Rituals

Most conservative Muslims reject certain public rituals of Muharram as being innovations, or *bid'a*. These Muslims consider the use of icons and processions in memory of the Prophet's family as un-Islamic. Moreover, they reject the idea of associating local pīrs with Allah, which they term *shirk* (forbidden). Conservative Muslims also point to the festive nature of some rituals during the month of Muharram, which to them is supposed to be a month of mourning. This opposition to the public celebration of Muharram can be understood within the larger context of Islamic reformism, which emphasizes the greater significance of the holy month Ramadan, and stresses observance of fasting and the reading of the Quran as obligatory acts for Muslims.

The Triangle of Local Islam

Likewise, I have observed three crucial aspects of devotional life in Gugudu, which accord with larger trends in South Asian Islam. These are: (1) the local pīr or Sufi master who represents both Shi'i and Sufi devotion, (2) the devotional stories shared by Muslims and non-Muslims, and (3) the public rituals of Muharram that privilege the power of the local pīr. I will introduce these three key aspects now as they occur in Gugudu, which will in turn give us a background of the village itself.

1. The Local Pīr

The idea of a Sufi holy person or pīr has long been recognized in scholarship as having a prominent place in popular Islam, and is visible in numerous religious practices. With regard to the usage of the term "pīr" in the context of Muharram, Richard Wolf has observed that "pīrs are properly speaking Muslim saints or spiritual leaders, but in this case they are casteless, godlike spiritual beings."[14] Most of these pīrs, including the family of the Prophet, possess a similar "casteless, god-like spiritual status" in public devotion in South India. In Gugudu, aspects of the cult of the village pīr are connected to both broader Muharram practices and the popular local pīr tradition.

Although various practices and teachings, legitimized through attribution to a pīr and celebrated in Gugudu, reveal this intermingling of broad and local trends, the representation of the pīr through the use of metal battle standards is typical not only of Shi'ism broadly but also Sufism. The battle standards as well as the rubric of devotional rituals are clearly adopted from Shi'ism. Yet through their adoption into the local pīr tradition, these practices provide opportunities for a range of caste groups to participate in various shared rituals of Islamic and non-Islamic devotion. As we shall see, this dual movement from the universal to the local and vice versa constitutes some of the most essential processes of the local pīr tradition in Gugudu. Dynamic processes of owning and disowning religious beliefs and practices suggest a self-conscious habit of selection that is highly influenced by local devotional traditions. Thus, this phenomenon of localization requires a nuanced approach if it is to be understood, in particular, the adaption of "Islamic" practices either directly or indirectly, different modes of reformism, and their relation to "local" devotion.

In the public events of Muharram, or *pīrla paṇḍaga* ("The Festival of Pīrs"), in Gugudu, this dual movement is recognized, at least in part, as a way of bringing together the use of metal standards as icons of the Karbala martyrs and more amorphous ideas of the pīr tradition in Muharram. In South Asia, the Muslim sainthood practices that comprise the pīr tradition are typically associated with famous Sufis like Abdul Qadir Jilani, Nizamuddin Awliya, Nagore Wali, and Khwaza Moinuddin Chishti. Along similar lines, the practices related to the twelfth- century Sufi saint Baba Fakhruddin of Penukonda, which is close to Gugudu, are popular among Muslims and Hindus in South India. According to local Muslims, Baba Fakhruddin spread the message of Sufism throughout the Deccan, and local pīr figures such as Kullayappa were the first generation of Muslim ascetics to carry the message of Baba Fakhruddin into remote villages and urban public spaces. According to this story, various pīr practices that are deeply embedded in the devotional life of Gugudu have a history of at least eight centuries.[15]

Describing Chishti Sufism, Carl Ernst and Bruce Lawrence explain, "It is both an experience and a memory. It is the experience of remembering God so intensely that the soul is destroyed and resurrected. It is also the memory of those who remembered God, those who were devoted to discipline and prayer, but above all, to remembrance, whether they recited the divine name *(zikr)* or evoked his presence through song *(sama)*."[16] Such statements also apply to local pīrs like Kullayappa, for they also play a significant role in evoking the presence of God and addressing people's spiritual needs, making remembrance of God an essential devotional act.

2. Shared Devotional Stories

As a means of sharing religious knowledge about the local pīr, devotional stories play a significant role in the Muharram tradition of Gugudu. Although various social groups in Gugudu take measures to try to "own" the pīr, their particular stories and memories must have sufficient resonance with other accounts of the pīr to have any validity in Gugudu. The stories told and shared in Gugudu are not just stories for entertainment or social prestige; they also impart locally valued religious knowledge and ethics. By circulating particular ideas about the public rituals of Muharram, a locally specific version of Islam is propagated. In particular, these stories spread the message of three dominant Muharram themes: *niyyat* (pure intention), *barakat* (divine blessing), and *faqīri*, a temporary ascetic practice performed to honor the pīr. These themes differ from those of the larger Shi'i world, revealing an extended or modified version of Shi'ism. When associated with devotional stories, even personal memories and everyday conversations can be used to inculcate the teachings of the pīr. Devotees and pilgrims who visit the pīr or undertake *faqīri* share their memories of the experience with their family members, and especially with children.

Both the Festival of Pīrs and the local version of Islam that is present in Gugudu are defined by the actions and perceptions of the devotees who enact these rituals and narrate the tradition, often while also asserting their caste identities. In Gugudu, several caste groups distinguish their own path of devotion from others, even as they acknowledge the validity of the stories and modes of devotion of others. Moreover, the many kinds of domestic and public rituals during the ten days of Muharram demonstrate the internal diversity of devotional life in Gugudu. However, localized Islam tries to counter this internal diversity by asserting a singular interpretation of the Muharram tradition. Many of the devotees in Gugudu distinguish reformist Islam as something that works against their beliefs, stories, and rituals, even as the number of reformists grows the importation of orthodox Islamic ideas grows. Neither side in this conflict is static and passive but evolves dynamically in response to the other.

3. Public Muslim Rituals

Devotional stories establish the imagined religious environment of Muharram, which public rituals then bring to life. Of course, public rituals vary among different groups. However, many of those in Gugudu, such as *faqīri* and the food rituals called *kandūri*, are enacted by devotees irrespective of religion, caste, and gender. During my research, I observed the activities of various reformist Muslim groups seeking to "purify" religious practices in Gugudu by privileging a fixed pattern of "Hinduism" and "Islam." Moreover, one section of younger religious activists, particularly Sunni Muslims, under the influence of the recent mosque movement in Andhra Pradesh, now work to promote a translocal Islam by circulating and reading bulletins and sermons on Islam and by attending orientation camps that teach what they call *asli Islam* (True Islam). However, the predominance of the public rituals that occur within the space of the shrine, supported by the thousands of devotees and pilgrims who participate in them, means that "True Islam" has made little headway to this point.

Introducing Gugudu

When I arrived in Gugudu in 2007 during the month of Muharram, I noticed immediately that the devotees who visited the shrine of the pīr Kullayappa celebrated Muharram in a very distinctive manner. Both Muslims and non-Muslims in this village differentiate their tradition of Muharram from the well-known celebration that takes place in and nearby Hyderabad, the capital of Andhra Pradesh. "Our Muharram is unique and *dynamic*. Are you ever going to see this *grand variety* in your Hyderabadi Muharram?" sixty-year-old Sattar Saheb challenged me one day, as we stood watching the thousands of devotees performing Muharram rituals much different than those I had grown up with in my hometown close to Hyderabad, less than 250 miles away.

When asked what made Muharram an event of such "unique, dynamic, and grand variety," Sattar Saheb repeatedly pointed to the way that both Muslims and Hindus tell stories about the pīr and perform public rituals together. He also emphasized the uniqueness of Muharram in Gugudu, so different from "Hyderabadi Muharram," which, according to local devotees, is considered to be a manifestation of more normative Islam. With a significant Shi'a population, the city of Hyderabad is well-known for its ten-day Muharram celebration and strict adherence to what Sattar Saheb described as "the Shi'i model exclusive to Hyderabadi Muslims."

By contrast, Muharram in Gugudu crosses these boundaries, being more inclusive while focusing on worship of the local pīr. Like Sattar Saheb and Lakshmi, many devotees and pilgrims distinguish local devotional practices as forms of "authentic" and "true devotion." In this way they are extremely self-conscious about possessing distinctive local practices and a unique devotional path. As Sattar Saheb said on several occasions, "There is no Hindu or Muslim. All have one religion, which is called 'Kullayappa devotion (*bhakti*).'"

Like many families in Gugudu, Sattar Saheb's family has lived there for generations. And like many, their Islam is deeply connected to their devotion to the pīr Kullayappa, who is also known as *Topi-walī Saheb* (literally, "Pīr with a Cap"). To them, devotion to Kullayappa has never been at conflict with their devotion to the family of the Prophet, or, at a larger level, with the idea of a single God, Allah. Every year, Sattar Saheb's family, along with thousands of Hindus and Muslims, participates in the public rituals dedicated to the local pīr.

A retired elementary school teacher, Sattar Saheb is known in the village for his gentle manners and knowledge of Islam and Hinduism. Pointing at the shrine, he said, "Here is the real (*asal*) Islam, and here is our way of practicing Islam. Here is the way "our land" (*vatan*) performs worship (*ibādat*), in which we have an immense faith (*imān*). These pīrs offer you a ladder to arrive at the peak of your faith." Sattar Saheb was referring to the same Five-Pillar model of Islam that any Muslim would. But when he connects his way of Islam to "our land," the model of normative Islam is translated into an alternative model centered instead on the figure of Kullayappa. This alternative model is deceivingly complex, with multiple forms of both Hindu and Islamic devotion being enacted in the ritual culture that occurs every day as well as during the celebration of Muharram in Gugudu.

In many rural places, local Islam clearly tends toward a pluralistic devotional context, and devotion either directly or obliquely distinguishes its performance from the Muharram rituals of Muharram in Hyderabad. Moreover, various Muharram practices in Gugudu point to a set of local and caste-based devotional narratives and rituals. These particular local practices revise certain established theological dimensions of normative Islam. For instance, as the eldest brother of the martyrs, Kullayappa displaces the authority of Husain, as part of a regional pattern of redefining the concept of *imāmate*. The notion of imam conventionally centers on the identity of the Imam Husain, but here he is replaced by a local pīr, in turn validating the shared rituals that are performed toward the pīr, irrespective of the Hindu or Muslim identity of his devotees.[17]

I will now introduce the actors that play a central role in local Islam in Gugudu.[18] The majority of the inhabitants of Gugudu are non-Muslims. Of its population of 2,600, only 10% of the families belong to the Muslim community, and none of those are Shi'a. However, among the thousands of pilgrims who visit Gugudu each Thursday and Friday as well as those who come during the ten days of Muharram annually, it is estimated that the number of Muslims has been increasing year to year. As many devotees told me in Gugudu, Muharram is the only public religious event that this and neighboring villages celebrate, when thousands of devotees come to worship Kullayappa.

Several villages near Gugudu help to put on the annual Muharram celebration. They do so by setting up the battle standards, performing daily worship, transporting heavy logs to the firepit, and making arrangements for the seventh- and tenth-day processions. What we see in Gugudu is not unique. In many villages across Andhra Pradesh, Muharram commemorates the founding of the village itself; the situation is no different in Gugudu. Villagers believe that the coming of the pīr Kullayappa laid the foundation for the construction of the village through his *niyyat* ("pure intention") and *barkat* ("divine blessing"), and the realm of the pīr is an embodiment of these two foundational Islamic notions.

Kullayappa: "God" with a Cap

As with most villages in South India, the story of Gugudu's origins also begins with local version of the Ramayana. Unlike many such place stories, however, this one centers on the life of a minor low-caste character in the epic named Guha.[19] The story of Guha, as told in Gugudu, turns the story of Rama into a larger story about an immemorial past, and one that is at heart actually about a Muslim pīr. The name Gugudu means "the nest of Guha" in Telugu, thus retaining the memory of Guha's immense devotion for Rama. But the local story does not end with the Ramayana story; after several centuries, Rama actually visits the village, but now as a Muslim pīr. As narrated by some caste groups, Rama's new birth as a Muslim saint transformed the devotional focus of this region toward this new *avatāram*, who was given the Persian name Kullayappa, literally meaning "a god with a cap" (*kullah* is Persian for cap, and *appa* is the local Telugu word for "god" or "father").[20]

More than the physical manifestation of this new incarnation, the saint's ideas of *niyyatu* (pure intention) and *barkatu* (divine blessing) are popular and widespread in this region. The term *niyyatu,* from the Arabic *niyyah,*[21] means "personal intention," and takes on a particular meaning locally as denoting the entire moral being of a person. Meanwhile, the term *barkatu* is considered the end result of the actions and practices of the entire community.[22] The term *niyyah* is foundational in Islam as it connects both the action and intent of the faithful. The pīr, in the form of a metal battle standard ('*alam* or pīr) of Muharram, is considered to be the embodiment of *niyyatu* and *barkatu*. In some regions, this pīr is called *pīru swāmi* (Pīr-Lord) or *turaka dēvuḍu* ("The Turk God;" Muslims are locally called *turakas*).

Most of the devotees perceive Kullayappa as a regional deity, and here the blending of religious practice works at two levels: (1) the blending of the metal battle standards typical of Shi'i Islam with the personage of the Sufi pīr that is attributed to these standards, and (2) the linking of the standards with typical modes of Hindu temple devotion, such as performing worship three times a day, walking around a fire, rolling wet bodies around the firepit, and breaking dry coconuts. Connecting practices from both traditions, Kullayappa functions as the anchor of the local Muharram tradition. For all these participants, Kullayappa provides a model for their moral life, and is a deity that fulfills the wishes and dreams of their families (Figure 0.2).

We can see a third layer of pīr practice at work here: Muharram functions as a ritual setting for the transmission of Sufi ideas and pīr devotional

FIGURE O.2 A procession of the metal battle standards of the martyrs of Karbala, including Kullayappa.

practices in Gugudu. Moreover, the public celebration in Gugudu connects it to a pīr tradition that has its roots in regional political history. Even now most of the local communities speak of the importance of the Qutub Shahis of Golconda (1518–1687 C.E.), Hyder Ali (1720–1782 C.E.), and Tippu Sultan of Mysore (1750–1799 C.E.), who ruled this region during medieval times and introduced the public rituals of Muharram.[23] In the history of South India, these periods are known for the expansion of various Sufi schools of thought that they witnessed, and these rulers were the grand patrons of the public rituals of Muharram. This suggests that the rituals of Muharram have been brought together with Sufi practices in a way that has consistently expanded the network of pīr practices in the region, resulting in a shared and pluralistic devotional culture.

Meanwhile, the hagiography of the regional saint Baba Fakhruddin suggests that the tradition of Muharram and the practices of wandering *faqīrs* in this region originated at least eight centuries ago. The public celebration of Muharram was one of the early means by which these Sufi notions were popularly introduced. Baba Fakhruddin, regionally called Babayya Swami, is known for his Sufi practices that have origins in Persian Sufism.[24] Although the saint is popular among both Hindus and

Muslims, some proponents of "true Islam" (*asli Islam*) point to the practices of this saint and his shrine as legitimate forms of the faith.[25] Specifically, at least one section of the local Muslim community strongly believes that Baba Fakhruddin used to send Muslim *faqīrs* in the four directions to spread the message of Sufism and, according to this version, Kullayappa was one of them.[26] This account claims that Kullayappa was a disciple of Baba Fakhruddin, and as a chosen disciple and *faqīr*, started the tradition of Muharram in Gugudu eight centuries ago.[27] With the arrival of Kullayappa, many practices came into being, including the creation of a local Karbala, which would become the central site for the public celebration of Muharram.

From Historic to Symbolic Karbala

"Let us go to Karbala first. Then you will come to know what the *real* Muharram is!" With these words, Tirupatayya directed me toward the local Karbala in Gugudu. Tirupatayya is no ordinary peasant in the village. His role as bearer of the metal battle standard of the pīr during Muharram is a family tradition that dates back five centuries, to when his ancestors first invited the pīr to this village. This event is foundational in the public memory of the village and the pīr tradition. Or, to put it differently, Tirupatayya's family history *is* the history of the village and the local pīr tradition. As he narrated several stories that gave the history of Kullayappa and Muharram in Gugudu, Tirupatayya walked me to the village Karbala in the southwest part of the village. This local Karbala is an open space surrounded by four hills, with an old well in the fields nearby that plays a central role during final rites of the pīr on the tenth day.[28]

Villagers believe that Gugudu is the actual site where the Battle of Karbala occurred, and where the martyrs including the local pīr shed their blood to save not only the supporters of Imam Husain but also the village. Yazid, the enemy in the conventional version of the story, is described as a local subordinate of the Mughal emperor in the oral history of Gugudu. According to the local story, the Mughals tried to capture and imprison the nine pīrs, including Kullayappa. In the final battle, however, the forces led by Kullayappa drove the enemy away. The Battle of Karbala was the final attempt of the pīr Kullayappa and his brothers, including Husain and Hasan, to reinitiate the tradition of Muharram, and to save their motherland of Gugudu from the clutches of the enemy.[29] This fascinating narrative is just one manifestation of the process by which larger religious stories and practices are reimagined in the local context.

The very usage of the term "history" (the locally used Urdu term is *tārīkh*) undergoes a thorough revision in the context of local Muharram traditions: several myths, epic stories, and caste histories intersect and produce an entirely local version of Muharram that highlights the acts of the pīrs.[30] As narrated in these stories, the local pīrs, including the grandsons of the Prophet, lived and walked in these local spaces. These devotees believe that the family tree of the Prophet has its roots in their own village, rather than somewhere in Iraq. Along with this narrative shift, local spaces associated with the events of Karbala reinforce the idea of blended practice in several rituals enacted within the premises of the pīr-house. In essence, global Islamic history functions as a tool for constructing a shared religiosity around the local pīr.

When Tirupatayya or any villager in Gugudu made me visit the local Karbala site, I understood their gesture as an effort to demonstrate the local origins of the Muharram tradition in Gugudu. The Muharram tradition of Gugudu includes other ritual sites as well, such as the house of the pīr, the graves of Muslims, and the local well or lake where the pīrs take their final ritual bath. Most of these ritual sites are busy on Thursdays and Fridays throughout the year as a huge number of devotees visit to worship the local pīrs and perform song and dance in the presence of the pīrs. In the month of Muharram, however, these sites are transformed into theaters where key public rituals are performed. These public rituals reenact the drama of the pīrs' life in order to reinforce the notions of *niyyatu* (personal intention) and *barkatu* (divine blessing) as lessons from the pīr's oral hagiography. As one popular saying in the village goes, "If there is no pīr, there is no *barkatu* for this place."

Fieldwork in Shared Devotional Spaces

Before visiting Gugudu, I had intended to focus mainly on the festival rituals that occur during the month of Muharram. When I arrived in Gugudu in September 2006, Muharram was still four months away, and yet the atmosphere was almost like that of the month of Muharram. Since it was Thursday, hundreds of devotees and pilgrims were arriving in Gugudu and visiting the pīr to fulfill their vows or perform regular obligatory rites. The phenomena of ritual and pilgrimage outside the month of Muharram contribute to why devotees believe this to be "a different Muharram." Even on this day outside of Muharram, the pīr-house was busy with villagers, some of whom visit the pīr-house every day to pay their respects and others who had travelled a long ways as a part of an annual family tradition, often considered a "little *hajj*" or "*tirtha*." The place was busy with ritual specialists as well.

Based on what I knew of Muharram in Hyderabad and various other nearby sites, I had two specific ideas in mind regarding the tradition of Muharram in Gugudu. First, though Gugudu is a small place geographically, its sacred geography is extensive. For thousands of pilgrims who venerate the pīr Kullayappa, Gugudu is the center of their devotion. In this way, they also consider it to be their home. This sacred map covers three South Indian states, meaning that my study would not be confined to the physical location of Gugudu. As a result, I travelled to the village with two groups of pilgrims from Karnataka and Tamil Nadu. These devotees shared with me their thoughts on the journey. This broad-based worship of the pīr takes the form of a tradition known as "Kullayappa devotion" (*Kullayappa bhakti*). Second, the realm of ritual practices of Muharram in Gugudu is also not confined to the month of Muharram. Outside of this period, we still find devotees and pilgrims visiting Gugudu and performing obligatory rituals at the shrine on a regular basis.

I planned for my research to focus particularly on *Kullayappa bhakti* in Gugudu. The idea of *Kullayappa bhakti* has two forms: as a place that gave birth to the pīr, and as a center that attracts pilgrims from many places. This extends to the consideration of time, since rituals are observed both within and beyond the month of Muharram. To be able to portray the full extent of religious life of Gugudu, I made the village my home for nine months, and traveled extensively to neighboring villages and pilgrim centers as well. While in Gugudu, I met with villagers, devotees, and pilgrims, and engaged in both formal and informal conversations with them. My most common source of information turned out to be those conversations I had over tea at the pīr-house.

I used various methods of fieldwork to collect data that would help me understand the pīr stories, everyday shared rituals, and the public celebration of Muharram, which constitute the three aspects central to *Kullayappa bhakti*.

1. Ritual Observation and Conversation

For the first few weeks after my arrival in Gugudu, I was an unknown entity, a stranger in the village. Because it is a small place and the community is very close-knit, when I walked along the main street of Gugudu I could overhear questions like, "What's this person doing here?" One evening when I was coming out of a house after watching a family video of a naming ceremony at the pīr-house, I observed a group of six or seven people discussing me. Sattar Saheb was among them, trying to respond to their questions.

"He is not a local but a native of Hyderabad. Why is he interested in our Muharram?" one woman was asking curiously.

". . . because this is a unique Muharram. What do they have in Hyderabad? Just beating their chests and spilling out their blood!" replied Sattar Saheb.

"But Hyderabad Muharram is *asli* ("true" or "proper") Muharram. That's at least what they say!"

"What is *asli*? That's *asli* for them, this is *asli* for us."

It was not difficult to overhear them, as they could not see me walking toward them. Later on I asked Sattar Saheb about the conversation.

"To all of us you're just a Hyderabadi and an urban person. Your Muharram is different from our Muharram and our people are curious to know what made you come here."

"What did you say?"

"I said Kullayappa has pulled you this far, even though you're a Hyderabadi!"

In many parts of Andhra, local devotees take pride in their own tradition of Muharram, and believe that public rituals are the main reason for the continuation of Muharram. Devotees in Gugudu add an extra point of attraction—their devotion to Kullayappa. They believe that their village has a "true" tradition of Muharram rituals as well. As the above conversation makes clear, my identity as a "Hyderabadi" made me an outsider to the tradition for the villagers, even though I am a Muslim myself. This did not change throughout my stay, despite all of the kindness I received in the village. At one point, after I asked several questions about the origins of the pīr, my informants seemed unhappy, and immediately commented that "You Hyderabadis never understand our pīr or our Muharram."[31] In spite of such sentiment, I decided to continue to participate and observe the rituals closely. I also tried to track down one or two devotees to ask questions of during teatime at the stall of Mumtaz Hussain, outside the pīr-house, or at the local Karbala.

I made it a point not to miss any of these public rituals. While in Gugudu, I attended daily worship, known as *nitya fātehā puja*, everyday inside the pīr-house. During this ritual, I began to observe the ways that devotees of different caste group participate in worship. During this time I would also briefly converse with Husenappa, the custodian of the pīr-house. Thursdays and Fridays in Gugudu are hectic days as hundreds of pilgrims join in the daily devotion, and since some pilgrims stay for as long as three days, I was able to talk with many of them about their family traditions of rituals and *faqīri* practices.

As the custodian of the pīr-house, Husenappa also had some knowledge of Shi'i rituals, which made it possible for us to discuss some of the crucial differences between the Shi'i tradition and the Gugudu tradition of Muharram rituals. After the daily morning worship, we used to walk together to the local mosque and perform *namāz* there. During these walks, we shared many conversations and stories about our families, villages, and specifically about Husenappa's views on various rituals inside and outside the pīr-house. After the morning *namāz*, Husenappa opens the doors of the pīr-house again to allow devotees to visit the pīr. I would sit for a while inside the pīr-house and chat with village elders about the history of the village, as well as other family matters. Finally, I would go and eat breakfast, which was usually *citrannam* (lemon or tamarind rice) and *bajji* (fried spicy fritters) at Mumtaz Husain's tea stall across from the pīr-house. I made use of this time to talk with devotees from various caste groups.

As people became timid in the presence of my digital voice recorder, I never used it except when recording folk songs about the pīr. Instead, I often relied on memory, or jotted down important points in shorthand. Back in my room, I would write down each conversation in my logbook, noting the conversations verbatim. This helped me to figure out the local devotional vocabulary. Initially, I tried to write down each word that devotees said, but after a while, as I became used to the practice and relatively comfortable with the local people, I started to conduct structured interviews with a handful of devotees. When speaking about their practices, most of these devotees turned to their family histories as well as personal interpretations.

2. Documenting Devotional Stories

At the very early stage of my fieldwork, when I started collecting stories in and around Gugudu, I realized the importance of learning about how the story of Muharram is being told in other places too. I visited villages in several districts of Andhra to document the variety of Muharram stories present, recording more than fifty stories in Telugu and Urdu that narrate various events in the story of Karbala. During my early visits to these places, several narrators declined to tell the story outside of the month the Muharram. One man, when pressed, told me, "I cannot tell the story at this time. It's a Muharram story and told only during the month of Muharram. Telling the story at other times would bring *lānatu* (Urdu term for 'destruction') upon the village" Others told their local narrative, but left the ending of it out. "That way we can avoid any inauspiciousness coming down upon us," they told me. These stories are so connected to the ritual efficacy of the month of Muharram that they are usually never told outside the ritual. Thus I had to wait until Muharram to record the endings of these stories.

This experience highlights the difficulties documenting devotional stories connected to a local religious calendar. Literally, one had to enter the temporality of the ritual to hear the story. During my early conversations with devotees and pilgrims in Gugudu, I found three types of stories surrounding the Kullayappa tradition: first, stories from the family of Tirupatayya; second, those which were about family of Tirupatayya, as heard from various groups of devotees; and third, stories about Kullayappa told by various caste groups, including both Muslims and non-Muslims. Though most of the caste groups in and around Gugudu pointed unanimously at the family of Tirupatayya as the source for the primary stories of Kullayappa, it was intriguing to learn that each caste group and family has its own story as well about the pīr. In the process, I met the family members of Tirupatayya and collected their ancestors' stories. Tirupatayya's family story is considered to be the story of Kullayappa and Muharram in Gugudu. Most of the stories feature a pattern of the themes of *niyyatu, barkatu,* and *īmān.* Many stories centered on the practices of Kullayappa also at certain points refer to the family of Tirupatayya. Specifically, these stories describe the practice of *faqīri,* for which the family of Tirupatayya is considered to be paradigmatic. The efficacy of the practice of *faqīri* itself features in many stories. Finally, some stories describe the interactions of diverse caste groups with the pīr. This became the most important subject of my fieldwork, and I spent the most time listening to, transcribing, and translating these stories.

The process of recording the pilgrim stories was an elaborate one. There are a wide variety of pilgrims in the Kullayappa tradition: pilgrims who come for devotional purposes, natives revisiting as pilgrims, and small traders who also join festivities to sell their wares. I traveled with two groups traveling on special pilgrimage buses, and had extended conversations with them throughout the journey. This experience helped me considerably in understanding their perceptions of an "imagined" Gugudu, their devotion to Kullayappa, and their thoughts about pilgrimage.

Recording these various kinds of stories provided me sufficient clues to understand the Kullayappa tradition as a collection of many stories that possess and set of underlying themes centered on the public celebration of Muharram. In some stories, a clear itinerary of the pīr's wanderings is given, with destinations like Narpala, Penukonda, Kadapa, Guntakal, and Tadimarri. I visited these places to understand their connections to the pīr's story, and met devotees and pilgrims I found there to learn more about the pīr, and to understand the variety of experiences and ideas surrounding devotion to the pīr.

3. Documenting the Public Rituals

I had an especially difficult time documenting the ten days of rituals during the month of Muharram, as this small village became tightly packed with the arrival of thousands of pilgrims. For those ten days, I tried to spend much of my time with the families of Tirupatayya and Husenappa. These two themselves were often busy with ritual arrangements, and I was able to participate in some of these rituals, including cleaning the ritual standards, reciting the first verse of the Quran with other Muslims, and distributing sugar *prasādam* at the pīr-house.

On the tenth day, during the funerary rites of the pīrs, the *muzāvar* allowed me to wash the symbolic bodies of the pīrs at the local Karbala. Such occasions afforded me opportunities for many conversations. After observing my work in these rituals, Tirupatayya and Husenappa would say, "You're doing fine now. By the next Muharram, you will be much better." By this time, many families in the village had begun to invite me for lunch or dinner to share the *prasādam* of the *kandūri*.

During the *kandūri* food rituals I had close interactions with the families of the devotees, meeting everyone and taking every opportunity to extend our conversations. Before each ritual, I met the main ritualists, and during the event I took notes on every detail. During conversations, I asked the ritualists to tell me about their previous experiences participating, and in so doing, I heard many family stories. Before the start of each morning during Muharram, I would read over these notes to train myself to be able to follow each ritual. And after the processions on the seventh and tenth days, I met the main ritualists and had long but informal conversations with them.

In addition, I made sure to pay attention to what was happening at the local mosque on these days, as an opportunity to observe the tensions between rituals at the pīr-house and the local mosque. I recorded the sermons each day on my digital voice recorder, and had detailed discussions with imams in Gugudu and neighboring places. Since these local imams were especially interested in discussing the value of reading the Quran, performing daily prayers at the mosque, and other forms of localized Islam, I conducted structured interviews with these imams and various Islamic scholars who visited Gugudu during Muharram. These interviews have offered me a clear idea of how *asli Islam* is understood and perceived in the devotional life of Gugudu.

Structure of the Book

In Chapter 1, I describe various ritual sites and sacred spaces in and around Gugudu. These tell the story of the local pīr Kullayappa as they are inscribed into local spaces. I will also introduce the village of Gugudu as it is portrayed by local devotees, pilgrims, and villagers of various caste and religious groups.

Chapter 2 introduces the pīr Kullayappa. While maintaining concern about the historicity of this local pīr, I describe the realm of the saint as narrated by the villagers. This chapter seeks to understand how the complex tradition that has built up around the pīr is perceived and interpreted by members of the diverse caste groups who practice rituals toward Kullayappa.

In Chapter 3, I focus on the major public rituals of the month of Muharram, and the place of Kullayappa within the larger religious tradition of Gugudu. Focusing on multiple aspects of Muharram as a public ritual, this chapter highlights multiplicity and contestation in caste stories about the Muslim holiday.

Chapter 4 discusses the individual rituals of various groups of devotees and pilgrims who visit Gugudu. The observance of *faqīri* reveals its practitioners' passionate devotion to the pīrs, and also their effort to refashion their personal lives based on an ethical model given in the life story of the pīr.

Finally, Chapter 5 discusses the recent tensions between the local Muharram tradition and the normative Islamic tradition. These observations are made in relation to three main issues: first, the continually changing situation of Muharram as a public ritual; second, recent efforts by a new generation of Muslim groups to "reform" local Islamic practices; and third, the ongoing effort to redefine various village ritual sites as part of the effort to establish a clear division between Hindus and Muslims.

CHAPTER 1 | Gugudu: The Emergence of a Shared Devotional Space

The village is there only because of the pīr. The pīr really gave us the village and without the pīr, there is no village. If there is no pīr, there is no divine grace or pure devotion.

—TIRUPATAYYA FROM GUGUDU

A New Village with New Devotion

Both villagers and pilgrims say that the village Gugudu is a gift from the pīr. Their story of the rise of this village now called Gugudu is connected with the fall of another village, called Chandrayana Peta. When narrating the stories of this latter place, villagers say that "that village Chandrayana Peta breathed its last as the new village took rebirth as Gugudu."[1] At the center of this "rebirth" was a new shared shrine, the pīr-makānam (pīr-house). This model of "rebirth" (punarjanma) is crucial, since the story of the "death" of the old village and the "rebirth" of the new village is replayed each year in the ritual fire-walks which occur on the seventh and tenth days during the month of Muharram.

The fire of the fire-walks simultaneously signifies the great fire which devoured the old village and the rebirth of the village.[2] As several fire-walkers and devotees explained, "When we walk through the fire, it reminds us all of that old story of the great fire, and it also reminds us of the arrival of the pīr who made this village his home and our home, too. It reminds us of the importance of niyyatu ("pure intention") and barkatu ("divine blessing") that the pīr brought to Gugudu." For the devotees residing in Gugudu and for the pilgrims who visit the pīr, these rituals of fire-walking continually remind them of the central value of *niyyatu* and *barkatu* as two aspects of devotion to Kullayappa. Many places in Gugudu are considered "pure" based on the notions of *niyyatu* and *barkatu*.

In this chapter, I will introduce the village of Gugudu as it is portrayed by local devotees, pilgrims, and villagers of various caste and religious groups. In other words, rather than describing the physical landscape of the village, this chapter will present different places in this sacred land-scape through villagers' and devotees' narratives as well as oral histories of village life, which though caste based are known by all. I will argue that the rise of the shared devotional space in Gugudu is ingrained in the local conception of religious experience, as that is conceived through the pīr tradition and the concepts of *barkatu* and *niyyatu*.[3]

By describing the physical spaces of Gugudu through the views of the devotees, this chapter undertakes to present Gugudu as a place that is ritu-ally made extraordinary through the constant intercessions of the pīr Kul-layappa. This chapter is divided into four sections: (1) an introduction to Gugudu as a typical South Indian village; (2) a description of local spaces as they are presented in local stories, especially those about the crucial moment of the pīr's arrival; (3) Gugudu as imagined by devotees as insiders/outsiders and pilgrims; and (4) a description of the extended realm of the pīr as understood by pilgrims.

Gugudu: From a Small Village to a Big Pilgrim Center

When I arrived in Gugudu in the fall of 2006 for field research, there was no Muharram ritual activity, but the pīr-house was busy with devotees and pilgrims. Many devotees were walking around a huge cone-shaped mound topped with a holy basil plant. After walking around the mound, the devo-tees proceeded into the pīr-house to pay respects to the pīr. Inside, the *muzāvar* (custodian), locally known as *"muzāvaru pujari,"* was busy recit-ing the *fātehā*, the first verse of the Quran. This act of recitation is called *fātehā puja*—from the term *fātehā* from Islamic devotion, and *puja* from Hindu devotion.

I met Husenappa, the custodian of the shrine, after the morning rituals to hear the story of the village. Even before telling the story of Gugudu, he began to talk about the old village Chandrayana Peta. He said, "This is not about one village, but the story of the two villages. You need to know the stories of the two villages to learn about the pīr. The early village was

Chandrayana Peta, and the present village is Gugudu." The story Huse-nappa told me I heard from many other devotees, and it is clear that the entire story of the local pīr is connected to these two villages: Chandray-ana Peta and Gugudu. Since Gugudu is more closely connected with con-temporary rituals, I begin describing it first, and then narrate the story of Chandrayana Peta.

Located eighteen miles east of the district of Ananta Puram, Gugudu is like any ordinary South Indian village, with one central residential area and a few surrounding settlements inhabited by various caste groups. The real center of the village is the pīr-house, considered by villagers to be the "navel" (naḍi boḍḍu in local Telugu) of the village. Most of the houses in Gugudu stand on opposite sides of one main road running through the heart of the village. Every vehicle and passerby going through the village must travel along this arterial thoroughfare. Local buses and jeeps pass through here before dropping passengers at the end of the main road, from which they can walk to the pīr-house, sitting amongst a cluster of the houses. Since the village is small and has barely any basic amenities, vil-lagers walk or bike to Narpala, the closest town, for groceries and govern-ment services.

According to the recent census, the village has a population of 2,620 people living in 551 houses. Of these, 182 Muslims inhabit 38 homes, whereas the large majority of the population—1,400 people—come from various lower castes (Table 1.1).[4] The most dominant castes are the *Bōya* and *Vaddera,* which subsist primarily as agricultural laborers, stonema-sons, day laborers working from day to day.[5] Since the village has no water resources and is constantly under the threat of drought, farmers have few options (beyond groundnuts and lentils) for farmable crops, and laborers must often rely on petty jobs like small-scale construction to earn their daily keep.

Migration due to drought has a significant impact on local life.[6] Many families migrate temporarily to nearby towns such as Narpala, Dharma-varam, or Battalapalli, or even to the neighboring state of Karnataka. For many such migrant families, Kullayappa is a connecting link and the public event of Muharram is an occasion for the reunion of the family. As Madar Sahib, who sold his lands in Gugudu forty-five years ago and set-tled as a small businessman in a town in Karnataka, told me, "We had a joint family with more than thirty members. Now we are all scattered in different directions just like migrant birds. But for those ten days we all visit Gugudu and spend time together. If there was no Kullayappa or Mu-harram, we would never get a chance to meet or connect with each other."[7]

Not surprisingly, the story of Gugudu that Husenappa and other villagers tell is also a story of migration from one village to another, or to a nearby town. When the earlier village, Chandrayana Peta, burned down, it took several years to build Gugudu. According to the local place story *(sthala purāṇam)*, the old village and new village have totally different devotional systems. The old village had a Vishnu temple known as Chenna Kesava Swami at its heart. In Gugudu, meanwhile, the pīr-house has taken over that central place. In most of the villagers' stories and conversations, the local pīr Kullayappa remains the connecting link between the two villages as a deity, playing differing roles as Muslim exemplar, regional deity, and personal spiritual guide and, to a certain extent, the incarnation *(avatāram)* of Rama. The oral narratives about the pīr also include the history of sixteen different caste groups in this region, both Hindu and Muslim. These narratives also map out the contours of a new religious vocabulary, including terms like *barkatu* and *niyyatu.* Devotees always use these two terms to define or describe this *ūru* (village). Gugudu and nearby places are considered to be the embodiment of *barkatu* and *niyyatu.* Villagers also say that the processional routes of the pīr during the seventh and tenth days of Muharram are blessed by the pīr's presence.

Local Places and Their Stories

Several stories describe places said to be blessed by the pīr, who visits them in his multiple manifestations. By his visit these places are established as symbols of the efficacy of *barkatu* and *niyyatu,* and also of the efficacy of the pīr's *barkatu* and *niyyatu.* The stories of these places are reenacted each year during Muharram. Various rituals are said to renew the *barkatu* and *niyyatu* of these places; this is especially the case with the ritual reenactment of the pīr's evening walks in a procession on the seventh and tenth days of Muharram. As has been noted, Gugudu is more than a village; it is a pilgrim center. The pīr tradition thus extends beyond Gugudu's territorial limits because thousands of pilgrims from other states join the villagers in worshipping the pīr. When pilgrims come to Gugudu, they often connect the pīr to their own network of deities and Sufis, further extending the spiritual genealogy of the pīr.

Both villagers and pilgrims tell stories and share religious experiences as they visit various Hindu and Sufi sites around Gugudu. Even those who come from far-off places to Gugudu claim the pīr as their own, just as much as do the villagers themselves. As one villager from Gugudu said,

"This air is sweetened by the sugar *prasādam* and incense sticks that we offer to the pīr every day. This sweetness further extends into our lives when all castes join to worship the pīr." For most of these devotees and pilgrims, Gugudu is not just a space; it is a doorway opened to heaven, as suggested by Muslims' use of the Urdu phrase *jannat kā darvāza* (the door to heaven) to describe Gugudu, and also Hindus' use of the term *vaikuṇṭham*, which literally means "heaven." People enact this vision of Gugudu as a heaven through the purification of their surroundings, such as by cleaning, whitewashing, and decorating their houses.

As I mentioned before, except for the veneration for the pīr, Gugudu is an ordinary South Indian village. When devotees visit this place for the first time, however, they often make a vow to the pīr that will require them to visit Gugudu each subsequent year. As one pilgrim, Lakshmamma from Karnataka, described it: "Each visit is a totally new experience. I have been visiting the pīr for at least forty Muharrams, each Muharram counting as one year. Each *ziyāratu darśanam* of the pīr is new and breathes new energy into my life." When pilgrims describe each visit as a different experience, they speak of each visit in new terms to acknowledge some new reflections on the pīr Kullayappa.

During the month of Muharram, both villagers and pilgrims prepare for their visit to the pīr. The way these villagers purify, prepare, and beautify their homes to invite the pīr as a guest demonstrates the importance of the space in their devotion to the pīr. In the month of Muharram, Gugudu practically transforms into a new village. This can be seen on two levels: first, the physical surroundings with whitewashed walls and dazzling design lights every night; second, each villager and devotee prepares himself or herself mentally to have the *ziyāratu darśanam* of the pīr. "We are inviting the pīr with a mind and body of pure intent. We are celebrating his arrival and the birth of our village, too," said Lakshmi Reddi, whose family is said to still keep a definitive memory of the first arrival of the pīr. This pure intention takes its practical and physical form when the entire village is cleaned and whitewashed, with some walls decorated with the hand-shaped icons that represent the pīr. This "purity" further extends into the realm of mind, when these devotees enact *faqīri*, a temporary ascetic practice that embodies other practices of purity. This will be discussed in Chapter 4 (Figure 1.1).

The physical purity of the village and villagers preparing themselves for the visit of the pīr, in fact, echoes something in the mythology of Gugudu. "First there was a deep forest and a huge river. . . ." Thus began Tirupatayya, as we sat inside the pīr-house, when he was asked to tell the

FIGURE I.I Purifying the village before the pīr's visit: Gugudu in the month of Muharram.

story of the village.[8] This story is told so often that every villager and every pilgrim basically tells the same story. About several hundred years ago, as both Hindus and Muslims tell it, the Hindu god Ram took a new *avatar* as a Muslim saint.[9] During this new age, as narrated by the villagers, the entire village was a part of huge mythical forest called *daṇḍakāraṇyam*, an impenetrably dense forest where Ram wandered during his forest life.

The birth of the new village is often described as a new beginning with a *barkatu*. Local legend narrates that the pīr granted the village a new life that was bright and prosperous for its inhabitants. For this, they use the term *barkatu*. According to the villagers, Chandrayana Peta existed several hundred years ago. But the memory of its existence, and of the great fire that ruined it, still lingers. Very often, doomsday stories in South Indian villages center around a great fire, by which a whole village is destroyed and the villagers have to migrate to new places. However, in the case of Gugudu, this story is actually connected to the establishment of a new village, and the memory of the great fire is now reenacted through a fire-walk ritual each year at Muharram. As portrayed by the villagers and devotees, walking through this fire reenacts the walking out of their old village and old life and entering into the new village and new life. The arrival of the pīr is the turning point of this story, and the way these villages perceive the shift from one village to another reveals their idea of devotion.

Both Gugudu and the site of old village Chandrayana Peta are surrounded by hills with names like Black Hill, North Hill, Eastern Hill, and Cattle Hill. The site of the old village is to the southeast, close to Eastern Hill and the Chenna Kesava Swami Temple, which was rebuilt there. One morning when I took a walk toward this site, I ran into a young man named Venkata Chalapati Rayalu. He had a red dot on his forehead and a small flower tucked behind his right ear, as if he had just come from doing puja at the temple. Rayalu usually leads devotional hymns with men and women in the pīr-house during Thursday night vigils. The day I met him, however, he was coming from the old temple at Chandrayana Peta. Rayalu belongs to the Telugu *Vaishnava* caste, and aware that his ancestors used to take care of the old temple, still continues to light lamps and offering flowers to the deity in the temple. He took me that day to the temple and explained the history of the temple as we toured the surroundings.

As Rayalu described it, the temple, known as Chenna Kesava Swami, was once the center of the village, and hundreds of devotees used to visit it. Once a solid structure, all that remains of the original temple is a half-broken *dhvaja sthambham* (flag pillar) (Figure 1.2).

FIGURE 1.2 Chenna Keśava Swami Temple and the broken long pillar.

In 1960, a small structure was built at the site to house the deity, but beside this the place is desolate, and no ritual activity takes place there. "It was only to save this temple from complete destruction. I'm the priest and the only devotee who comes here," Rayalu commented, with a look of irony. According to him, the temple was once the heart of the old village. "After the great fire that devoured the entire village, this temple became a broken structure. Devotees stopped visiting this place then, and all the inhabitants of the village moved to Gugudu."

Inside the small structure now sits the idol of Chenna Kesava Swami, said to be an avatar of Vishnu, and once the familial deity of Rayalu's family. However, this deity's former popularity was not the same following the arrival of the pīr Kullayappa. Rayalu's family now pledges allegiance to the local pīr and were responsible for starting the tradition of singing devotional hymns to the saint. In one of his devotional hymns, Rayalu stretches the genealogy of the pīr to Vishnu. He also believes that some of the rituals—such as wearing the sacred thread in *faqīri*—originated from a *vaishnava* practice.

The story of how Chandrayana Peta came to a tragic end, and how Gugudu rose up in its place, centers around the hand-image, which was supposedly thrown into a well as the old village burned by two goldsmith brothers, and later rediscovered by a peasant named Koṇḍanna when his cattle grazed near the well. When Koṇḍanna found the image—which would eventually be called Kullayappa—he brought it to the village and began to perform *fātehā*, reciting the first line of the verse of the Quran as he had learned it from the pīr. The story of Koṇḍanna, the first devotee of the pīr, is so important that that his story has practically become the story of the Guguda as a whole. Even now Koṇḍanna's heirs—Lakshmi Reddi and Tirupatayya—take a lead role in performing the pīr-related rituals and in Muharram in the village. Moreover, they are the main source for the pīr narratives in Gugudu.

As the image entered the village, it is said that life began anew as things fell into their proper place. As local devotees put it, "Everything came into an order which defined the new village life: new duties for each caste group and a new source of devotion for every caste group." Most importantly, the village under the spell of the pīr began to experience new prosperity and progress, which they call *barakatu*. Lakshmi Reddi said, "There was no looking back once the *pīru swami* entered the village. We almost forgot the old lifestyle. We entered into a new arena of rituals and responsibilities which made everyone happy. It was like we found the right direction of life. We found a new value—*niyyatu*—for reaching the *pīru swami*."

Most non-Muslim devotees, like Lakshmi Reddi, call the pīr *"pīru swami,"* a term that blends the Islamic term pīr and Hindu term *swami,* meaning "god" or "lord."

Muharram became the time for expressing many of these ideas through public ritual. Since the founding of Gugudu, the village is said to have seen five hundred Muharrams, each one renewing faith in the local pīr and reinforcing his efficacy. The hand-image that Koṇḍanna re-discovered is now considered the body of the pīr. Wanting to make the village the home of this pīr, the villagers came up with the idea of building a pīr-house, which is now the center of everyday religious activities as well as Muharram.

In the ensuing pages, I will describe (1) the pīr-house, followed by (2) the firepit, (3) Lord Anjaneya and Peddamma Temple, (4) Karma Yōgi Brahmam on the hill, (5) the local mosque, (6) the graves of the Muslim muzāvars (the custodians of local Muslim shrine), and (7) the local Karbala.

1. The Pīr-Makānam (Pīr-House)

According to the villagers, the pīr-house (*pīr-makānam*) has a history of at least a few hundred years. When Kondanna brought the hand-shaped icon (*panja* in local Urdu, though non-Muslims always use *dēvuḍu* (god) or *pīru swami*) to the village, it was immediately installed at the entry point of the village, which was to become its center or navel. The present building was built in 1922 as a mosque-like structure. The actual home of the pīrs is about four hundred square feet, with an entrance facing to the east. On the right side of the structure lies the temple of Anjaneya, while in the back are small sheds where free food is distributed. Recently, the temple committee has built a new *maṇṭapam* (pandal), enabling the devotees to perform night vigils. Across from the building, there is a raised platform under which lies the small abode of a village goddess named Peddamma.

The feelings that devotees have toward the pīr-house are strongly connected to their purpose in visiting the pīr. The structure of the pīr-house itself is said to have done miracles (*karāmatu*) for some of those who make a return visit because of a previous vow. For many families, it is traditional to visit the pīr before significant new undertakings, such as new business ventures, large purchases such as a house or vehicle, marriages, and the beginning of a child's schooling and other family events. New parents bring their babies to perform a name-giving ceremony inside the pīr-house. Gifting sugar is the most important ritual during non-Muharram days. Each devotee makes a vow that he or she will gift certain amount of sugar when his or her wishes are fulfilled. As one approaches the pīr-house, he or she sees many shops and roadside vendors selling sugar packets, coconut, incense sticks, and other ritual paraphernalia. Some devotees offer the pīr huge bags of sugar, though most bring two or three one-kilogram packets. Thursdays, Fridays, and Sundays are especially busy days for the vendors, as hundreds of devotees visit the pīr-house. On Thursdays and non-Muharram days, the pīr-house doors are open by the *muzāvar* after the morning prayer (*fazar*). At 5:00 a.m. every morning, the local *nādaswaram* group begins their concert for half an hour. The *muzāvar*, meanwhile, begins his day at 4:00 a.m. when he takes a purifying bath and attends morning prayer at the local mosque. Typically, the pīr-house remains open until 10:00 p.m., but during Muharram it is always open, as devotees visit continuously.

Inside the pīr-house, devotees take *darśanam* of an image of the pīrs, which rests on a raised platform. On the right side of the entry is a huge donation box, awaiting the donations or gifts from devotees. The beautiful silver-plated pillars inside the pīr-house resemble those of a typical Hindu temple. Yet the atmosphere is more like that of a Muslim shrine or *dargāh*. Similar to patterns of behavior common to any mosque, women are not allowed to enter into the pīr-house, and they must wait outside while men receive the blessing of the pīr. However, on Thursdays and special days such as Muharram, even men must stay outside the pīr-house. As such, the *darśanam* of the pīr that occurs on the seventh and tenth days of Muharram is a rare occasion. The *chakkera fātehā* (literally "sugar *fātehā*") is the basic ritual inside the pīr-house (Figure 1.3). Devotees give gifts of sugar to the *muzāvar*, who then brings it before the images of the pīrs at the center of the pīr-house. He burns incense and places some sugar before the images, then reads the first verse of the Quran. The *muzāvar* then returns the sugar packets, which are now, to use Diane Mines's words, "transvalued" as *prasādam* through the contact with the deity.[10] Devotees finally distribute the sugar outside.

The pīr-house is also the abode of Anjaneya, the monkey-god in Hinduism. To the right in the temple, there is a huge stone, carved and painted red in his image. A *Vaishnava* priest performs daily rites to him, but very few devotees actually visit Anjaneya, as their primary loyalty is to the pīr. Those who do visit Anjaneya break coconuts at his feet as an offering.

2. The Firepit: A Symbol of Passionate Devotion

Any spatial or ritual description of Gugudu should actually include the firepit. According to the villagers, the firepit is the oldest ritual site in the village. They believe that it was originally built during the mythical time

FIGURE 1.3 Inside the pīr-house: as devotees bring sugar for the pīr, the *muzāvar* recites the *fātehā*, the first verse of the Quran. The pīrs are seen in the picture frame on the left.

of Ram. As this story goes, when Ram did not show up, his lower-caste devotee Guha built this firepit and jumped into it to show his devotion to the god. According to the villagers, now this firepit is the same one that is used for devotion to the pīr Kullayappa. On the seventh and tenth days of Muharram, devotees walk across the firepit. This is considered first an act of "purifying past mistakes;" to use local words, "the fire washes off all the dark sins," and the devotees enter into another birth (*janma*). Second, the fire is the meeting point between the devotee and the pīr. Lakṣhmi Reddi told me, "The names of the gods change, but intense devotion remains, that devotion which is so intense that devotees prepare for union with the god."[11] Although he did not offer the same image of rebirth, Khasim Saheb, a local Muslim, defined devotion (*ibādat*) in much the same words: "I don't believe much in this Ram story, but I believe in the basic idea of devotion which makes the devotee sacrifice everything and join with the creator. It is like what we say, '*ibādat me fanā hōnā*' (annihilating the self in devotion)." Few of the pilgrims who visit Gugudu during Muharram fail to walk through the fire, as they consider it a ritual cleansing of their mistakes and a reentering into a space of new *niyyatu*.

Most of the pilgrims who visit Gugudu make an obligatory visit to the firepit to perform water and food rituals. It is not uncommon for villages in South India that have Muharram traditions to build a temporary firepit for the occasion, around which devotees dance and tell the story of Karbala. But the firepit in Gugudu is unique in that it is not temporary. It is always there before the pīr-house. For the ten days of Muharram the firepit glows red with flames. For the rest of the year, one sees a large mound topped by a basil plant with tender green leaves. When devotees visit the pīr-house during these days, they walk around the fire-mound (*pradakṣiṇa*) before they enter the pīr-house. In the evenings, villagers join to perform various dances and songs. Usually they sing about the pīr and dance for the pīr. On Thursdays and Fridays, dancers and musicians from other villages also come to perform and show their devotion for the pīr.

3. Anjaneya and Peddamma Temples

For Hindus, two particularly important spaces around the pīr-house are the temples of Anjaneya and the village mother goddess, Peddamma. The temple of Anjaneya lies to the right of the pīr-house, separated by a wall. Meanwhile, the idol of Peddamma, which means "elder mother," or "great mother," sits a few steps away from the temple. According to the oral history commonly told in the village, Anjaneya was the first deity to visit the village. Anjaneya's image, carved in stone, is typical of other images of him found in Andhra villages. Usually sculpted on huge stones and then painted red, the images of Anjaneya are believed to protect the villages from evil. In Gugudu too, Anjaneya protected the village from impending danger after Guha's death. Thus, Anjaneya saved both Guha and the village.

Across the street, the idol of Peddamma sits under the raised platform across the pīr-house. Since women are not allowed to enter into the pīr-house, after performing the *sugar fātehā* at the pīr-house, they walk around the firepit, and then go straight to Peddamma and light lamps and offer bangles to her. During night vigils on Thursdays and Fridays, women usually spend most of the night performing various rituals such as praying, lighting lamps, garlanding the idol, and offering bangles to Peddamma. This part of the pīr-house premises is specifically reserved for women. However, both Anjaneya and Peddamma's rituals remain at the lower strata of the local divine hierarchy. Devotees who visit Gugudu still focus primarily on the pīr Kullayappa (Figure 1.4).

4. Yōgi on the Hill

There is another sacred space in Gugudu normally categorized as "Hindu": the temple of the deity locally known as *Karma Yōgi* Veera

FIGURE 1.4 Women visiting Peddamma: during the night vigils for the pīr, women spend most of the night praying to Peddamma by lighting lamps, breaking coconuts, and gifting bangles.

Brahmam, whose prophecies, known as *kāla jñānam* (The Knowledge of Time) have been popular in Andhra since the premodern period. For this he is also called *"kala jñāni."* Regionally, Veera Brahmam's asceticism and devotional practices are popular for their non-Brahmanic ways, and the deity in particular seems to signal a shift in premodern village life in Andhra, when the artisan castes made an effort at upward mobility. Contesting the Brahminic claims to asceticism and purity, Veera Brahmam developed a subaltern version of religiosity in the rural areas of Andhra.

Veera Brahmam's teachings and sainthood practices also represent the growing intersection of Hinduism and Islam. Verses of his are still popular in villages, with a mixture of Sufi and Hindu mysticism, a mixture also predominant in the Kullayappa tradition. Veera Brahmam also welcomed Muslim disciples, and in his verses he takes ideas from the Islamic and Hindu canons and erases the boundaries between them. Lying on the hill where Guha supposedly performed great *tapas* (austerity) by stepping into the fire, Veera Brahmam's temple in Gugudu draws huge numbers of devotees, drawing especially from women and lower castes. In spite of Veera Brahmam's encouragement of Muslim disciples, his temple is now largely

FIGURE 1.5 Brahmam's idol on the hill.

a "Hindu" space. Lower-caste devotees and women visiting the pīr-house make sure to visit the Veera Brahmam temple. In particular, newly married couples make an obligatory visit and light a lamp inside the tiny dwelling where Veera Brahmam resides (Figure 1.5).

The hill upon which the abode of Veera Brahmam sits is a busy place during Muharram. On the tenth day, the group of devotees circles the hill before gathering to watch the procession led by the standard of the pīr Kullayappa. "On the tenth day of Muharram, the hill looks like a jasmine hill (*mallela guṭṭa*) as hundreds and hundreds of devotees, holding lamps and huge garlands, wait for the pīrs," said Tirupatayya. When the pīrs walk closer to them, devotees excitedly throw the garlands toward them and then walk to the temple to light the lamps. Tirupatayya told me that the hill functions as a convenient spot to take *darśanam* of the pīrs.

5. Local Mosque

Like the above two rituals sites which are specific to Hindu devotees, the local mosque is a space exclusively for Muslims. This small building with four small towers (*minar*) has one big room capable of seating thirty people. Yet except during Ramadan and other Muslim festivals, most days see only four or five people attending daily prayers. The local imam visits with neighborhood and nearby Muslim families almost every day, hoping to make them attend the prayers. Still, attendance remains about the same.

Each morning at 5:00 a.m., speakers transmit the morning call to prayer, and as three or four people arrive, the imam begins the prayer. He performs five prayers, and recites chapters from the Quran or the *Faza'il-e-'amal* (The Merits of Practice) after every prayer.[12] Through donations, local Muslims recently built a cement platform and water pipes to be able to perform ablutions (*vajū*) before the prayer. During my fieldwork, the imam was also trying desperately to collect donations to purchase a coffin so that Muslim bodies could be carried to the graveyard. During our meetings, he explained to me how important it is for Muslims to depart this world with respectable final rites.

According to the imam, this mosque has at least twenty-five years of history, but until recently no one ever visited the mosque. He said, "Now at least four or five people are coming every day. It's a big change in itself. But we have a lot of Muslim families in and around Gugudu. They're all under the influence of image worship now, forever haunted by these local pīrs. The day will come when the mosque is going to have a full assembly, and we will develop this mosque as the main ritual center for local Muslims."

6. The Graves of the Muslim Muzāvars

The *muzāvar* who takes care of the pīr-house plays a crucial role in local pīr traditions. In many villages, the graveyard of *muzāvars* is located in a fixed place close to the pīr-house or *dargāh*. Very clearly these graves also demonstrate the power of specific *muzāvars* and remain symbols of their life stories. Very often, devotees and pilgrims make visits to the graves and pay respects to these ancestors by covering the graves with silky *chadars* (blankets) or sprinkling red rose petals. As elsewhere, in Gugudu these graves are close to the pīr-house, and devotees who visit the pīr-house traditionally visit these graves, too. During the tenth-day procession, the pīrs are also made to be carried into the cemetery to pay respects to the *muzāvars*. On non-Muharram days, especially Thursdays, devotees visit the graves and pay respects either by offering an embroidered blanket, sprinkling rose petals, or simply leaving some sugar at the foot of the grave. These rituals demonstrate that graves play a dominant role in the making of the religious ethos of Gugudu, and the graves remain important to the continuation of the pīr culture.

As one non-Muslim devotee named Lakṣhmi said, "I come here when I feel lonely and sad. I come all the way from my hometown, Narpala. When I come here and enter into this area, my sad feelings begin to go away, making me feel lighter. When I take the names of the pīrs, they make me remember the worst suffering that the pīrs themselves underwent. Before their suffering, mine is nothing. Even gods and saints suffer and face challenges!" For Lakṣhmi, the visit is a personal deliverance from suffering. However, for many people who visit Gugudu, the visit to the graves serves different purposes. For the village as a whole, the graves constantly remind the villagers of their local history and the history of the people who mediated their devotion to the pīr. The present *muzāvar*, Husenappa, proudly remembers the legacy of their pious ancestors who were first chosen by the pīr to perform everyday rituals and recite *fātehā* in his home.

7. Local Karbala

Many villages in South India have their own local Karbala, which is usually a local water tank, river, or well that functions much like a *tīrtha* in the Hindu tradition. This specific ritual site plays a crucial role in the enactment of the final rituals of Muharram. On the tenth day, devotees perform the final rites toward the standards of the pīrs. Usually known as *ashura* or *ṣhahādat* (the Day of Martyrdom), this ritual serves as a farewell to the pīrs until the next Muharram. Gugudu's local Karbala is an old well, the very place where the pīrs were said to have been retrieved five hundred years ago. Located at the southwest end of the village, this well is set amidst the fields which belong to Kondanna's family. Usually a desolate place, on the tenth day of Muharram this site becomes crowded, though not noisy. Thousands of devotees arrive at the well with small pots of food and juice to serve the final supper to the pīrs. They come here with sad and grief-stricken faces, and remain silent throughout the ritual. When the pīrs are given the final bath, thousands of devotees at once shout *dīn gōvindā*, another mixed term that echo the ethos of Kullayappa tradition—*dīn* means "Islamic faith," while *gōvindā* is another name for Vishnu in Hinduism.[13]

Local Karbalas have another significant ritual role. After completion of the temporary ascetic practice of *faqīri,* that had begun on the seventh day with the wearing of a red thread, on the tenth day devotees cut off their thread and throw it into the well. However, like the pīr-house, this local Karbala is not a site for everyday rituals. Except on the tenth day of Muharram, this place remains desolate, and I would usually only see Kondanna's heirs sitting there in the evenings, or village peasants stopping for a while to rest. But the place turns into a sea of people on the tenth day of Muharram, as almost every devotee and pilgrim attends the final rites of the pīrs. Failure to attend is considered inauspicious. As Tirupatayya said, "That's one reason for an increasing number of pilgrims on the ninth day. They visit Gugudu to spend one night close to the pīr and stay with the pīrs during their last hours."

Every Inch of This Village Is Pure: Routes of the Ritual Procession

Though Muharram is celebrated in many villages, with Karbala always the central narrative theme, storytellers in the different villages tell unique versions of the narrative to highlight their local pīrs, spaces, and practices. In Gugudu, this narrative practice takes on an entirely local color when Kullayappa is imagined as the pīr who wandered through each part of the village. Many local spaces are described in detail. The narrative prominently positions places like the firepit, pīr-house, Karbala well, and the *kurla guṭṭa* ("hill of the sheep") and the old temple. The most intense festival activity during Muharram occurs on the seventh and tenth days, when processions of the pīrs occur. During these processions, the pīrs visit each neighborhood in the village and provide each devotee an opportunity for *darśanam.* Villagers treat the pīr like a guest visiting their homes.

However, the processional routes travel by particular places to connect them to key moments in local history. Both processions start at the firepit, clearly linking the old and new ritual practices. From there, it moves toward the old fort on the eastern side of the village. Next, it follows a road to the graveyards of the *muzāvars,* where devotees pay respects to the family of the Muslim priest. The procession goes through every neighborhood, irrespective of caste association. Kullaya Reddi, chairman of the present temple trust committee, said, "These processional routes are fixed, and we are following an age-old practice [by taking them]. My father and grandfather told me that each route was decided by the pīr himself."

According to the *Muzāvar* Husenappa, "Most of these places—the firepit, Fort Street, the graves of the Muslim priests, the Eastern Hill, and the local Karbala—were "purified" with the *fātehā,* the first verse in the Quran, and each place is as sacred as the pīr-house." Thus the processional routes, in a way, reinforce the idea of *niyyatu* ("pure intention") and the importance of *fātehā.* The villagers undoubtedly believe that all these routes—including the starting and ending points of the procession—are, to use Narsimhulu's words, like "the boundaries of devotional experience.[14] As the procession begins from the firepit and ends at the local Karbala, we experience different levels of devotion."[15] However, if these processional routes and sacred places, in defining the boundaries of the new village and its new devotional life, give meaning to this particular locale, how do the thousands of pilgrims who visit Gugudu each year during Muharram perceive the village? Where do these pilgrims locate Gugudu on the map of their religious life? Having described the spaces of the village, we now turn to the people who consider Gugudu as *vaikuntham* or *jannat* (heavenly abode), and discuss their relationship with the village.

The Imagined Gugudu: Pilgrim's Paradise

I observed early in my research that villagers made a clear distinction between insiders and outsiders, and yet pilgrims who came from far-off places such as Tamil Nadu and Karnataka never felt out of place in Gugudu. This section of the chapter endeavors to understand the various perceptions of Gugudu of local devotees and pilgrims. I argue that sacred geography redraws normal spatial boundaries through rituals and devotional practices that pattern the map of the mind. In essence, rather than physical boundaries, devotees are tied to devotional boundaries, in turn redrawing the divide between insider (*mā ūri vāḷḷu*) and outsider *(bayaṭi vāḷḷu)*.

The above descriptions of each place and its ritual role in the village should provide a clear sense of how rituals sanctify each of those spaces. But the sanctity of these places, as well as their related narratives, also reinforces the ritual efficacy of *barkatu* and *niyyatu*. At Muharram, villagers reenact that historical memory for many purposes, including remembering the past and passing that memory to the next generation.

A feeling of "ours" is the first sign that marks this collective historical memory. In the context of this festival, local villagers assertively stake out their insider status by saying, "our festival," "our pīrs," and "our practices." This is especially significant since each village perceives a need to outdo others in terms of performing these rituals. Folk groups in the village say that their particular narrative is powerful and that other village narratives are less so. During several recording sessions, folk groups from other villages asked me to come to the ritual site in their village, because they cannot tell the story of their Muharram and their pīrs in other places. These groups attribute enormous powers to the Muharram narrative and assert that the actual power of the story originates from the pīrs as well as sacred local spaces, such as *dargāhs*, pīr-houses, the graveyards of local pīrs, and local Karbalas. Attributing these powers in such a way strengthens the feeling of "self" in terms of place and pīrs. Hence locally constituted ritual sites play a major role in the making of boundaries of insider and outsider.

Geographical boundaries are also given considerable attention during Muharram. At the end of each procession on the seventh and tenth days of

Muharram, the standards of the village pīrs are walked to the boundaries of each village and made to meet the pīrs of the other villages. Typically, the processions on the seventh and tenth days function as boundary-affirming rituals, subtly differentiating insider and outsider spaces. However, due to financial restrictions from a lack of patronage, some villages have recently begun performing the public rituals together. Many villages consider not performing Muharram as a "sin" and, an "inauspicious act" and "the sign of a bad omen." This fear of ritual failure constantly haunts them. In such cases of shared celebration, four or five villages join together, and each village installs two or three pīrs. On the seventh and tenth days, most of these pīrs meet at the borders of the villages, and all begin a joint procession from there. In such cases, the feelings of insider and outsider are erased, as the processions become a collective ritual for the participating villages.

Pilgrims and Traders

The population of Gugudu is no more than 2,700, but each year three hundred thousand pilgrims visit Gugudu on the seventh and tenth days of Muharram. They begin arriving in Gugudu on the seventh day and stay until the tenth day, departing from the village after having the final *darśanam* (Muslims use the Urdu term *ākhri*, Hindus the term *ākhri ziyāratu darśanam*) of the pīrs. What does Gugudu mean to these many pilgrims who visit during Muharram? While still celebrating Muharram in their own villages, how do these pilgrims interact with Gugudu's pīrs? (Figure 1.6.)

Recordings of various pilgrim narratives in 2007 reveal that the Kullayappa cult centered around Gugudu is a regional tradition which encompasses several hundred villages from Andhra, Tamil Nadu, and Karnataka. Though each village has its own celebration of Muharram and its own pīrs, Kullayappa has a special status among these village pīrs and impacts thousands of families who visit Gugudu each year. Of course, pilgrims who arrive in Gugudu make sure to take *darśanam* of their own local pīrs too, but on the crucial seventh and tenth days of the month they attend the processions in Gugudu. Even those pilgrims who come from Tamil Nadu and Karnataka consider Kullayappa to be a family deity, suggesting that Kullayappa transcends the status of local Hindu deity.

Though often making the pilgrimage for several generations, travelers to Gugudu are still considered outsiders. Some families stay in the old Ram Temple or rent a house temporarily. Due to the lack of basic amenities, these outsiders have to deal with many health and water issues. Most

FIGURE 1.6 Pilgrims arriving to Gugudu.

of the pilgrims pitch tents in fields outside the village, under trees or wherever they find some space. Middle class families even bring portable gas stoves, while the poor build ovens with stones or bricks. Walking through the fields on these days, one can smell the sweet flavors of biryani and spices everywhere.

Besides devotees, there are two other categories of outsiders that typically visit Gugudu during Muharram: small-scale business people and entertainment groups. On the seventh day of the festival, when huge numbers of devotees begin to arrive in Gugudu, business people set up tea stalls and tents to sell goods like toys, pictures of the pīrs and the pīr-house, and sweets. On the main road running through the village, at least hundred business stores are crammed together in a small space. Close to the temporary bus station, a big circus company occupies a huge ground with large tents. This company plays three shows every day and almost every show sells out during these ten days.

However great their profits might be, we cannot underestimate the devotional aspect also of these business people. Khaja Hussen, a small-scale businessman, said, "First we come here to pay our *ziyāratu darśanam* and do the *kandūri* food ritual, then comes business." He has been visiting Gugudu during Muharram since his grandfather took him as a boy. Various categories of these insiders and outsiders who make a trip to Gugudu clearly show their devotion to the pīr Kullayappa. For them, Kullayappa is not just a village deity; he possesses a regional importance that encompasses several thousand villages in three South Indian states, many of which they also visit for business.

Beyond Gugudu: An Extended Realm of Kullayappa

Sacred spaces within the pīr tradition, such as Gugudu, are not isolated places. A basic argument of this chapter is that the pīr devotional tradition is deeply tied to place and to local laborer and artisan caste groups, and thus it has also developed a network of relationships that spreads far and wide. As the next chapter explores, local pīr narratives tell a story of the emergence of regional sacred spaces too. Specifically, the stories about Kullayappa and local Karbala martyrs establish a sacred geography that connects many sacred shrines in the region, such as Penukonda, Guntakal, and Kadapa. As one pilgrim told me, "Gugudu is like a center that is surrounded by various sacred sites. We begin our devotional journey at Gugudu and then travel to other places like Penukonda, Kadapa, Narpala, and Guntakal. In a way, most of these sites, one way or the other, are connected with Kullayappa."

Among the many sacred locales in the region, Penukonda, Kadapa, Narpala, and Guntakal are prominent for their various sacred places and sainthood traditions. Those who tell stories about Gugudu also mention these spaces and the saints who lived there. In a way, they represent a network of village sainthood traditions, with Kullayappa as the connecting node. Lakshmamma, a seventy-year-old pilgrim who traveled all the way to Gugudu from a remote village in Karnataka, told me, "I go to all these places after my *ziyāratu darśanam* of Kullayappa. I respect all those saints, but worship only Kullayappa, who is like a thread that connects all those great pearls."

Stories about Kullayappa are what connect the personal devotion of pilgrims and devotees to the sacred shrines mentioned above. This section tries to understand the specific points where these sacred shrines connect to each other in these stories. We begin with Narpala, which is typically considered a "Hindu" ritual space. As a geographical and economic unit of administration, Gugudu falls under Narpala, which is the closest small town. Normally, since Gugudu has limited bus service, devotees visiting Gugudu arrive in Narpala by bus and then go the rest of the way by shared jeeps. Narpala also connects various other towns, such as Dharmavaram, Battala Palli, and Ananta Puram, from where hundreds of devotees come to Gugudu. But more so than this, Narpala is famous for the sacred site of Tikkayya Swami Avadhuta (1832–1952), a religious ecstatic who lived from 1900 to 1924 in Narpala.[16] In a small temple recently built near the bus station, devotees perform various "Hindu" rituals to the idol of Tikkayya Swami. Since this figure was a direct disciple of a yōgi from Karnataka, devotees from Karnataka also visit the place. Interestingly, many devotees travel to Gugudu after various rituals in Narpala to take *ziyāratu darśanam* of Kullayappa.

Seshananda Swami, the present trustee of the Tikkayya Swāmi temple, told me, "Tikkayya Swāmi used to walk to Gugudu every Thursday, and his role was very crucial in the construction of the present pīr-house in Gugudu. Each Muharram Tikkayya Swami used to donate bags and bags of sugar to the pīr." Furthermore, Seshananda Swami during our conversations tried to draw similarities between their teachings. As he explained to me, "They taught the same thing from two different aspects: intense devotion. During his lifetime, Tikkayya Swami was well-known for his intense devotion to lord Shiva. But Tikkayya Swami was also influenced by the pīr swami's teachings. In a way, Tikkayya Swami was also a disciple of the pīr. But when I was at this temple during several visits, I observed that only Hindu devotees visit and perform rituals there. Though local Muslims know about Tikkayya Swami and his stories, they consider him a "Hindu yōgi."[17] Known especially for his devotion to Shiva, Tikkaya's devotional hymns are now popular in the region.[18]

Muslims in Gugudu also tell stories about the Sufi pīr, Babā Fakhruddin, who made Penukonda his home. The shrine is said to have been popular for at least eight hundred years.[19] During the sixth century, Penukonda was famous for its Jain temples, and even now it is considered among the four most famous Jain sites in India (the others being Delhi, Kolhapur, and Jina Kanchi). In spite of its Hindu and Jain background, Penukonda is now mostly known for its *dargāh* and for the miracles of Baba Fakhruddin, who is popularly called *Babayya Swami*, and known among Hindus and Muslims as the *badshah* (emperor) of the *faqīrs*. The ritual site itself is known as the *darwaza* (door) of the *faqīrs*. Commonly both Hindu and Muslim devotees visiting Gugudu also stop at Penukonda to pay respects to Babayya Swami. The saint is popular for his *karāmatu* (miracles), and many ritual sites in Penukonda are associated with his miracles. Many spaces within the *dargāh,* too, are associated with a miracle story.

Finally, many pīr narratives in Gugudu specifically mention that traveling east is auspicious, and when I asked local devotees about this, they specifically referred to the Sufi *dargāh* in Kadapa. Many devotees who walk along the route between the two villages believe that the pīr might have walked this path too. At Kadapa, they visit a Sufi shrine. Well-known for its Sufi practices, the Kadapa *dargāh* is now the most popular Islamic shrine in the region. However, similar to any Sufi shrine, both Hindu and Muslim devotees visit the site and perform typically Sufi rituals such as gifting flowers at the graves of the pīrs. Those pilgrims who visit Gugudu from places such as Tamil Nadu and Karnataka also visit Kadapa to seek blessings from the local pīrs. However, their primary allegiance remains with Kullayappa.

The close links among these shrines reveal a shared pattern of regional devotional practices. Despite many variations, Muharram is the thread that connects most of these practices. Pilgrims who make visitations to the various sacred sites particularly chose the month of Muharram and try to cover most of these shrines during their journey, considering it as a "little *hajj*" in an appropriation of the normative Islamic pilgrimage to Mecca. Most of the Muslims from this region are small-scale businessmen who run small tea stalls, textile stores, cotton-related and tailoring shops, and auto repair shops. Due to economic limitations, they cannot afford to undertake a true *hajj,* and visiting these local shrines serves as a partial substitute. However, many non-Muslim caste groups consider local pīrs to be family deities, and make obligatory annual visits. In spite of these different goals, Hindu and Muslim devotees alike perceive continuity among these shrines and understand these practices as serving similar functions. This serves to locate the shrines in one network with a shared tradition.

CHAPTER 2 | The Pīr with a Cap: Narrating Kullayappa

Our stories become our actions
Our actions become our stories
They're all paths to reach . . . Kullayappa.

—TIRUPATAYYA FROM GUGUDU

Introduction

In many places such as Gugudu, the annual Muharram holiday does not just serve as a memory of the grandsons of the Prophet. Crossing the boundaries of normative Islamic practices, this holiday blends with local religions and thereby becomes inflected at different levels. This mode of creative blending reveals a dynamic quality to local Islam. This puts it in constant conflict with the static version of localized Islam vigorously promoted by various reformist Muslim groups. For every devotee, whether Muslim or not, a visit to Gugudu means visiting the pīr-Kullayappa. In Gugudu, it is primarily a public ritual honoring the memory of Kullayappa. Devotees tell Kullayappa's stories, remember his martyrdom on behalf of the community, and invoke his name in everyday conversation.

This chapter examines the place of the pīr in Gugudu's devotional life in order to understand how the complex tradition centered on the pīr is perceived and interpreted by the diverse caste groups whose devotional lives center around Kullayappa. To this end, this chapter will describe the origin and arrival of the pīr Kullayappa to Gugudu using stories drawn from various sources: family stories, caste stories, informal conversations with various villagers, and stories told by pilgrims visiting from various

South Indian states. The chapter has three sections: (1) a survey of the persona and ritual status of Kullayappa as depicted in family, caste, and local place histories as well as pilgrims' stories; (2) an account of how the Kullayappa cult in a general sense is perceived by diverse caste groups; and (3) stories told by pilgrims coming to Gugudu from elsewhere, which affirm the outsiders' relationship to Kullayappa as a family deity connected to their own native places. I conclude the chapter by summing up the specific interpretations of Kullayappa given by various key groups in Gugudu.

Though the basic outlines of most of these stories can be traced to a single family of Tirupatayya whose ancestors supposedly brought the standard of the pīr to the village several hundred years ago,[1] I have also collected stories from various neighborhood devotees and pilgrims who frequent Gugudu and perform various rituals at the pīr-house outside the public festivities of Muharram. Almost every village and town connected to Kullayappa observes strict pīr rituals and *faqīri* practices that evoke key events in the hagiography of Kullayappa. In Gugudu, however, ritual and story are so inseparable that enacting a ritual seems also to be a way of recollecting the hagiography of Kullayappa. Telling the story is also a way of invoking an authentic model for the performance of a ritual, enabling one to imagine a connection between one's own experience of the pīr and the experience of others who have sought the saint's blessings.

Many stories about Kullayappa invest him with an exemplary personality and even divine qualities. But the local and outsider stories which circulate among the devotees of diverse caste groups are not only about Kullayappa. They describe the intensity of ritual practices undertaken during Muharram and the memories of the hardships experienced as a result, such as working day and night to pay for the travel expenses necessary to visit the pīr. When pilgrims and devotees tell stories about Kullayappa, they also talk about their family's devotional legacy stretching back centuries, and how for them the pīr, as they explain, "opened the great door to a world of piety and prosperity."

These stories have become part of Gugudu's religious life through storytelling, dance, music, and familiar forms of folklore. In many other villages, the stories about pīrs are told by a group of narrators and folk performers in a semistructured narrative performance of a fixed time and location. The same group tells the story of Karbala each year during the ten-day Muharram. Locally called *pīrla katha ceppē vāḷḷu* ("those who tell pīr stories"), this fixed group is usually made up of performers from diverse caste groups. Devotees believe that the group's storytelling ability is itself the result of a "divine blessing" (*barkatu*) bestowed upon each member of the group. As one Muslim devotee said, "if you're not blessed by the pīr, you don't get such knowledge. Once you get that art of storytelling, you are not supposed to ignore it. Since this story is the key that keeps the village protected, the storytellers also have a certain charisma."[2]

The situation in Gugudu is different. Not only is there no group of performers, but the structure of the pīr-narratives also shifts as family stories and caste histories are combined with the story of the pīr. Moreover, the performance of the story about Kullayappa is not the main element in the observance of pīr practices in Gugudu. Rather, there are specific rituals—setting of ritual standards, obligatory prayers, the distribution of sugar *prasādam,* and practices—that are more prominent in Gugudu's practices. There is also a patterned set of Hindu rituals which includes *pradakṣiṇa,* the ritual of walking around the firepit, and *porlu daṇḍālu,* or rolling wet bodies around the firepit. Pīr observances in Gugudu also give a prominent place to vow-making, fire-walking, a certain style of preparing food (*kandūri*), fasting (*vokka poddu*), and the tradition of *faqīri.* As devotees tell stories about Kullayappa and exchange accounts of their interactions with the metal battle standards that represent the pīrs, the details of these stories legitimize and further encourage these pīr rituals. Every ritual has a story that connects it to the life of Kullayappa and his authority as a local pīr.

That authority attributed to Kullayappa raises several questions about the pīr's status and his religious role in Gugudu. Seen more broadly, it has strong religious implications for, and causes tensions with, various forms of localized Islam in Gugudu. Kullayappa is considered the heir of the Prophet and is given a spiritually higher status than the grandsons of the Prophet in the religious narratives and practices of Gugudu. His popularity complicates the concept of *pīr* and religious authority in localized Islam as well.[3] In a way, the place of Kullayappa in Gugudu seems to be an adaptation of the role of *imam* as described in Shi'i traditions, particularly in so far as the *imam* is considered a vital link between the divine being and devotees. This adaptation forces us to ask how the local community understands and interprets Muharram when such a vital link is now filled not by the *imam* as explained in localized Islam, but by a local pīr. In various forms of localized Islam, the role of an *imam* is usually given and attributed to the grandsons of the Prophet, but in places like Gugudu that role is taken by a local pīr.

With this question in mind, we can ask how local stories about families, castes, and place histories along with pilgrim stories help us to understand the religious persona of Kullayappa as analogous to the *imam* in Shi'i

Islam. Using various stories as ad hoc frames of reference, local devotees appropriate the ritual rubric of Muharram to elevate and empower their pīr.

The Host Family of the Pīr

As mentioned above, the story of Kullayappa preserved in Tirupatayya's family is a basic part of Gugudu's pīr tradition. According to numerous local accounts, the story begins several hundred years ago when a cow herder named Tirumala Koṇḍanna met a Muslim pīr in the wild forest of Gugudu. Later on, this Muslim pīr was given the name Kullayappa since he had a cap on his head. Heirs of Tirumala Koṇḍanna still live in this village and perform each Muharram ritual as their ancestor promised to the pīr. Tirupatayya, in imitation of his ancestor Koṇḍanna, plays a central role in the Muharram celebration as a "carrier of the metal god."[4] Tirupatayya's role is significant in various rituals. His role as a ritual specialist also reverses the dominance of the Brahmin caste typically found in a localized Hinduism.[5] The question of ritual purity usually identified with a Brahmin takes on a different pattern in Gugudu through the idea of *niyyatu*. Contrary to the idea of bodily purity as typically understood from a Brahminical perspective, the term *niyyatu* emphasizes the importance of "personal intention."

When I first met Tirupatayya it was not easy to make him speak, since he is a man of few words, and when he speaks he does so quietly and with an economy of words. For him, words perhaps also have a kind of magical power. At least villagers and devotees who visit Tirupatayya believe that Kullayappa speaks through him when he carries the metal battle standard of the pīr. In ordinary conversations, it seemed that he uttered no word which lacked clear purpose. Several times he declined to talk about the pīr, in spite of my persistent efforts to draw him out. When I insisted, he simply said, "Not that I don't want to. Simply, it's not coming out of me." It took a long time to convince him to tell me his family's story. Since the pīr's story is deeply connected to his family, and many pīr values are embedded in this family story, we begin with the story of Tirupatayya himself.

A Person with "Pure Intention"

As I gathered from various conversations with villagers and pilgrims, Tirupatayya is a sincere, hard-working farmer and a true family man. He is never a public person except during the seventh- and tenth-day processions of Muharram. Working hard for several hours a day, he tends to few things in life other than his only property: his fields and his cattle. He would often connect these personal matters with the idea of *niyyatu,* which he considers the hub of his life. In trying to explain what *niyyatu* means, he repeatedly came back to the idea of striving to be pure and having good intentions in one's life. Within the limits of Tirupatayya's life, practicing *niyyatu* begins with basic everyday issues such as food, marital relations, and community service.

Tirupatayya eats only homemade *rāgi mudda* (boiled cereal ball) with *pappu* (lentil soup). He has never touched alcohol in his life, "since the *pīru swāmi* never liked it," he said once during our conversations. This expression is a common one. In many villages, when people talk about personal prohibitions they often end their explanation by saying that, "going against *niyyatu* is going against the *pīru swāmi.*" The use of such an expression is a way of affirming that all their actions, whether in everyday or festive life, take their rationale from the values of the *pīru swāmi.*

In terms of other practices, carrying the metal standard of the martyr-saints is such a key practice in Tirupatayya's life that he hopes to carry the pīr till his last breath. Others notice this deep spiritual respect; during the procession devotees come running in groups to him and strain to hear his every utterance. While the procession of the well-decorated metal standard walks through the lanes of the village, devotees come and pay respects to him, while the *muzāvar* Husenappa walks in front of the pīrs. When the devotees bring sugar packets to offer to the standard, called "the metal god," the Muslim *muzāvar* recites the *fātehā,* breathing the first verse of the Quran over the sugar and then returning the sugar to the devotees. Devotees believe this Quranic utterance to have enormous magical power. They bring their sick children to the feet of the pīr, and have the *muzāvar* recite the first verse of the Quran over the body of the child. Most of the time, new-born babies are given names on this occasion. Almost every baby gets the same name: Kullayappa, if it is male, and Kullayamma, if female. Parents consider themselves fortunate if Tirupatayya utters that name and give the child a little sugar *prasādam.*

As I mentioned earlier, it was difficult to persuade Tirupatayya to tell the story of the pīr. But after a month of pressing him, Tirupatayya came one morning on his own, and began to narrate the story. While talking, we walked out of the village and took a narrow path that led us to his field. Tirupatayya spends much of his time taking care of his cattle. He is a poor and simple farmer, having just a piece of land and a few cattle. Yet he seems content with his life, his wife, and his physically disabled son. Even though Tirupatayya is eighty years old, old enough that he should stay home and rest for the remaining few days of his life, he has to work in the fields to make ends meet for his family. He says that such hardship has been common in his family ever since it came into contact with the pīr. As Tirupatayya put it, "We are supposed to live in poverty forever. We are *faqīrs* forever." He said that the *pīru swāmi* had told his ancestor, Tirumala Koṇḍanna, that the family would never have a surplus of food to save, but would barely earn its daily bread. He said,

> Whatever you get, you get it for today, and poverty is your way of life. You'll be a *faqīr* forever. That was what *pīru swāmi* told my grandfather. It was always like that. Once I got like 20,000 rupees by selling my land. That money, though a lot, didn't last for even twenty days, and then I fully realized that the pīr's words are always true, that money won't stay in our hands. With all that money, as if some bug entered my head and scratched my brain,[6] I went on a pilgrimage and returned after twenty days with only a single coin. That's it. The money was gone and I was a pauper again. Poverty remained our way of life. We're destined to get food only for this day. Living in poverty is the blessing that we received from the *pīru swāmi*. My ancestor Koṇḍanna gave the *pīru swāmi* a promise and we are keeping it. Whatever I get to eat today is enough, no worries about tomorrow. And I really enjoy poverty, though I also don't really feel like living in it.

Then Tirupatayya narrated two stories that connect his family history to village caste histories and to the oral hagiography of the *pīru swāmi*, Kullayappa. Before each segment of the story, he made the following disclaimer: "See, I'm not telling it; *pīru swāmi* makes me say these things. I truly don't know anything." At other times Tirupatayya was not a good conversationalist. For him, the moment of storytelling was almost like a possession or, to use his own words, something "coming down from the pīr into my body." As he said, "when I say something about the *pīru swāmi*, it's almost like I am being possessed by the *pīru swāmi* and he is telling the story." Switching back and forth from the personal to the communal and then from the communal to the personal, Tirupatayya's version of his family's story about the pīr has never been just personal. When I asked several caste groups in the village to tell the story, in spite of each group having its own distinct narrative, most responded by saying, "Who would be better than Tirupatayya to tell the story of this village?" Tirupatayya's story is thus story of the village, and also its Muharram celebration.

Many villages around Gugudu tell the same story about the pīr. In Gugudu's religious life, every caste group, whether Hindu or Muslim, believes that these stories teach them about the *pīru swami*. In addition, there are many secondary level narratives in circulation which are told from the viewpoint of different caste groups. Devotees are never tired of telling stories about the *pīru swami,* and in every family one finds that the same names have been given: Kullayappa, Kullayamma, Kullayi, Kullayi, Kullaya Saheb, Kullaya Bi, and Kullaya Reddi. The naming of every child has at least one personal story connected to the pīr's story. But the stories of Tirupatayya's family have now become popular far and wide, since they address many issues related to these villages and to Muharram.

Understanding Kullayappa

The current manifestation of the pīr Kullayappa is a replica that receives worship everyday in the pīr-house. For non-Muslim caste groups, Kullayappa is both a pīr and god (*pīru swāmi*), while Muslims envision him as a pīr and a *walī*, or "friend of god." Yet these differing perceptions have little effect on how the rituals are enacted either at the pīr-house or the local Karbala. As mentioned before, both local devotees and pilgrims call the pīr "*pīru swami,*" combining both Muslim and Hindu terms. In many places in Andhra, Muslim pīrs are popularly called *sufi dēvullu* (Sufi gods).[7] This naming of Kullayappa itself, as "*pīru swami,*" shows the blending of practices from Islam and South Indian Bhakti Hinduism in Gugudu.

In Gugudu, the pīr is the creator of the village, and the stories about him function as a thread connecting various caste groups to the early days of the formation of the village.[8] He is considered "*appa*"—father or lord—by all castes. Muslims, too, call him "*tōpi-walī sāhib,*" which is a literal translation of the term "Kullayappa" in Urdu. Such an image is, to use Gananath Obeyesekere's words, "an idealized father figure, who expects total filial piety, submission, and devotion. For others he is a guide directing the devotee through the tangled paths of human existence."[9] Whether Muslim or non-Muslim, lower or upper caste, the functional role of the pīr is similar in many ways and for every caste.

Devotees understand the various terms and themes in these stories in various ways, but their interpretations generally assert the legitimacy of their local identities. For example, some Vaishnavas and other non-Muslims consider him the final incarnation of Vishnu, while at least one group of orthodox Muslims in the region explains the origin of Kullayappa based on the Quran.[10] This group points to the key verse in the Quran—*al-Ikhlas,* popularly known as *khul sūrā* among local Muslims. When I asked one Muslim, he opened the Telugu translation of the Quran and read and interpreted this verse. Since Kullayappa has been a major influence in the lives of these villages for several generations, his story reveals multiple aspects of local life. The making of the pīr is deeply connected to the making of the local community.

Before the appearance of Kullayappa, the villagers were in a state that like that described by Victor Turner, as "likened to death, to being in the womb, to invisibility, to darkness, to bisexuality, to the wilderness, and eclipse of the sun or moon."[11] These images of Turner's, while describing a different context, also explain the mental state of Kondanna when he was in the wild forest which local villagers call "*daṇḍakāraṇyam,*" a mythical forest in the *Ramayana.* This story is tied to the history of Gugudu, and tells us about the transition from old to new village, and Kullayappa's role in this process. When asked about the old village, Tirupatayya and Sattar Saheb immediately said, "It's all death. There was no sun or moon there." Indeed, our earlier conversations with Tirupatayya began with him mentioning the old village.

These stories tell of the village's past, going back several generations to its beginnings with two goldsmith brothers. Goldsmiths and woodcutters are commonly stock foolish characters in the stories that local Muslims tell domestically and in public. Typically, these characters have selfish or greedy motives that drive them to the point of destruction. In one of the stories about Gugudu, the goldsmith brothers yearn for greater fame and to this end begin working on an incredible artifact made from all kinds of precious metals. Thinking about it constantly, they also dream about it, and find it miraculously standing before them the next morning. In Muslim stories, dreams are often the sphere of an intense interaction with God or a pīr. Interpretations of these dreams typically offer a resolution to a long-standing search either for practical or spiritual needs. In the context of the story of the goldsmiths, the resolution comes through the creation of a beautiful replica, which demands purity and clear devotion, but which the brothers fail to maintain. Failing to value such a miraculous object, they throw it into a deep well in the old village.

These stories about the object emphasize the importance of pious objectives in the village context. As the narratives increasingly incorporate Sufi and Shi'i symbols, the story of Kullayappa provides an "image" and an example of how the tradition of Muharram was gradually and silently changed by localized Islam in Gugudu even as its connections to Hinduism have been preserved.

Most importantly, these stories as understood by various castes in the village touch upon the Islamic notion of a single god, the intercessory powers of the pīrs, the Islamic lunar calendar, sacred visits (*ziyāratu*), and the Hindu notions of *viśva rūpam* (cosmic form), *darśanam* (sight), *punarjanma* (rebirth), and *avatāram* (incarnation). The most important aspect in the stories is the conflict between Brahmin and non-Brahmin devotional practices and the emphasis on the lower castes' simple and direct accessibility to God.

These stories also describe very specific pīr themes along similar lines to those commonly found across villages in Andhra. The themes here are tensions between old and new devotional practices, the rise of artisan communities such as goldsmiths, stonemasons, cotton carders, and peasant communities, the difference between dream and reality, the intriguing question of *niyyatu* (in the form of purity), the concept of *karāmatu* (miracle), fire as a dominant metaphor for destruction and rebirth, the importance of specific sacred places on the eastern side of the village, and of sharing the ritual meal known as *kandūri*, and finally the local usage of *dīn gōvindā* as a *mantra* for shared devotion.

Another vital aspect of these stories is the references to the origins of local pīr rituals. Furthermore, they provide a detailed framework for Muharram rituals, assigning each caste a specific role in the Muharram festivities. The narratives mention the authority that castes like Reddy and Muslims have to carry the pīrs and protect the pīr-houses.[12] Though a clear-cut division of labor is given in the stories, devotees use the words of the pīr himself—his supposed words, "the village community does this its way"—to legitimize the particular social arrangement. With these words, the pīr seems to offer a license to the people of Gugudu to perform these tasks in their village's particular way.

The greedy goldsmiths are a recurring motif in many Muslim stories. Yet in the local narrative of Gugudu they were not greedy about money matters, but sought a non-materialistic goal, though the goldsmith brothers were not clear about that goal. Their quest for that unknown goal brings the village to a point of destruction, from which an entirely new village settlement arises. This dramatic aspect of destruction by fire is now replayed every year in Gugudu. Such a desire for closer interaction with the pīr also raises questions of authority and hierarchy in sacred spaces. The story as told by the pīr, and the ritual framework that is prescribed by the pīr in the story, continue to define the public space and the Muharram festivities.[13]

Moreover, when I met these caste groups, including Muslims and *dudēkula* (a Muslim subcaste of cotton carders), they always emphasized their authority and their importance in the ritual process. Muslims, though very few in number in Gugudu, claim that Kullayappa is the heir of the Prophet. Some go so far as to point out the architectural layout of the pīr-house, in which Anjaneya's temple is constructed to appear subordinate to the pīr by being located several inches back from the pīr-house. These Muslims referred to the popular local Muslim saying that "all idols are kept twelve feet away from the mosque and the pīrs."[14] In a similar vein, the *sātāni vaiṣṇava* caste group in the village claims Kullayappa as the final avatar of Vishnu, and sings devotional hymns attributing a Vaishnava identity to him.

Between these sectarian extremes are the lower castes and artisan groups in the village, to whom Kullayappa is the one and only God. Though caste hierarchy plays a dominant role in rituals, and several of the untouchable castes are denied access to the pīr-house, Kullayappa remains the only spiritual outlet for these groups in Gugudu. Irrespective of these varied perceptions and claims, Kullayappa devotees share public devotional space by confining certain personal practices to their homes. When different caste groups visit the public space of the pīr-house, they enact the various rituals prescribed to them by the conventional narrative of the pīr. As one upper caste Hindu devotee, a Vaisya of the traders' community, put it, "Within those four walls [of one's home], he is our family deity, *kula daivam* and *iṣṭa daivaṁ* (chosen deity)."

But this does not mean that what is done in public space during Muharram is understood in the same way. In the next section, we will look at different castes' interpretations of the religious expressions and rituals done during Muharram at the pīr-house, by returning to the stories about Kullayappa.

Kullayappa and Stories of Group Identity

In this section, I will provide an analysis of various caste groups' stories about Kullayappa. These caste stories include those of: (1) local Muslims who consider Kullayappa as a mediator; (2) Vaishnava spiritual connections between the pīr and Viṣṇu; (3) various lower caste groups, including the Dalits' understanding of the pīr as a god; and (4) *dudēkula,* as a caste that facilitates the intercession.

The Embodiment of Dīn: Muslim Stories

The term *dīn* is used to denote "Islamic knowledge" in Gugudu. In most cases, either in a ritual or textual context, this term is used to limit religious discourse to the five pillars of Islam. Muslim devotees consider the image of Kullayappa an embodiment of *dīn*. As mentioned earlier, Muslims often refer to the *khul sūrā* from the Quran to explain the etymology of the term "Kullayappa." This reference functions as a way of reinforcing the Muslim-centered nature of the Kullayappa tradition. In this section, I will show some of the other ways that explain how Muslims affirm their version of the pīr Kullayappa, or "Tōpi-Walī Sāhib," as an Islamic figure.

The verses of the khul sūrā are as follows:

In the name of God, the Compassionate, the Caring,
1
Say he is God, one
God forever
Not begetting, unbigoted,
And having as an equal none
2
Say he is God, one
God the refuge
Not begetting, unbegotten,
And having as an equal none
3
Say he is God, one
God the rock
Not begetting, unbegotten,
And having as an equal none.[15]

Reciting this verse is fundamental to Islamic religious identity, and even ordinary Muslims with no extensive training in the Quran recite this verse in everyday life. In many Muslim houses, this verse can be found printed in a calligraphic design, and beautifully framed and hung on the walls. In addition, the ritual use of this verse gives it a deep resonance among Muslims. Before every new change in life, Muslims utter this verse. For instance, during marriage rituals a bridegroom utters this verse when for the first time he looks at the face of his bride. This verse serves as a similar marker of a new beginning in the case of certain public rituals.

References to the *khul sūrā* in Gugudu also touch upon the Prophet's life stories. As one Telugu Islamic scholar explained to me, "When the Prophet Mohammad was trying hard to convince the pantheists about the existence of Allah, they asked him several questions, such as: 'Who is your Allah? What does he look like? From what kind of material is he made? And who is his heir?"[16] Interestingly, the *muzāvar* Husenappa used the same questions while explaining the early stages of the life of the pīr. Remembering his ancestor's words, the *muzāvar* said that people used to ask him: "Who is Kullayappa? What does he look like? From what kind of sources did he come? And, how did he get the status of pīr? How does this local tradition fit into the history of Muharram?"

I asked these same questions of various groups of local devotees, pilgrims who had spent considerable money to travel and see Kullayappa, and temple authorities who make arrangements for the worship of the pīr, not only during Muharram but also every Thursday and Friday. At first local devotees misunderstood these questions as challenges to the existence of the pīr himself, just as was the case with those who questioned the Prophet in this way. A Muslim devotee even sarcastically pointed at me and said, "Hyderabadis like you never understand the pīr," thus condemning me to a realm of misunderstanding.

One evening I walked to a local mosque with Sattar Saheb, a local middle-class Muslim and retired teacher. During the conversation, when I asked him about the origin of the name Kullayappa, he began to describe the way the pīr first appeared in the nearby forest. From the way he told the story I knew that he had the *khul sūrā* in mind. He explained that the pīr had recited the *khul sūrā* for the first time in that village and had therefore became "Khullayappa." As Hindus cannot properly pronounce the Urdu glottal sound "*khu,*" they spell it "*ku.*"[17]

Sattar Saheb said, "We read *khul sūrā* when we are midway through a change, a shift, switching over to some new thing. Muslims read this verse at every turning point, if the turning point is by choice or by chance. Kullayappa read this verse when the old village caught fire and everything was lost. He read this *sūrā* when he led us into the new village of Gugudu. Just imagine the *shift* (here he used the English word); if there had been no *shift*, our forefathers would have died of utter poverty. When Kullayappa recited this verse, our forefathers came into this new village. They raised their families here and went back to their work. All this happened because Kullayappa recited the *khul sūrā* with pure intention (*niyyatu*). These *dēhāti* (rustic or village) people, they don't know anything about spirituality, they don't have *dīni mālumāt* (religious knowledge). Kullayappa opened their eyes to *dīn*; that's why during Muharram when they do fire-walking they say, "*dīn gōvindā*" (*dīn* is "Islamic knowledge" and *gōvindā* is equivalent to Hindu term "dharma"). In order to convince Hindu devotees, the pīr might have also used the utterance *gōvindā*. But as you can see there is nothing Hindu here. For the first time in their life even these non-Muslims were exposed to a new world of *dīn*. Indeed, *khul sūrā* opened this gate to *dīn*."

Since Sattar Saheb worked as a secondary school teacher in several villages around Gugudu, he remains well-acquainted with both Hindus and Muslims. Although his explanations are primarily Muslim-centered, and to a certain extent mosque-centered, he makes an effort to acknowledge non-Muslim viewpoints that support rituals like observing *pradakṣiṇa* (walking around the idol) and *porlu daṇḍālu* (rolling wet bodies around the firepit) at the shrine. He clearly knows that idolatry is un-Islamic, yet he argued that the metal battle standard of the pīr is not an image, but a symbol to support the memory of Muslim sainthood practices. Several conversations with him during Muharram and non-Muharram days helped me to understand this Muslim-centered argument. Here is one segment of our conversation:

AM: What is the purpose of using a material symbol or image for the pīr? How do you understand this symbol?

SS: We definitely need symbolic objects to keep our memory fresh. It is not like the Hindu notion [of idols]. For me, even a mosque is a symbol and everything in a mosque is symbolic. In a mosque we have *qibla*, we have the book, we have incense sticks, we have rosary. Similarly, we have the Muharram metal battle standards, and we give different names to them that keep their memory alive.

AM: Do you think the object makes your prayer or devotion perfect?

SS: It depends. But having an object before you helps you to focus on your devotion. You know, in devotion, one should become "*fana.*" If not, it is no devotion at all.

AM: What do you mean by the term "*fana*"?

SS: It is the same thing that Hindus call "*aikyaṁ*" (union). Of course, Muslims have five daily prayers to become "*fana,*" and various other ways. Hindus just go to the temple. Just being there is not going to help them become *fana*. Topi-Walī Saheb provided more opportunities, from *fātehā* to *faqīri,* to become *fana*. And his icon allows you to focus on every aspect of this devotion continuously.

Sattar Saheb used another commonly used term—*fana* (annihilation)—to indicate deep and passionate devotion to the pīr.[18] However, in the case of pīr-worship, non-Muslims use similar terms. While Muslims used "*fana*" and Hindus used '*aikyaṁ*' (union) to explain this process, I noticed these terms being used in several neighboring villages, and by pilgrims, too. Not surprisingly, various groups of Reformist Muslims firmly reject this idea, yet most local Muslims agree with Sattar Saheb's view. Whether Hindu or Muslim, almost all segments of the local community unquestioningly accept that as a pīr Kullayappa has an exemplary personality. Most of the metal battle standards in the village context attain similar personal and community significance.

Next, I present another interpretation, this given by the local *sātāni vaiṣṇava*, a Telugu Vaishnava caste.

Kullayappa: The "Eleventh Vishnu"

With intense devotion, surrendering totally,
They prostrate their bodies and stretch their hands towards his feet
Coming from Kambam, Garudadri, and Kadiri
Never tired of chanting *dīn gōvindā*
They utter every word for Kullayappa
. . . only Kullayappa
And their all acts culminate in Kullayappa
. . . only Kullayappa.[19]

When thirty-year-old *sātāni vaiṣṇava* Venkata Chalapati Rayalu recites the above lines from a hymn to Kullayappa, he is explicitly connecting devotees to three sites—Kambam, Garudadri, and Kadiri—which have profound Vaishnava histories and ritual traditions in Andhra.[20] Before discussing the terms "total surrender" (*prapatti*) and "intense devotion" (*kaḍu bhakti*) in this hymn, it is very important to trace the spiritual itinerary Rayalu is providing from Kambam to Kadiri, covering three Vaishnava temples from three different directions in Andhra. Kambam, Garudadri, and Kadiri are well known for their massive Narasimha (an avatar of Vishnu) temples, which attract large crowds of devotees each day. As the above hymn suggests, all those journeys end at one point, in Gugudu, at the house of Kullayappa.

Rayalu explains that his ancestors belonged to a lower caste, and converted to Vaishnavism under the influence of Ramanuja, the Vaishnava reformer in South India (1017–1137 CE). Earlier, Rayalu's family took care of a local temple, where they performed everyday rituals like *nitya puja*. Before Kullayappa, the temple had already lost its prominence, and soon had neither devotees nor protection.²¹ Even now, however, Rayalu goes to this temple every morning and evening to light a lamp and put flowers before the deity Chenna Kesava Swami. From the debris of this temple, with its broken flagpole (*dhvaja sthambham*), and from the stories told by Rayalu himself, we can assume there was once a sizeable group of devotees, before the arrival of Kullayappa to the old village.

In spite of this, Rayalu's family found the shift to the new cult easy, as they drew continuity between their own intense devotion (*bhakti*) and total surrender (*prapatti*) and their new pīr practices. Interestingly, Rayalu said, "Even after we became Vaishnavas, we never had the privilege of wearing the sacred thread, but Kullayappa gives us that privilege at least for ten days during Muharram. We wear this sacred thread that shows our intense devotion." In addition, as was narrated in the local stories, the pīr himself had assigned the task of singing hymns to the Vaishnava community, thus specifying their place in the ritual cosmos of Gugudu's Muharram. As told by Rayalu, along with the Islamic *dīn*, the *pīru swāmi* also allowed the use of *gōvindā* in the chanted mantra. *Gōvindā,* an epithet of Krishna, is the same mantra that devotees chant while on their way to the "seven-hills god" Sri Venkateswara Swami in Tirupati, one of the most popular Vaishnavite temples in South India. Interestingly though, Rayalu's family and other rural Vaishnavites focus more on Narasimha in their hymns. This specific aspect becomes evident in the above hymn, which exclusively mentions three Narasimha temples in Andhra. Most of the other villages in this region also have a strong connection with the Narasimha cult.

Describing Kullayappa as "the Eleventh Vishnu," the hymn glorifies the role of Kullayappa and explains how he finally landed in the remote fields outside of Gugudu, and impacted Tirumala Koṇḍanna, who is often characterized as a "fool and illiterate" (*mūḍhamati*) in oral narratives. Even now, villagers point out that Konḍanna was totally illiterate, and that Kullayappa visited his family only to enlighten them. Rayalu's family story tells us that before the entry of Kullayappa as the eleventh Vishnu, there was an established Vaishnava tradition in the village. However, this family's journey from Vaishnavism to the local Kullayappa cult demonstrates the centrality of Kullayappa in Gugudu. Their family never considered this cult as conflicting with their Vaishnavism, and they continued to use the same Vaishnavite rituals and vocabulary when they talked about Kullayappa.

The above hymn uses two striking Telugu terms: *bhakti* and *prapatti,* or "intense devotion" and "total surrender," respectively.[22] Whenever Rayalu tried to explain these terms, he reminded me of their place in the Vaishnava tradition. According to Rayalu, "Either in the devotion of Vishnu or Kullayappa, *prapatti* is the basic prerequisite. Just *bhakti* is not enough; it should be an intense passion for *bhakti* and then *prapatti*—absolute surrender with unwavering *niyyatu*. That's why when we go to the pīr-house we prostrate our entire body and pay respects to the pīr. And both *bhakti* and *prapatti* reach their high point when we observe *faqiri* in Muharram." When Rayalu talked about intense *bhakti*, he referred to a line in his hymn: "They get a good hold of his feet, circling their hands around the feet of the pīr, and then pay their vows."[23] However, *sātāni vaiṣṇava* are not supposed to enter the pīr-house, as they are still considered untouchables in the local caste hierarchy. They are also never allowed to touch the deity except during the Muharram procession. Explaining this, Rayalu said, "That's why those ten days of the Muharram are very important for us. If we go to the pīr-house we never get a chance to touch him, but when he comes out for evening walks on the seventh day and the tenth day, the pīr is a guest at our place. We pour water at his feet and pay respects to him by holding his feet." In spite of their lower caste status, Rayalu's family remain active participants and performers in local pīr practices, by, for example, singing hymns every Thursday night at the pīr-house during a night vigil called *jāgaraṇa*. Participation of women is high in this important temple ritual. They participate in return for the fulfillment of wishes, such as getting married and having babies.

"Drum Till You Drop Dead": Tales of Untouchable Devotees

A key part of ritual life at the pīr-house involves a group of drummers walking toward the shrine, beating their drums vigorously. This group of young and middle-aged *Mādiga*, an untouchable caste of leather workers joins the Muharram procession, particularly on the third day when for the first time devotees from various villages begin to move logs to the firepit in front of the pīr-house. As devotees from various villages transport the logs on their bull carts, the *Mādiga* drummers walk in front of the cart beating their drums. However, the real emotional force of the drumming comes into play on the seventh day of Muharram, when the firepit is lit and flames stretch toward the sky. While the drummers pour all their energy into the drums, beating them heavily and rhythmically, a group of young devotees begins to dance around the fire, moving their bodies to the rhythm.

Every Thursday evening, Gugudu becomes the center of several folk performances, and many groups from various villages come and perform dances and songs for Kullayappa. Yet the performance of drumming occurs very specifically on the tenth day of Muharram. Usually, Thursday mornings in Gugudu begin with the sound of melodious clarinets, locally called *nādaswaram sannāyi,* as the devotees begin to arrive for the morning *fātehā* ritual. Each Thursday morning, *fātehā* rituals begin at a slow pace and in a quiet mood, as the *sannāyi* musicians sitting before the pīr-house begin their concert in a manner that is highly melodious and a little melancholic. Most of the morning ritual activities seem in tune with *nādaswaram* music, which has been played by a local barber caste for several generations.

On the seventh and tenth days of Muharram, however, *Mādiga* drummers take full control over this usually quiet ritual environment, and draw the entire gathering toward them with their vigorous drumming. On the seventh and tenth days, the drummers drum relentlessly, sometimes madly, as the pīr walks past every section of the village before the procession finally arrives at the local Karbala. Thirty-five-year-old Narsimhulu said about this: "I just felt that it was my *ākhri* (final day) too." He told us this while we were having a cup of tea in the evening of the long night of the drumming. On the night of the seventh day we observed his fierce drumming. His friends danced around him, shouting, "Drum, drum, and drum till you drop dead." Responding to their shouting, Narsimhulu drummed even harder. The performance was so emotional that at certain points it seemed he would break down and fall unconscious.

Through his grandfather who taught him how to do it, Narsimhulu has a family connection to this ritual drum performance. Many of the ritual drummers told a similar story. Yet these days, more young boys join the group irrespective of caste status. For many of them, it is like an apprenticeship, with no family history of such performance during Muharram. As Narsimhulu said, "They do it for fun. I can't see drumming as fun. It is the force of devotion, and I drum because I don't have another way to pray to the *pīru swāmi.*"

Ethnomusicologist Richard Wolf, observing that Dalit communities have developed their own rhythm and dances to commemorate Muharram, states that drumming itself is "emblematic of Dalitness."[24] In a similar vein, recent initiatives between Dalit and Muslim groups have focused more on drumming as a bond among the dispossessed, building on this notion of the symbolic significance of drumming.[25] Most important, the art of drumming in Gugudu is, as Narsimhulu aptly put it, the only arena in which the untouchable castes can express their devotion to the pīr. While most villages have *pīr* performance groups which include *Mādiga* caste performers who sing together in Muharram, in Gugudu singing is completely absent; the *Mādiga* caste depends wholly on drumming to express their passionate devotion for the pīr. In many ways, the act of drumming helps these untouchable castes reinforce their identity at Muharram festivities and in village life as well, as they can openly contest local caste hierarchy.

At Muharram performances in Trinidad, anthropologist Frank Korom found that drumming has a communicative quality through which one can locate "what phase the procession is [in]."[26] By contrast, drumming in Gugudu functions as an intense devotional tool by which the devotee begins to "see" the pīr and seek a conversation with him, all while subverting the usual caste hierarchy. Narsimhulu explained this state of translating his devotion into drumming:

> It's absolutely like possession (*pūnakam*), and I perform as if the pīr possesses my body and the pīr himself is drumming inside. Ordinarily if I had to beat like that I would need enormous alcoholic support. In Muharram, while observing *faqīri*, I can't drink and can't even touch the liquor. However, *imān* (faith) and *bhakti* are more important than anything. Sometimes it is surprising even for me. The next day, when friends or villagers mention how ferocious I was the previous day, and when they begin to describe it, I am surprised and shocked. An incessant force flows into my fingers when I beat the drum before the pīr. It's the only way in which I can speak to him, and it gives me a chance to converse with him. [But] really my performance is nothing when I hear villagers remember my father and tell stories about him. So it's in my blood.

As evident from the above words, Narsimhulu sees his drumming as a strong protest against his lower status in the village. At the same time he sees the performance as a powerful expression of Gugudu's identity. As he once claimed, "Without drumming, there is no Muharram at all in this village." These two elements are so connected that when he begins to perform in front of the pīr-house, he feels like he controls that sacred space. His understanding of the pīr is closely connected to his family's own history with the pīr and with drumming. He once told me, "When I beat the drum, I'm no longer their slave. I am no longer that untouchable who just lies there like some leather *chappal*. At that point I get a feeling that I'm very powerful and directly connected to the pīr. The pīr comes out through my drumming and responds to my drumming before he moves on to any big neighborhoods." A group of untouchables was present with us as Narsimhulu was explaining this. They began to speak about various aspects of the drumming, and this eventually led one to claim that drumming is a subversive devotional tool. Yet the difference for Narsimhulu is that, as he put it, "It's in my blood." We heard from people in Gugudu and in neighboring villages that his father and grandfather, besides being great drummers, had a strong element of protest in their personalities, and they too never tolerated inequality. As Narsimhulu put it, "my parents and grandparents would always tell me that the pīr is our pīr and he came for us, the *Mādigas*, all the way."

In many villages, low-caste devotees and untouchables go so far as to deny the mediating role performed by saints and priests. They consider Kullayappa to be a god who interacts directly with his devotees. Yet to a certain extent, they still accept the authority of the local Muslim "priest," since they believe in his knowledge of the pīr. Narsimhulu said, "They know about the pīr, hence there is a point when you pay respect to the Muslim priest." Like many other caste groups, Dalits also certainly heed the words of the Muslim priest for practical devotional needs. Thus let me now describe the role of this Muslim "priest," known as a *muzāvar*, who belongs to the Muslim subcaste Dudēkula, the cotton-carders caste.[27]

Facilitating the Intercession: The Dudēkula "Priest"

My first visit to the Gugudu pīr-house was on a Thursday morning in September 2006, five months before Muharram began that year. When it is not Muharram, devotees would go directly inside the pīr-house, though rules of caste hierarchy works were in effect. Dalits do not even attempt to touch the steps of the pīr-house. Women sometimes try to touch the inside doormat, as if touching the pīr himself, until male devotees yell at them, "Hey, lady, don't touch. Go back, back!" We often heard these warnings on Thursdays and Fridays, when a large number of female devotees swarm around the entrance of the house. Devotees bring sugar, which the *muzāvar* takes to the framed photograph of the pīr (original metal battle standards are installed only during the ten days of Muharram). Reciting the *fātehā*, he then returns the half packet as *prasādam* to the devotee. Afterward, the devotee distributes the sugar to other devotees gathered around the pīr-house. Like any priest in a South Indian Hindu temple, the *muzāvar* performs all the ritual activity inside. Devotees believe that he conveys their message to the pīr by invoking the *khurānu mantram* (the chanting of the Quran), or rather, the *fātehā*, the first verse of the Quran. In essence, the *muzāvar* serves as the facilitator between devotees and the pīr. The *muzāvars* belong to the Dudēkula Muslim subcaste, which is present in many villages in Andhra.

Though most of the villages in Andhra have pīr-houses, they typically only function ritually for ten days during Muharram.[28] By contrast, the Gugudu pīr-house has an administrative system similar to many Hindu temples, though the rituals are similar in nature to any Sufi shrine. Reciting the *fātehā* is a crucial ritual inside the pīr house since it functions to connect the pīr and his devotees. Fifty-year-old Husenappa now holds the *muzāvar* position as an inherited position. Thus Husenappa's family story is the story of this particular Muslim subcaste, and his ancestor, known as Budan Saheb, performed Islamic rituals when the pīr entered the village for the first time.

Reformist Muslims consider Dudēkula Muslims as "intermediaries" (*naḍimi vāḷḷu*), oscillating between Hindu and Muslim practices. Thanks to the localization process underway, there has been an effort lately to bring them back to the "Islamic" fold, where they are given the high-status label of *nūr basha*. Husenappa's family looks like any other practicing Muslim family. Husenappa claims that his ancestors were not Hindus at any point in time, and he always emphasized to me the orthodoxy of his family's Islamic practices, such as reading the Quran, performing prayer five times a day, and practicing all the Muslim rituals of family life, from daily ones to those connected with special days like marriage and death. Husenappa and his family are very particular about fasting during the month of Ramadan, too. Husenappa never misses a single prayer in the local mosque. As a result of all this, the new groups of various reformist Muslims hold him in high regard. Husenappa's day usually begins with the morning prayer at the local mosque and ends with the night prayer. However, during Muharram, endless visitations of the devotees keep him busy at the pīr-house.

In spite of various popular and "un-Islamic" elements in many stories and anecdotes about Kullayappa, Husenappa still sees them as preserving something important of the conventional Shi'a Karbala story. According to him, the local Muharram and pīr practices are the recollection of that memory. Though he did not denigrate the stories told by Tirupatayya, Husenappa always tried to read those stories in light of the battle of Karbala, as narrated in the history of Shi'i Islam. Husenappa's perception is similar to other Muslim interpretations described above, and his life is so closely connected to this ritual process that we cannot at any point separate him from his role as a *muzāvar* or the expert in these rituals whether during Muharram or the rest of the year. During everyday rituals he performs *fātehā,* and during Muharram his role is central, from the installation of the pīrs to their final destination (also known by Muslims as *ākhri,* the "final"), in the local Karbala. For him, Kullayappa is a pīr who brought the message of Islam to the village.

When asked about *hussēniyat,* a theme that universally encompasses almost every ritual of Muharram, and about Kullayappa taking place in Gugudu, Husenappa explained:

> Everything is for Husain, but local pīrs are important too. It happens in every village. Pīrs are powerful in many ways, and these pīrs are their local messengers. People believe more in local pīrs, since they have a direct attachment to them and learn directly from them. Kullayappa pīr has such an attachment to local people. I have been an active participant in Muharram since my childhood. When my father was the *muzāvar,* he used to tell me that Islam taught him reason, and that reason led him to the pīr who provides access to Allah. I believe in the pīr, too. Devotees out of passion might be emotional and at some point tell different stories. Yet they have their own reason. For most of the devotees who come here from far and wide, it is a spiritual need. They need a guide to direct their lives. The pīr entered into this village amid groundbreaking changes in the village. Most of the people here are artisans, hard laborers, and belong to the lower caste. They didn't have spiritual access for several centuries, and the pīr opened that great door to Islam.

While explaining the specific aspect of the "door to heaven," Husenappa stressed the importance of the "great door," for which he used the Urdu term *buland darvāza.* At this point it is relevant to note that he does not use the name Kullayappa often, but rather uses the term pīr or Topi-Walī Sahib in his conversations with both Muslims and Hindus. While Hindu devotees who come to him always use the term Kullayappa or *pīru swami,* even then Husenappa consistently uses the term pīr or Topi-Walī Sahib.

In many ways, Husenappa is in charge of ritual life in and around the pīr-house and the local Karbala. Those who visit the pīr-house pay attention to his words carefully and follow his instructions strictly. He said:

> From the things I've heard from my father, the pīr's presence made this village prosperous. Before the pīr, there was nothing. It was all huge dense

forest into which even ants could not enter and crows could not fly. After the pīr, it has become a fertile land. People began to learn what's good and what's not. That's a big change which *īmān* (faith) brought into village life. That's one reason why this village has only one public event: that is Muharram. Though Hindus have several public religious festivals, like the wedding of Śrīrāmanavami or Dasarā, on their calendar, in this village they don't celebrate even a single Hindu public festival. It's only Muharram because of an intense *īmān* (faith) in Kullayappa.

Husenappa understands the arrival of the pīr as a significant shift both economically and ethically, under the Islamic term *īmān*. During our several conversations at his home, the pīr-house, and the local mosque, his emphasis was on *īmān*, which Frederick Matthewson defines as "a religious virtue that is more highly regarded by the Qur'an than Islam, 'surrender'."[29] Most of the interpretations offered by Husenappa center on this concept of *īmān*.[30] For Husenappa as for other Muslims in the village, it does not really matter if Hindus consider the pīr as a god or Vishnu's eleventh incarnation, as long as Muslims stick to their interpretations when approaching the pīr. "We still go by the *shahādā*," he says, showing a calligraphic depiction of the Quranic verse on the wall of the front room of his house. Personally, however, he would not privilege his position as a *muzāvar* in any way when at the pīr-house, openly saying that, "before the pīr, everyone is the same and equal." Positioning himself as a facilitator in the ritual process, Husenappa stated, "Their idea of my role in between them and the pīr comes from their very basic belief that the pīr is god."

Pilgrim Stories

According to the latest figures, it is estimated that three hundred thousand devotees visit Gugudu annually. As I have already mentioned, the population of Gugudu is not more than three thousand, which means that most of the devotees who visit Gugudu come as pilgrims. Gugudu is part of a network of several popular shrines, including Penukoṇḍa and Guntakal, which are also well-known for their Sufi practices. Thousands of devotees from Karnataka and Tamil Nadu visit these places as pilgrims. From the British gazetteers, we know that these places have a history of pilgrimage that stretches back several hundred years.[31] Pilgrims who visit Gugudu commonly continue their pilgrimage on to Penukoṇḍa and Guntakal.

However, the pilgrims seem to feel a special affinity for Gugudu, as can be seen in the way they speak about it in their family stories and conversations. For many of them, Gugudu is almost a home. How do they define "local," and what is local for them? I will respond to these two questions as I present various pilgrims' perceptions of Kullayappa. As in Chapter One, which describes Lakshmi Reddi and other villagers using the term *maa* or *mana* (our) in the context of the pīr, pilgrims who visit Gugudu also use such terms when talking about Kullayappa. Specifically, there are three types of pilgrims: (1) pilgrims who come for devotional purposes; (2) natives revisiting Gugudu as pilgrims; and (3) small traders. Though these three types all ascribe to common religious beliefs, there are slight differences in the way they perceive their journeys to Gugudu. For many pilgrims who visit Gugudu, this village is the home of their family deity or the pīr Kullayappa. Gugudu is not connected to their livelihood. They live with gratitude that the pīr has blessed their lives with enough resources to sustain their families. In a way, a visit to Gugudu is an obligatory vow for them. When they move through various pīr-connected places in Gugudu, they are emotionally connected to those places by various rituals. These aspects of their pilgrimages can be seen in the following examples of pilgrims.

"Devotion Is the Goal"

The first group of pilgrims visits Gugudu only for the *ziyāratu darśanam* of the pīr. This is not to say that the other pilgrim groups do not also come with devotional intentions. I learned some of the views of this group about Gugudu and their visit to the pīr when I traveled with some of them on a special bus for the hundred-mile journey from Bellari in Karnataka to Gugudu. Here I narrate two family stories from this group, one from a Muslim family and another from a non-Muslim family.

Fifty-five-year-old Mastan and his family are long-time pilgrims to Gugudu from Bellari. They come during the month of Muharram. Mastan, who now teaches at a primary school nearby to Bellari, started visiting the pīr in 1980. He said, "I was twenty-eight when I made the first *ziyāratu* to Gugudu. Since then, Gugudu has become part of our life and rituals thanks to our everyday prayers in our domestic shrine. When we arrive in Gugudu, we do not feel as if we are outsiders, but as if we are at our home. We feel the constant presence of the pīr here at every step. We know that here was the place where the pīr walked and was martyred for the *ummah* (community)." When I asked him to explain the Islamic term *ummah*, he stated: "*Ummah* is a devotional community that has faith in the Prophet and venerates the heirs of the Prophet. We perform Muharram in our village; every village does it. But coming to Gugudu is like *ziyārat* and *hajj* for our family." Pointing at the special bus by which he and seventy other devotees of different caste groups had traveled to Gugudu, he said, "When we come here, we feel that we are meeting a big *ummah* of devotees. You've seen them throughout the journey. This is the most crucial journey we make every year: during Muharram for the pīr."

During my day-long journey with these devotees, I overheard them sharing their experiences, including some miraculous stories about the pīr. Seventy-year-old Lakshmamma, one of the pilgrims, belongs to the *Lingāyat* caste in Karnataka. She has been traveling to Gugudu since her twentieth year, when she was first introduced to a Shaiva saint named Tikkayya Swami, whose shrine is located in Narpala, a town close to Gugudu.

> Devotion means reciting the hymns sung by Tikkayya Swami to me when I was twenty. Though originally from Karnataka, Tikkayya Swami visited Gugudu and was blessed by the pīr. When I heard the pīr's name from Tikkayya Swami, I turned to Kullayappa, too. When I recite the hymns of Tikkayya Swami, though they're for Siva, they also teach me about the pīr. Specifically, the ideas of *niyyatu* and *śuddhi* are the same for me. Tikkaya Swami's hymns are about the importance of purity of mind and pure intention. When I realized this connection between Tikkayya Swami's devotion for both Siva and the pīr, I began to understand his hymns more. Now I also began to understand why Tikkaya Swami, though having traveled to hundreds of places, settled close to Kullayappa.

For Lakshmamma, the shrine of Tikkayya Swami at Narpala and the shrine of Kullayappa at Gugudu are as local to her as her native village, Chellikeri, in Karnataka. As she explained, going to Gugudu is like going to a *tīrtha* (the local term used for a Hindu pilgrimage). However, when she talks about devotion, she also talks about a different kind of landscape. For her, devotion is not about land or space. She said: "Wandering saints and *faqīrs* never lived in only one place. Their death at one place might be a mere chance; they are always beyond that place. We visit Gugudu or Narpala to remember their last moments of death. Wherever these saints resided, that's my home too. That's what I learn from wandering saints such as Tikkayya Swami, who never settled in a single place, but settled in Narpala only to die after a few days. Just like Tikkayya Swami, Kullayappa was also a wandering saint, but was martyred at Gugudu."

Migration Stories

The second category of pilgrims is that of Gugudu natives who are returning for a family reunion, or visiting their family deity Kullayappa. At least
a small percentage of these pilgrims are natives of neighboring villages of
Gugudu, who migrated to far-off places in search of work. As mentioned
in Chapter 1, drought and migration are defining factors in the lives of
local peasants, farmers, and artisan castes in the district of Ananta Puram
and the many places surrounding it. Many families from villages migrate
to nearby towns and states in search of work and a livelihood. As a result,
the population of many villages in Ananta Puram district has decreased
gradually since the late nineteenth century.[32]

Before 1880, Ananta Puram and Kaḍapa districts were famous for their
weaving, and the gazetteers estimate that there were more than eleven
thousand looms operating in the early 1880s. The areas around Gugudu
were well known for silk-weaving too. By the 1880s, the market for
handloom-woven products was undergoing widespread changes as the colonial British government encouraged mercantilism, which uprooted the
caste-based handloom production of woven goods. This in turn destabi-
lized rural areas, as urban centers became key in the production process.
Thousands of villagers who used to live by handloom-weaving migrated to
the cities, and when the market began to move toward mechanization, they
completely lost their livelihoods. The constant drought and famine affected
the lives of rural agricultural societies as well. As two of the most important sources of work in the rural economy came to an end, both agricultural
and artisan groups suffered heavy losses and were forced to migrate to new
places to take up new professions.

The family of sixty-year-old Yusuf Basha is among them. His ancestors
were handloom weavers who were forced to leave that profession and turn
to petty jobs to earn their livelihoods. Yusuf Basha himself, however, has
an interesting rags-to-riches story. When his family lost their only source
of income in weaving, they almost became beggars in their own village.
He said: "Economically, our family sank to the lowest depths. Literally,
we had to beg for each meal. Then, I made a decision to become involved
in the scrap business, selling used metals. This business actually grew so
fast that we migrated to Goa after ten years and are now settled in Goa."
Yusuf Basha is now a well-settled businessman, but he has never entirely
lost his connection to Gugudu, even though the family now is limited
mostly to visiting for Muharram and the pīr Kullayappa.

Each year during the month of Muharram he and his family visit Gugudu and actively participate in local rituals such as *kandūri*. Yusuf's family also helps fund the maintenance of the local mosque, and thus they help promote localized Islam in the village, too. Yusuf's family is deeply devotional, and they sincerely believe that their *imān* in the pīr saved them during hard times. "Only *imān* saved us. Whatever our condition was, wherever we were, we never missed a single *namāz,* and we never fail to remember Tōpi-Walī Sāhib." For Yusuf's family, the mosque and the pīr-house are equally important.

Even though Yusuf's family can now afford to go to Mecca for the *hajj,* they still believe that coming to Gugudu is their *hajj*. Yusuf's wife said: "This is our annual *hajj,* since Tōpi-Walī Sāhib is our family pīr. In our family, we all perform regular *namāz* and our men go to mosques. This idea of making a choice between the mosque and the pīr-house never existed before. As pure Muslims, we do both." She repeatedly emphasized that they are "pure" (*asli*) Muslims. During our conversations, she did not make any distinction between the mosque and the pīr-house. She said: "They are not different for me or for our family. If you're differentiating between them, why should you go to *hajj* to visit a sacred shrine? For us, visiting the pīr-house is like a little *hajj*. If performing *hajj* is obligatory, visiting the pīr-house is also obligatory."

Pilgrims of Business and Devotion

Two days before the seventh-day Muharram procession, Khaja Basha arrived in Gugudu and set up his food stall on the main road of the pīr-house. He has been visiting Gugudu for at least ten years to sell food items like sweets and snacks. Khaja Basha's family in Karnataka lives on the profits from this food business. But coming to Gugudu is not just a business affair for him.

> To be honest, I never feel at home in Gugudu. But when I perform rituals for the pīr and participate in the final rites of the pīr, I feel the pīr is an intimate friend (*walī*). Many of these illiterate villagers consider the pīr as their god, but God is God (*dēvuḍu*),- none can be equal with God. If you visit my food stall in Gugudu, you can see the *shahādā*, which says "Allah is my one and only God." Kullayappa for me is only a pīr, but nonetheless an influential pīr in my life. Earlier, we used to go to Ajmer to perform the *ziyāratu* for Khaja Moinuddin Chishti. My father used to visit Ajmer each year and our family carries the name of Khaja as our

middle name. For every occasion, it was our family tradition to visit Ajmer, or perform food rituals in the name of Khaja. When I came to Gugudu by chance ten years ago, my family tradition took a new turn, and I began participating in the rituals of Tōpi-Walī Sāhib. Gradually, my food business also took a new turn, and every Muharram we began opening a store here for three days. In that way, we began to believe that Tōpi-Walī Sāhib had shown us a means of livelihood too. In a way, my livelihood and piety are connected. If you ask which comes first, it's difficult. But our family has a long tradition of piety, and after turning to Tōpi-Walī Sāhib we stayed there. Gugudu is a busy place in the month of Muharram, just like any pilgrimage place.

When Basha's family visits Gugudu, it travels to Penukonda and Guntakal to visit local Sufi shrines as well. But their allegiance remains with Tōpi-Walī Sāhib. Basha said: "We visit many places actually; I think visits are different from following one way of practice. It's not unusual that many Muslims visit several pilgrimage places and shrines in order to perform various rituals. But when we come to Gugudu and visit the pīr, we feel that this is our family tradition."

As we can observe in the above pilgrim narratives, visiting Gugudu has been a tradition for many Muslim and non-Muslim families for several centuries. These three groups of pilgrims who visit Gugudu help extend Kullayappa devotion beyond the spatial limits of the village. They also redefine the village's Muharram celebration as a coming together of a broader devotional community. Moreover, they often introduce or promote elements of localized Islam. For all those, either Muslim or non-Muslim, who visit Kullayappa, their devotion to the pīr defines the parameters of this devotional practice, which has is based in a mixture of Muslim and non-Muslim concepts.

Conclusion

Before concluding this chapter, I will sum up the various interpretations of the local pīr Kullayappa. These include the pīr as (1) village deity, (2) Muslim exemplar, (3) caste deity, and (4) martyr-saint. Though these categories are not entirely distinct from one another, it is nonetheless possible to distinguish them individually. In this section, I will elaborate on each of these specific but overlapping categories, which shed light on the multiple manifestations and interpretations of the pīr in Gugudu.

It is clear that most of the lower-caste groups perceive Kullayappa in the framework of a village deity tradition, and many of them unquestioningly consider him as their one and only deity. For such devotees, it is not unusual during Muharram to worship Fatima, the mother of Hasan and Husain, as a village goddess. In some narratives, her role is similar to Sita in the Rāmāyaṇa, and they tell stories about Fatima that portray her as the daughter of the Earth goddess.[33] In some parts of the Rayala Sima region of Andhra, the ritual events of Muharram are focused on Fatima.[34] In many villages in Telangana, Husain is considered to be a god, and some of the villages have a Hindu-style temple system, too.[35] Located centrally in these villages, these temples have even more modern facilities than Gugudu. The terms *sufi dēvuḷḷu* and *pīru dēvuḷḷu* (*dēvuḷḷu*: gods) are used for Muslim saints in most of the villages in Andhra.[36] In Muslim houses, along with Kullayappa one also finds posters of Tajuddin Baba[37] and other Quranic calligraphy, which include the *ṣhahādā* and *khul sūrā*. This is very significant, since it also shows us where these villages locate Kullayappa in their divine hierarchy. In many villages around Gugudu, Kullayappa is always prominent, even in everyday domestic rituals like *nitya pūja* and family ceremonies. However, on certain special occasions such as marriages, buying new vehicles, constructing new houses, starting a new business, signing a contract or taking up new jobs, devotees' first step is to receive the blessing of Kullayappa through recitation of the *fātehā* and distribution of sugar at the pīr-house. These specific personal rituals demonstrate the villagers' unwavering devotion to Kullayappa.

As village devotees sometimes explained to me, the difference is that the great Hindu gods Viṣhnu and Shiva inhabit the heavenly world and oversee the universe, while Kullayappa inhabits this world and oversees the universe. This significant distinction makes Kullayappa closer to them than Viṣhnu or Shiva, and in that way many castes which previously had no access to religious spaces have in Kullayappa an intimate and friendly god.

Along similar lines, each devotee and each family has an imagined past that includes the pīr at a personal and a family level, and they articulate this in various narrative forms, as well as everyday conversations and anecdotes. Most of these conversations reveal that every devotee has a very specific "image" of the pīr's appearance and personality. As in the caste narratives, these personal and family stories also try to authenticate their own version of the personality of the pīr. Each devotee strongly believes that the pīr visits his home to save his life, and devotees therefore tend to weave several personal stories around the pīr. These personal stories are mostly of three types: miracle stories, moral stories, and fire stories. In general they characterize the pīr as a generous, ethically admirable person.[38] Pilgrims tell personal stories about their access to the pīr. Many times these stories are endless and in some way connected to the firepit. Since most of the devotees give the pīr's name to their children, they also tell a wide variety of stories about this naming, and these stories are important within their kinship group. Similarly, parents tell stories about the pīr to their children about the pīr's miracles and morals.

The local story about Kullayappa as a martyr-pīr begins with the reimagining of the historical Karbala battle in local space and time. Tirupatayya told me this story when we were walking to the local Karbala one evening. The site is located toward the southern end of the village. Whereas in many other villages such a place is only symbolically significant, people in Gugudu believe that it was right there that the Karbala martyrs shed their blood and breathed for the last time. In addition, the Gugudu version of the Karbala story revises the conventional Karbala narrative, significantly displacing the historical role of Imam Husain.

For ordinary devotees, their diverse devotional practices climax in the ten-day Muharram celebration, which in Gugudu has Kullayappa at its center. How do the participants in Gugudu's Muharram connect their diverse practices and ideas during Muharram? In the next chapter, I will discuss this aspect of the holiday, where all devotional approaches to Kullayappa manifest at once in public.

| Kullayappa and the Public Rituals
of Muharram

Without Kullayappa there is no Gugudu, and without Kullayappa
there is no Muharram. Though every day is like Muharram for this
village, still the month of Muharram is the greatest public event in the
life of this village.

—KULLAYA REDDY, A FARMER FROM GUGUDU

Introduction

Since the Muharram holiday in Gugudu is grounded in the pīr traditions
and practices of Gugudu's devotional life, we cannot separate an account
of the pīr Kullayappa from a description of Muharram. This chapter explores the interrelatedness of the pīr tradition and the event of Muharram
by describing the thirteen days of ritual practices in the village, as well as
the daily ritual activities performed during non-Muharram periods, particularly on Thursdays. Together these descriptions will give an idea of the
extent to which pīr practices occur in daily non-Muharram life.

The Muharram festivities that attract hundreds of thousands of pilgrims
to Gugudu for a few days of the year are "persistent and alive" because of
the underlying local pīr tradition, and the practices associated with it that
shape locals' lives throughout the year.[1] Men practice temporary renunciation, known as *faqīri,* outside of Muharram. Women tell stories about the
pīrs during non-Muharram days too, recollecting the sacrifices made by
the pīrs: young women invoke the name of 'Ali, the father of Karbala martyrs, as their only savior, and they seek his intercession in removing their
domestic suffering. Children also sing about the pīr during their evening

playtime. Through these various narratives, rituals, and conversations, the pīr takes on multiple manifestations in everyday life. This chapter argues that without understanding these everyday practices surrounding the pīr, our perceptions of the pīr tradition and Muharram would remain incomplete, and that this more festive occasion can arise only because of this ongoing local religious commitment.

This chapter's argument has three sections: (1) an account of the thirteen-day public rituals in Muharram; (2) a survey of some of the everyday practices which are related to those done at Muharram, performed at various sacred spaces in Gugudu throughout the year; and (3) a discussion of the major themes in both everyday and public ritual practices of the pīr tradition, as they relate to Muharram.

Muharram Public Rituals: Thirteen Pure Days

During the thirteen "pure" days of Muharram, devotees participate in many types of public rituals. These culminate on the tenth day in a final ritual *ākhri* that recalls the martyrdom of the pīrs. We might call this an umbrella ritual, since most public rituals leading up to it point toward this final ritual, and since it remains the overarching frame for other aspects of the Muharram celebration. This final ritual also raises many questions about martyrdom, death, and resurrection in the context of local Muharram celebrations, and these themes are seen in each ritual through metaphors of fire, water, and graves. Each year this ritual drama of martyrdom, death, and resurrection unfolds against the backdrop of a tension between these public rituals as markers of local Islam and localized Islam as a pattern of global Islam.

Gugudu has several-centuries-long history of Muharram performances, and it is consequently of little surprise then that much of its ongoing social life is focused on the annual rituals of Muharram. So important have these performances become that other villages compete with each other and with Gugudu to host the best rituals. Because the event involves several rituals, and because there are multiple interpretations of each ritual by devotees and pilgrims, the event of Muharram in Gugudu is an extremely multifaceted event. I will present a detailed description of each day in order to capture the flavors of the event and its overarching framework. My account comes from what I heard talking to people who participate in Muharram in Gugudu. I met hundreds of devotees, including men, women, and children; farmers, peasants, artisans, teachers, mineworkers, business people. I met them on their way to Gugudu; in their own villages; in local pīr-houses that are also called *āshur khānā*;[2] in mosques, temples, and public places such as *raccabaṇḍa* (village-level informal roundtables or village squares); in tea-shops, barber shops, and at bus stops; and I met them while they were work-ing in their fields, grazing their cattle, traveling in buses or carts, and teach-ing in primary schools. I met them on ordinary days and on festive days such as Muharram and *Sri Rama Navami* (The Wedding Ceremony of Rama). Whether Hindu, Muslim, or Christian, irrespective of their religion and caste they depicted themselves as passionate devotees of Kullayappa and made it clear that Muharram is a big event in their lives. Though they know little about either Shi'a or Sunni Islam, their knowledge about Muharram or *pīrla paṇḍaga,* as handed down to them through their family and place histories, is vast, and their participation in this tradition is engaged and multifaceted.

Central to their participation is their knowledge of Kullayappa, whom they perceive in much the same way as the people of surrounding villages and towns understand the saints Shirdi Sai Baba, Tajuddin Baba, Mastan Wali, Babayya Swami, and Kullayappa. However, Kullayappa stands apart from these intercessors because of the popularity of the Muharram rituals strictly observed by both Muslim and non-Muslim groups. As I have al-ready mentioned, both Muslim and non-Muslim groups believe that Kul-layappa belongs to the *ahl-e-bait,* or what is known as the *panj-e-tan pak* (the holy and pure Prophet's family). Though non-Muslim devotees never use the common Muslim term *panj-e-tan pak,* their stories and veneration of Kullayappa and the other Karbala martyrs still identify Kullayappa as having a prominent place in the Prophet's family. They also observe Shi'a rituals, irrespective of their religion/caste backgrounds, including per-forming the vow of *faqīrs* for the final three days of Muharram.

Even before the month of Muharram begins, there is a continuous en-actment of the obligatory rituals at the pīr-house, and an attendant endless flow of pilgrims and devotees to the pīr-house. During my stay, there was a festive rush in the village two weeks before the Muharram: the pīr-house was busy with devotees performing various rituals; vehicles were arriving and departing, dropping off devotees in front of the house; children were anxiously watching the activities in the pīr-house; and devotees were handing over their packets of sugar and their incense sticks to the *muzāvar,* who took them inside and recited the *fātehā* before the framed photograph of the metal battle standard of the pīr. Soon after receiving the sugar *prasādam* back from the *muzāvar*, the devotees distributed the sugar to the people outside, and they in turn touched it to their eyes in devotion before consuming it. Then the devotees walked around the unlit firepit as they do in a Hindu temple, and women rolled their wet bodies around the firepit.

All these regular rituals took place very fast, while hundreds of devotees continued to wait outside the house for the pīr's *ziyāratu darśanam.*

"Is this not almost like Muharram for them?" I asked a pīr-house official who was overseeing the arrangements in front of the house. He replied, "Not actually. The activity you're watching now is not even 1 percent of the *huge* event of Muharram. In the month of Muharram you never get a chance to get so close to the pīr. People wait all night till the doors are opened in the morning. I can't even describe in words that rush in the Muharram month. You will see, anyways. The *pīr makānam* looks totally different in Muharram, as the real pīr will come down and you can see him directly. Direct *darśanam* makes a big difference."

Though rituals such as *ziyāratu* and *kandūri* continue into the month of Muharram, the first days of Muharram remain the center of all ritual activities in Gugudu. Beginning at the first sight of the moon on the first day, up through the tenth day of Muharram, Gugudu becomes a intense devotional center, and this activity and devotion lasts until the thirteenth day, when the pīrs again give a final *darśanam* to vast numbers of devotees. Most of these rituals are confined to the traditional rubric of Shi'i Muharram, yet interpretations and meanings change as the different groups of devotees enact each ritual. At a personal level, most of the devotees and pilgrims who visit the pīrs observe practices associated with a *faqīri* vow. Those devotees wear a red sacred thread and observe *faqīri* as a symbol of their rejection of all material and physical pleasures and luxuries. They live on bare necessities and abstain from sexual activity, enacting purity rituals as well during this time.

In 2007, the local newspapers reported that 300,000 pilgrims visited Gugudu to attend the Muharram public rituals.[3] With such crowds, many pilgrims now prefer to visit before Muharram to avoid heavy traffic and the crush that occurs during the thirteen days of the holiday. Yet thousands of devotees still believe that visiting the pīr-house during the thirteen days is auspicious and meritorious for many reasons. One commonly stated reason is that the family of the Prophet is believed to stay in the pīr-house until the tenth day's final ritual. Most of the devotees believe that this is the only occasion for the direct intercession of the pīr that is believed to "bring all good results." Most of the arrangements begin one month before the first day of Muharram. In 2007, a new *maṇṭapam* was constructed beside the pīr-house, and arrangements were also made for free meals to be served every night during the ten days.[4] The *maṇṭapam* construction was quick: the goal was to complete it by the first day of Muharram to provide enough space for the pilgrims who wanted to perform their three-day vigil rituals. However, as one temple official told me, "It is becoming highly impossible to provide three days of shelter now. Usually pilgrims rent a room some-where closer to the pīr-house, and the rentals are also going up. Some pilgrims pay even 1500 rupees for ten days, which is very expensive. For those who cannot afford those rentals, we want to make arrangements for at least one night's sleep." Though the *maṇṭapam* is relatively large, it barely accommodates more than fifty people.

During my visit, the pīr-house was decorated with colorful electric lights and the streets were cleaned. The residents of Gugudu had white-washed their houses and decorated walls with colored papers. The temple committee publicized the upcoming event by distributing posters, pam-phlets, and invitation booklets throughout the region, which is a fairly new tradition. The temple authorities, however, told me that this kind of public-ity has very little impact, since most of the pilgrims who visit Gugudu are following their family traditions. The 32-page booklet gave the details of each day's rituals at the pīr-house. But the most important part of the book-let was the list of donors from three South Indian states: Andhra, Karna-taka, and Tamil Nadu. Donations ranged from 116 rupees and to 60,000 rupees. Some donations, however, went directly into the *hunḍī*, a huge iron locker box at the entrance of the pīr-house, without public recognition.[5] The booklet briefly gives the following history of the pīr Kullayappa:

> Previously this place was the *āśramam* of Guha. As the place legend ex-plains it, it became Gugudu afterwards. It was said for several generations that the metal image of the pīr Swamy Kullayappa came into the hands of one Reddy caste devotee in a well close to this village. And then the Swamy became popular for teaching about a community that is beyond religious differences and discrimination. Since then, all communities irrespective of religion come here and perform various rituals. Every year 100,000 devo-tees visit Gugudu during the Muharram *Brahmōtsavam*.

The booklet has the picture of the ritual standards and Anjaneya on its title, and provides the details of the rituals on its third page. Though the official schedule of the rituals primarily follows the usual Muharram schedule as practiced in cities such as Hyderabad, the local practices differ in that more local temple and deity practices are included in the repertoire. Yet as I have noted earlier, the rubric of the Shi'a rituals remains the same; the devotees color it locally by calling it a form of *jātara*, a term com-monly used for a village public festival.[6] Not surprisingly, in some villages they use the term "Muharram *jātara*" too. In Gugudu, Muharram takes on this *jātara* character through entertainment and market or commercial aspects, as in the variety of food places that emerge throughout the village. During every Muharram, one big circus company pitches its tents on huge grounds on the outskirts of the village. Even many pilgrims who visit for spiritual reasons sell goods like handicrafts and pictures of the pīr, in hopes of earning money for their return fare.

To explain this complex of activity clearly, I will group the rituals that occur there into three types: (1) regular rituals, (2) special rituals, and (3) final rituals. Regular rituals have a continuity with everyday rituals done during non-Muharram periods. Called *nitya pūja* or *nitya fatehā,* these rituals continue even during the thirteen pure days.[7] Outside of Muharram, regular rituals are performed on weekdays, when it is said that "the pīrs are resting" or "taking a nap." During these resting days, devotees are not supposed to disturb the pīrs, unlike on the special days when folk performances are done.

Special rituals are performed on specific days during Muharram. Out of the thirteen days, seven are considered special days, when the pīr-house becomes the site of particular rituals like fire-walking, night walks, and other practices involving food and water. These rituals are public, and this is the time when one can see the heights of intensity to which devotion can reach.

The third type of ritual is *ākhri*, the final rituals, when it is time to bid farewell to the pīrs. At these times, mourning and sorrow engulf the whole village.

As is the case elsewhere on the subcontinent, in Gugudu, too, the Muharram observances begin on the day of the first sighting of the moon. In 2007, this happened the night before January 21. Devotees began to arrive in the evening, awaiting the presence of the moon. Since it is the first opportunity for *darśanam* of the pīr after one year, all waited for this auspicious moment.

The First Day and the First Moon-Sighting: Pradhama Darśanam

It was the night of January 20, 2007. Hundreds of devotees were waiting outside the pīr-house to witness the auspicious moment that would allow the first sight of the pīr that year. They were gazing into the sky for the crescent moon, and then anxiously looking at the entry of the pīr house for the first *darśanam* of Kullayappa. The pīr-house was bright with colorful electric lights arranged in the shape of a chariot, pulled by three horses, racing into the battlefield as if the pīrs would be riding them. Sitting before the pīr-house, a group of ten musicians played the clarinet *nādaswaram,* just as they provide ceremonial music for most of the rituals at the pīr-house, and at other ritual sites during Muharram.

Before the moon sighting, hundreds of devotees had gathered to find a place to sit or stand at the pīr-house. By 9:00 p.m., the entire place was so filled that there was hardly any space to stand. Inside the pīr-house, the sweet smell of fresh incense sticks was in the air. The *muzāvar* Husenappa, Tirupatayya, Lakshmi Reddi, and other temple authorities were actively engaged in a ritual called "bringing down the chest of the pīrs." During a prior meeting with the *muzāvar,* he had told me that he and the others had to observe strict purity rituals before they could touch the pīrs. "We are all very particular about it. All those who participate in bringing down the chest of the pīrs and opening it have to be strictly pure."

At 9:30 p.m. sharp, the *muzāvar* brought down an old chest containing nine pīrs. The pīrs were covered in heavy cloth mixed with sandalwood powder. When he opened the chest, the smell of the sandalwood filled the air. As we watched, the *muzāvar* took out all the metal standards one by one, and finally took out the tall, heavy metal image of the pīr himself. Then he handed the standard over to Tirupatayya, who was in a ritual costume specially worn for this occasion. As soon as Tirupatayya took it out, he brought it out to the front door of the house and showed it to the public, who was excited to finally have direct *darśanam* of the pīr. It was the first sight of the *pīr swami,* and people shouted slogans like, "*Yaah,*" "*Kullayappa,*" "*Dīn Gōvindā,*" and "*Dīn Shah Husain.*" The ritual of the *pradhama darśanam* had not lasted even five minutes when the replicas were again bundled into the box, where they would remain until being removed for cleaning the following day.

Day Two: Fire Rituals

Digging the firepit is an important ritual because it brings together various caste groups in Gugudu. Many castes participate and tell diverse stories about their activities related to the firepit. When devotees visit the pīr-house, they first pay their respects to the firepit. Muslims recite the *fātehā* when they approach the firepit, while Hindus circumambulate and prostrate in front of it. Both Hindu and Muslim devotees poke incense sticks into the pit and light them. The second-day digging acquires community significance, as all castes actively join hands and share in this activity. In a way, fire rituals replace the well-known urban Muharram ritual, *mātam,* self-flagellation.[8] As Hyder observed it, "Just like the *mātam,* fire-walking is a spectacle in which individual men show off the strength and resilience of their bodies in the face of real or imagined threats to their devotion and to their community's existence."[9] In many places in Andhra, Muharram devotees consider the ritual of fire-walking as a test of their devotion, too. Hyder has pointed out that the participation of Hindus "transcends the exoteric Shi'ism,"[10] and Muharram devotees see themselves as belonging to a single community irrespective of caste, class, and religious distinctions. Many aspects of story-telling and ritual practice richly contribute to this sense of a special community identity, and in the case of Gugudu, the pīr-Kullayappa becomes the unifying focus.

Still clearly conscious of their caste and class variations, these members of the Muharram community share their devotional experiences in songs, stories and memories. But they continuously claim their close access to the pīrs in a playful and competitive way.[11] Villagers blend personal and place stories within the broader narrative of Karbala.

The fire rituals begin on the second day of Muharram. As described in the official brochure quoted above, there are three types of fire rituals in the thirteen-day festival, including the digging of the firepit on the second day, the small fire-walk on the seventh day, and the final long fire-walk on the tenth day. Each fire-walking day has a clear connection to something in the Karbala story. In addition, I found during my fieldwork that a fourth type of fire-walk occurs on the fourth day in many places. This ritual is performed by women on this day which commemorates the martyrdom of the new bridegroom, Qasim. This is not mentioned in the brochures, and the ritual remains "unofficial and private," with most devotees never considering this as a main ritual. Few even talk about it. In this ritual, women meet at an open place in their neighborhood, imagine it as a firepit, and play around it in a circle. Many women sing songs and tell stories during this ritual. Devotees say that they feel the constant presence of Fatima at this firepit, in a mode similar to what happens in the urban *majlis,* the religious sermons during Muharram.[12] As one performer, Saidamma, explained to me, "Fatima is always there," pointing to the belief among these women that Fatima visits them during such imagined fire-walks. Referring to the presence of Fatima is a very common motif in Karbala narratives. In many villages, Fatima (locally called "Fatamma") acquires the significance of a local deity. The women decorate a handlike symbol similar to any ritual standard and perform rituals for Fatima.

Day Three: Installing the Pīrs

On the third day of Muharram, while some devotees were still busy digging the firepit outside the pīr-house, a group of ten devotees began the process of cleaning the metal battle standards. This cleaning ritual is called *śuddhi*. It begins early the morning after the first *darśanam*, after the group of ten have had a pure bath. Then, they enter into the house while the *muzāvar* recites the *fātehā*. There were at least ten people who began to work on each pīr, first cleaning them with water, then scrubbing them with dry coconut and tamarind husks. Husenappa was continuously reciting *fātehā* during this cleaning process. It was a long process, but when they were done with this cleaning, to use the words of Husenappa, each metal battle standard was as shiny as a mirror. Finally, red and green clothes were put on each metal battle standard.

Only "pure" castes, such as Muslims and the Reddy farming caste, were allowed to enter into the house to participate in this specific ritual. But standards of purity went beyond just caste status during the cleaning process. Throughout, Husenappa was giving instructions regarding purity to the cleaners. All of the ritualists had to take a complete bath, and then when they entered into the house, had to pay their respects to the pīrs. While they did this, Husenappa recited the *fātehā* over each of them. Husenappa told me, "If you're not pure, you cannot even enter and touch the pīrs."

Each standard was carefully and respectfully handled while being cleaned. Though each has a very specific identity—Kullayappa, Husain, Hassan, Qasim, Abbas, and so on—and devotees call them by those specific names, for newcomers it is impossible to differentiate one standard from another. But those devotees who make frequent visits to the pīr-house clearly know the identities of each, and could easily differentiate Kullayappa from the other standards. Once in their ritual costumes, the figures of the saints become easier to identify. Husain wears a red costume and Hassan a green one. Kullayappa wears both colors. After being wrapped in heavy costumes, the metal battle standards are installed in a horizontal row, with Kullayappa at the center and each family member of the Prophet arrayed beside him. Now the pīrs are ready for regular rituals like *nitya fātehā* or *fātehā puja,* as they are to be performed during Muharram.

Day Four: Nitya Fātehā

As I have mentioned before, five of the thirteen days of public rituals during Muharram are set aside for regular rituals like *nitya fātehā* or *fātehā pūja.* These regular rituals begin on the fourth day and continue on the sixth, eighth, eleventh, and twelfth days. These are considered the resting days for the pīrs after each day of hectic public rituals. During these regular rituals, devotees are not supposed to disturb the rest or sleep of the pīrs.

However, regular rituals such as reciting the *fātehā* and burning incense sticks continue. As soon as the devotees arrive in Gugudu, they find a place under a tree or in a field to pitch a tent. As the final fire-walking day approaches, more and more tents and temporary arrangements are put up around the village. Even with this apparently endless flow of devotees, the rituals inside the pīr-house continue just the same. As Husenappa said, "The only difference is that we have more devotees coming to the pīr-house, and sometimes it is really hard to control the crowds. Ritually, nothing changes, but we strongly believe that the pīrs are resting for the day and getting up in the evenings. Inside the pīr-house, it is a quiet and calm environment, while outside the house, a lot of activity goes on. Since we have a lot of devotees coming to perform the *fātehā*, I take the help of other Muslims, too, in reciting the *fātehā*."

Public Processions: Sarigettu, or Walking Around the Village

As the days of the public processions approach, the intensity of emotion increases in the village. Villagers call these public performances during Muharram *sarigettu* (*shahar gastī* in Urdu), meaning "cordoning off the city." It is a common term in cities for Muharram public processions, but in Gugudu, it is altered into *sarigettu* colloquially. *Shahar gastī* is an Urdu expression, and village Muslims commonly use it on other occasions, but when it comes to Muharram public processions even Muslims use *sarigettu*, which now is used only in the context of Muharram. When I tried to use the original Urdu word with Muslims, they were confused (or rather, they thought I was confused) and told me to say "*sarigettu*" instead of "*shahar gastī*." This experience made me realize that the precise use of religious vocabulary in Gugudu is often crucial. Though these terms have both an ordinary meaning in everyday life and a technical meaning in localized Islam, they acquire another exclusive and specific meaning in the context of the religious rituals in Gugudu during Muharram.

Sarigettu processions are common practice during the public events of Muharram in Gugudu. They begin on the fifth day, and are performed on the seventh and tenth days as well. These days correspond to the sequence of the battle of Karbala, and mark the memory of the Karbala martyrdom. Historically, the fifth day is significant as the day when the first martyrdom took place at Karbala. On this day, Shi'as in Hyderabad and other urban areas pay tribute to the two sons of Zainab, who were martyred on this day, by narrating this story and performing a brief procession in their memory.[13]

Day Seven: Rituals in Memory of Qasim

The seventh day is significant as the day of the martyrdom of Qasim, the thirteen-year-old son of Imam Husain and newly married bridegroom.

The first *sarigettu* procession ritual, which is known as *chinna sarigettu* ("brief walk around the village") takes place on this day. Besides the death of Qasim, the seventh day of Muharram marks the day that water was cut off at Karbala. For the warriors and Karbala martyrs, this meant that they were without sustenance. In Gugudu, by performing various food and water rituals, devotees believe that the hungry and thirsty Karbala martyrs visit the firepit to receive food and water. This is also the day when the pīrs visit the homes of devotees for the first time.

In honor of the Karbala martyrs, locals distribute food and water to the pilgrims. The morning rituals begin with the recitation of the *fātehā* as devotees visit the pīr, along with the distribution of food and sherbet to pilgrims. It is one of the busiest days during Muharram. Every hour of this day is considered pure, and various places in Gugudu hummed with the activities of devotees, including the pīr-house, firepit, the graves of *muzāvars*, the holy well, the Brahmam's temple on the hill, the local mosque, and the local Karbala. After visiting the pīr-house, during my visit, I went around the village, which was filled with devotees. During non-Muharram days, many places in the village are totally empty, but on this day, I could not even remember that quietness, as thousands of devotees filled the village. Every space was full, including the fields and hills. Pilgrims pitched their tents wherever they found a little space. They had also set up little ovens, and some even brought gas cylinders and stoves, where they prepared their lunch and dinner between visits to various sacred spaces in and around the village.

The rituals on the seventh day require stricter observance than other days, since this day prepares everyone for the final rituals on the tenth day. Devotees observe four specific rituals on this day: (1) offering of sherbet and water to the martyrs, (2) taking the *faqīri* vow in memory of the martyrs, (3) beginning a three-day fasting (this is done only by women), and (4) a brief fire-walk.

By the afternoon, the surroundings of the firepit were busy, as Muslim women from local and neighboring villages began to bring sherbet-pots for Qasim and other Karbala martyrs. The women came in large processions accompanied by drumming, reciting the *fātehā* before they put the sherbet-pots in front of the firepit. Small red and black pots, covered by leaves, tied by a red thread, and decorated with sandalwood paste marks, carried the sweet offering made of brown sugar, coconut, and basil leaves. This is one of the most popular rituals for Muslim women, and they play a key role in it. After this water ritual, Muslim women begin their three-day fast.

This is also the first day of the *faqīri* vow. Men buy a sacred thread, and after pure baths they go to the pīr-house, where the *muzāvar* recite the *fātehā* over the thread before they tie it on to mark the start of the vow. Some Hindu and Muslim women begin a three-day fast (Muslims use the term *satāve ke rōje,* meaning "the seventh-day fasting," while Hindus call it *okka poddulu,* or "fasting days"). Finally, the first public procession, which remembers Qasim and Abbas, occurs late at night. The procession starts after 9:00 p.m. and continues for three hours. Compared to the tenth-day procession, this is a relatively brief affair.

Final Rituals: Farewell to the Pīrs

"I can't believe that we are doing these funerary rites for our beloved pīrs" said one non-Muslim devotee on the tenth day. Those who visit Gugudu undergo a similarly ambiguous and intense feeling of separation when they participate in the final rites for the pīrs. This feeling is ambiguous because most of the devotees consider these final rites to be technically funerary rites, even though they also certainly believe that the pīrs are with them forever. As one devotee put it, "They're always there, alive and receiving every aspect of our devotion. If they're not alive there, how are we going to survive? They have no death. So performing funerary rites for them seems to me to be unfair."

As the tenth day begins, the emotional intensity increases in the village, as devotees begin to arrive in even greater numbers to attend the final rituals of Kullayappa and the other Karbala martyrs. It is a day of mourning and the funerary rites for the martyrs. Before the moment of the final departure, the other rituals specified for the tenth day are performed: fire-walking, folk performances such as drumming, dances, and music, and finally *sarigettu* and *meravaṇi* (the public procession around the village). When I was there, the place bustled with activity that day, as several folk troupes had joined to commemorate the Karbala martyrs. The transporting of logs and firewood by heavy vehicles, trucks, tractors, and carts, which had begun a couple of days before the beginning of Muharram, continued all the way to the tenth day. At 5:00 p.m., as thousands of devotees anxiously waited, the *muzāvar* read the *fātehā* and lit the firepit. Afterward, everyone joined him in saying the *fātehā* as the flames went up. Folk groups began dancing and singing.

Though music and dance are the most active part of weekly Thursday rituals, on the seventh and tenth days of Muharram more folk performance troupes from different villages joined the endless chain of performance of various folk genres. Most of the performances combined diverse folk forms of music and dance. Several of these folk groups have been performing at Muharram for several generations, and they all claim that they represent a legacy of several centuries.

The performances continued for hours, until it was time for the pīr's final procession. As the drumming continued, I walked into the pīr-house. Inside, the pīrs were being decorated for the great procession. Meanwhile, a group of people with long, heavy, red royal umbrellas and torches burned with a lot of coconut pieces, walked toward Tirupatayya's home to invite his family to the pīr-house in a ceremonious way. I recalled the moment told by Tirupatayya when five decades ago he had to carry the *pīru swāmi* for the first time:

> As that night was coming closer I began to feel like I was shivering. I took my bath. One should really have a complete bath and observe total purification before touching the *pīru swāmi*. I had my dinner early. I barely ate anything. It was the evening, . . . a great evening in my life. It was a new beginning in my life. How did this beginning turn out? When it was midnight, a long procession with *nādasvaram* flowed towards our place, and the elders of the village were present before me. They took me to the *pīr-makānam* with all the traditional formalities. It was wonderful to see all the village walking behind me with great respect and expectation, too, respect since I would be continuing the ritual tradition and expectation that I successfully continue the ritual.

The scene in 2007 was more formal than he described in this earlier story. The welcoming procession, carrying long, burning torches and playing *nādasvaram* music, reached the house of Tirupatayya to formally invite him and his nephews to the holy well near the entrance of the village. It was customary that one must take a ritual bath in the well before he can hold the pīrs. As the long torches showed the path and the procession followed them, Tirupatayya and his family bathed in the holy well and returned to their house. It took them more than an hour to put on their costumes. When they came out of the house, dressed in heavy clothing and wearing fabulous red and green turbans on their heads, I barely recognized them. I felt like I had never seen these people before, they looked so different in their festival costumes.

The auspicious and magnificent moment of the carrying out of the *pīru swāmi* had arrived. Huge gold-embroidered and red-colored umbrellas were waiting outside the pīr-house, the firepit was burning red, and the drumming and *nādasvaram* were competing with one another. The devotees continuously shouted, "*Dīn Gōvindā*," and "*Shah Husain Dīn*," as at least ten people carried the heavy *pīru swāmi* out. It was like a royal procession. Tirupatayya picked up the *pīru swāmi* and handed it to his nephew.

The great procession then began from the pīr-house, as the *muzāvar* recited the *fātehā* before the firepit. A number of policemen and local security volunteers with red turbans kept the crowds in order, as devotees anxiously waited for their turn to take *darśanam* of the pīr. The procession moved forward, Tirupatayya walking in front of the pīr, distributing sugar *prasādam*. The devotees came forward to touch the pīr. Women tried to touch their newborn babies to the saint. Many prostrated their wet bodies in front of the pīr. The procession took the pīrs through the major streets and to the major sites; at first they went to the holy well, the mosque, and Fort Street, then down the eastern street to the graves. Finally, they returned to the firepit before the early morning. The *muzāvar* recited the *fātehā* again, and the pīrs were taken back into the pīr-house.

Many ritual elements of Muharram reached their culmination when this final day approached. The procession on the seventh day seemed a preparation for the final walk on the tenth, which is clearly the most important day of celebration in the village. The number of devotees into Gugudu multiplied on the eighth day. As the Public Road Transport Corporations from various states increased the frequency of bus services, tens of thousands of devotees began to arrive. Despite the large police force and youth volunteers present, it was hard to control the rush of devotees at the pīr-house. When I walked up the hill and looked down, it looked like a sea of people flowing into the village.

Each devotee walking into the village went straight to the pīr-house, where several thousand others had already been waiting for many hours to take *darśanam* of the pīr. Each devotee strives to get a clear view of the pīr. However, as on regular days no one was being allowed into the house. As they stood at the steps of the house, folding their hands with devotion, volunteers came and took the sugar packets from their hands Along with the *muzāvar* Husenappa who was now inside the house, there were four or five local Muslim elders reciting the *fātehā* before the pīr. On this day, state-level political leaders and officials also visited the pīr-house. When they arrived, they were taken directly to the house and given special *darśanam.*

Nevertheless, the most important ritual activity of the day is the fire-walk, since this is the first time the pīrs walk over the fire. Tens of thousands of devotees swarm around the firepit to watch this fantastic moment. Then the pīrs arrived and stood before the firepit, getting ready for the fire-walk.

The fire-walk began with the recitation of Quranic verses starting with the *fātehā.* While the *muzāvar* recited the verses, with sugar in both hands, volunteers with long wooden poles flattened the heavy fire blocks and paved the way for the walk. At the end of the recitation, the *muzāvar* sprinkled the sugar over the fire and then walked over it for the first time. Then others, carrying the ritual standards, crossed over it with their bare feet. While this was going on, devotees chanted *"Dīn Gōvindā"* in high-pitched voices. This continued for a long time as many groups of people began to walk across the fire happily. As the fire-walk came close to an end, finally the pīr Kullayappa, sitting in the lap of the nephew of Tirupatayya, crossed the fire amidst loud chants that echoed around the village. After this final fire-walk, the standards were once again carried into the pīr-house, where they were put to sleep by being covered with a red cloth. After this, the pīrs are considered to be martyrs.

Akhri (The Final Day)

As the sun rose over the eastern hill of the village, the day began with *kandūri* rituals in front of the firepit. When I arrived there after breakfast, the firepit was surrounded by a huge pool of blood. It turned my white sneakers to red. I walked slowly past hundreds of people who were busy sacrificing goats and chickens. I could not escape from the blood spraying onto my clothes. Almost every Muslim in the village was here, performing the ritual of *zubah,* surrounded by hundreds of non-Muslims who were bringing sacrificial animals to the pīr-house.

After the *kandūri* meals, devotees waited for the last rites of the pīrs, which began at 4:00 p.m. As the sun went down, the village felt like it was covered in a shroud of sorrow. Without a trace of festivity or celebration, it was as if there had been a death in one of the families. The pīr-house made preparations for the farewell to the martyrs. The *nādasvaram* slowly filled the air; its happy melody had gone, replaced by the quiet, sad tune of the *sannāyi.* As the chanting of *"Dīn Gōvindā"* filled the air, the pīrs walked over to the firepit. The *muzāvar* recited the *fātehā*. Now the saddened procession continued through the streets. Devotees eagerly came forward to take final *darśanam*. They would not see the pīrs again until next year, so they stayed as long as possible for the chance now, straining to see up close or touch the pīrs. One additional ritual occurs during the final walk: as the pīrs walked through the streets, women brought several pots of water and poured them at their feet. Along with the water, they brought incense sticks and burned them before the pīrs. As some women poured the water, several women rolled their wet bodies around the pīrs.

Final Bath

As the procession reached the local Karbala, there were already several thousand devotees sitting or standing, eagerly waiting with food to give to the pīrs before they are given their final bath. Local Karbala is the final ritual site in any village Muharram, where the last rites for the pīrs are performed. Usually, these local Karbalas are close to a water source like a well or river. The final ritual has two activities: removing the pīrs' costumes and giving them a final bath, symbolically of their dead bodies. Most of these rituals are reminiscent of Islamic death rites. This ritual is called *ākhri* (the final) in Urdu or *jaladhi* (to immerse in water) in Telugu.

The imagined battlefield of the local Karbala is spread amidst the four hills across several acres. A dried-up well in the middle of this place remains the center of the Gugudu's Karbala. It took at least three hours for the procession to reach there. When the pīrs reached the well, again there were loud chants of "*Dīn Gōvindā*" and "*Shah Husain Dīn.*" As soon as the pīrs arrived, the *muzāvar* recited the *fātehā*. Devotees uncovered the food they had brought as a symbolic gesture that the food had now been given to the pīrs. The *muzāvar* and other Muslims from the village removed the costumes of the pīrs one by one and placed them in a specially prepared swing with colorful flags. It took more than an hour to complete this. As devotees sat or stood somberly around the local Karbala, the *muzāvar* took each pīr into his hands while reading the *fātehā*. He began to remove the costumes and wash each standard carefully as if he was washing a dead body. The place was filled by scattered clouds of sweet incense. The devotees prepared to finally say goodbye to their beloved pīrs.

During this ritual, non-Muslims are not allowed to touch the bodies of the pīrs, and even Tirupatayya's family stays away from this ritual. The work is done by the *muzāvar*, with the help of other Muslims. The entire process took more than two hours, with three or four Muslims carefully taking out each pīr and removing their costumes while reciting verses from the Quran. After the cleaning, and some further recitation, the *muzāvar* distributed a special kind of bread made specifically for this occasion. After eating the bread as *prasādam,* each devotee opened the food he or she had brought for the pīrs' final supper. They all offered a pinch of food to the pīrs and took the remaining food with them.

The procession left the local Karbala and walked with the swing to the pīr-house. As we turned back, Muslim women began singing *alvidā* (farewell songs for the Martyrs). At the house, the *muzāvar* recited *fātehā* over the food the devotees ate, and the *ākhri* ritual came to an end. Devotees paid a final visit to the house and the firepit. Though most of the devotees strongly believe that the pīrs have no death and argue that the pīrs are present in their everyday life, all participated in these final rites in a sorrowful manner. It felt as if a cloud of death hung over our heads, and every devotee's face looked thin and grave, as if they had indeed lost their *appa*, their father and their only deity.

In the public ritual of Muharram, we encounter a wide variety of religious themes, and many of the interpretations given by devotees help us to comprehend the contours of their worldview. In spite of their differing conceptions of life and death, these devotees share many pīr narratives and notions of devotional practice. Both local practices and localized Islam come into play in these public rituals.

Most of these devotees feel that the pīr visits their home during this procession. Though the pīrs also take a walk around the village on the tenth day, for most of the devotees, the seventh day walk is more auspicious, and they consider a personal visit paid by the pīr to shower *barkatu* (blessing) over their place and family. Though surrounded by thousands of other devotees, people being visited experience these little moments in the presence of the pīr in an intimate and reflexive manner. As they prostrate before the pīrs, they shut their eyes for a few moments, allowing themselves to experience the presence of the pīr. This procession, which seems to function at an external, communal level, becomes an internal experience at each doorstep. Even though the pīr is taken on a fixed route, to set destinations, each devotee who is visited feels as though she is paid a personal visit to her home.

During the procession, I also observed that as volunteers cleared the way for the pīrs, at times the carriers of the pīrs just stopped. Elders would push the carrier, and tell him again and again, "move, move." But he did not move even an inch forward. Several people told me that this was due to the stubbornness of the pīr. In many instances, devotees would attribute this to particular emotions of the pīr. They said, "the pīr is mad," "the pīrs are sulky," or "the pīrs are happy now." Attributing human emotions to the battle standards is a common feature in almost every village Muharram, since in a village life ritual standards transform into "live" pīrs.

Everyday Practices and Muharram

This section offers an attempt to understand daily ritual activity during Muharram. My argument is divided into three sections: (1) a description of the ritual, (2) local interpretations of the ritual by actors involved, and (3) analysis of the ritual as it relates to the pīr tradition. Much of this section is based on informal conversations I had with devotees at these daily rituals during Muharram. I have also included material from observations of these rituals at the pīr-house; structured and unstructured interviews with the priests at the pīr-house, Anjaneya Temple, Veera Brahmam's temple, and the local mosque; interviews with regular ritual performers such as the *nādasvaram* musicians; and interviews with small business owners selling goods like sugar packets and dry coconut near the pīr-house.[14] I will begin with one everyday ritual, *nitya fātehā pūja*, the act of reciting Quranic verses and burning incense sticks.

Everyday Rituals: Nitya Fātehā Pūja

Common terms for the daily ritual activities of the pīr tradition include *nitya fātehā, nitya pūja, nitya namāzu,* and *nitya malidaa or kandūri. Nitya pūja* is familiar as a Hindu term used for daily ritual activities either at a temple or home shrine. In his study on Sri Lankan Munneswaram temples, the anthropologist Rohan Bastin has emphasized the importance of *nitya pūja* and has argued that by performing this "barest minimum" act, the priests try to maintain the potency of the temple.[15] In many places in Andhra, where there has been an attempt to save old temples from destruction, a Brahmin priest lights a single lamp before the deity at least twice a day as just such a "barest minimum" act. When I asked a seventy-year-old Brahmin priest, "What is the point of just lighting a lamp when not even a single devotee visits the temple?" He replied: "I'm doing this for myself and God's sake, not for everybody. I sincerely believe that this God and his abode deserve at least *nitya pūja*. And this is good for the village, too." The practice of *nitya pūja* means constant offering and constant puja, but practically speaking it refers often to just the daily lighting of lamps. However, in Gugudu, the pīr-house *nitya pūja* acquires a slightly different connotation. It is called *nitya fātehā pūja,* that is, lighting incense sticks and also reciting the *fātehā.*

The daily rituals at the pīr-house may also include *nitya fātehā* and *nitya namāzu,* which translate into "daily recital of *fātehā*" and "daily prayer" respectively. *Namāzu,* as prayer, of course, is a practice of localized Islam, but interestingly, non-Muslim devotees use *nitya namāzu* in their everyday conversations, too, making it clear that the action is just as much about devotion to the pīr as about prayer in any conventional Islamic sense. However, usage of religious vocabulary can still be very careful in this context, as Muslims use the Arabic term *namāz* to specify Islamic prayer.

Pilgrims visit the pīr-house and do *nitya fātehā* inside by offering several packets of sugar. This specific ritual is also called *fātehā cadiviṁpu.* The term *cadiviṁpu* is a term with deep associations with gifting. It is a common ritual in marriages, when parties from both sides participate in a specific gift-giving ritual. In Gugudu, non-Muslims use the expression in combination with *fātehā.* Devotees often visit the pīr-house with their entire families. While women wait outside the house praying to the pīr, men go inside and offer the sugar packet on behalf of the family. The *muzāvar* takes the sugar packet to the photo-image of the pīr and recites the *fātehā* after placing some sugar before the pīr. He then returns the remaining sugar to the man who offered it; these actions are similar to any Hindu temple, and the *muzāvar* is often called a *"Muslim pujari."* Those who make the offering might further distribute the sugar as *prasādam,* first among their family members and then to the other devotees gathered around. Devotees generally save some of the sugar to take home and place before the images of Kullayappa in their home shrines.

After offering sugar at the pīr-house, the entire family walks around the firepit. Called *pradakṣiṇa,* this ritual is also the same as what can be seen at a Hindu temple. After this circumambulation, the devotees take a pinch of ash from the firepit and apply it to their forehead, an action also typical in Hindu practice. Next they visit the shrine of Anjaneya and break a dry coconut and receive *kumkuma,* sacred red powder, from the Vaishnava priest. These actions are markedly Hindu, and nothing comparable is done at the pīr-house. Indeed, breaking a coconut or applying the sacred red powder is considered un-Islamic. The third step in this ritual routine is to put a lamp at the image of the village goddess, four or five feet away from the pīr-house. This offering is typically performed by women.

The residents of Gugudu also engage in this daily ritual routine. As the call for morning prayer echoes from the distant mosque and slowly awakens the residents of the village, many begin the day with a formal visit to the pīr-house, while others turn toward and face the pīr-house as a way of paying respect to the pīr. As those who go to the pīr-house arrive, they go straight to the entrance and pay respects to the pīr by folding their hands in *namaskaram*. If they are Muslims, they recite the *fātehā*. If they are Hindus they go to the firepit and take a pinch of ash from the firepit ad apply it to their foreheads. Some of the villagers who do not go to the pīr-house daily make it a point to go on Thursdays and Fridays, undertaking this same ritual routine.

Thursday: Ziyāratu Darśanaṁ, or Visiting the Shrine

Many Muslim shrines are busy on Thursdays and Fridays, and this day is called *ziyāratu darśanaṁ rōju* (the day of visiting the shrine). On Thursdays, one sees pilgrims arriving to Gugudu from all different directions by carts, jeeps, cars, tourist buses, and on foot. Most of the pilgrims reach the pīr-house by morning, and proceed to make arrangements to offer a ritual meal, or *kandūri*. By the afternoon, they will have the food ready for the *fātehā*, when the *muzāvar* will come to the pīr-house after his noon prayers in the local mosque. The *muzāvar* Husēnappa told me while we were walking toward the local mosque for the early morning prayer (*fazar*), "Some days, I couldn't even fulfill my noon and evening prayers. Usually I would attend the early morning prayers, and then reach the *pīr makānam*, where I would stay for the entire day until midnight. I never miss the *fazar namāz*. It's the only *namāz* that I can perform with a peaceful mind in my everyday life. It gives me enough energy to get through my daily chores."[16]

Thursday is the day when devotees are busy enacting various rituals in memory of the pīrs. I will discuss the three most important activities: (1) *kandūri*, (2) *ziyāratu darśanam*, and (3) evening folk performances.

Kandūri, or the Food Ritual for the Hungry Pīr

In Gugudu, a visit to the pīr-house serves two functions—paying respect to the pīr and fulfilling vows (*mannat*).[17] Devotees begin to arrive in specially arranged buses, and by the afternoon the place smells of spicy, hot *biryāni* and other dishes prepared in metal pots over temporary mud or stone ovens. When the food is ready, devotees form a small amount of the dish into the shape of a horse[18] and place it in a covered plate. This is then carried toward the pīr-house in a small procession accompanied by *nādasvaram sannāyi* music.

Kandūri is a lively ritual of sharing meals. Men, women, and children express happiness as they perform the ritual, since most of them have been fasting for at least three days. Several premodern classical Telugu verses describe these *kandūri* rituals, suggesting that the *kandūri* has been popular for at least several centuries.[19] In earlier times, this ritual space was reserved for women, and men were not even allowed to see the food. Nowadays, while women still play an active role in the ritual, men participate in many ways such as building the oven, preparing the meat or vegetables, and even cooking.

According to Amina, a middle-aged Muslim woman from a neighboring village, "Bodily purity is the prerequisite for *kandūri* ritual. When Hindu women begin to perform this ritual, they take a complete bath in the holy well close to the pīr-house, while their men go to the firepit to perform a goat sacrifice." This act of sacrifice by Hindus is done according to the Islamic ritual called *zubah*, in which the throat of an animal is cut while reciting Quranic verse. Non-Muslims consider it "forbidden food" (*haram*) if they did not have the *zubah* done by a Muslim. So the purity emphasized by Amina is accomplished at two levels in this context: first, by purifying the bodies of women who will prepare *kandūri*, and second, by purifying the body of the animal that is to be offered to the pīr.

After cooking the *kandūri* meal, devotees serve it first to the pīrs, by making the *muzāvar* recite the *fātehā* at the pīr-house. Some families also make a vow to serve food for a certain number of poor, and fulfill this vow on Thursdays or Fridays. But generally only family members share the food that remains after the offering. Most of the families consider *kandūri* the first step toward visiting the shrine, *ziyāratu*. The ritual commemorates a specific event from the narratives of the pīr. As explained by many devotees, the current practice of *kandūri* originated from this story.

A visit to a holy place is locally called *ziyāratu darśanam* or *zaaratu*, and it is an everyday occurrence in Gugudu, with many also devoting all of Thursday to this ritual. In the Kullayappa tradition, the concept of *ziyāratu* overlaps with concepts of *darśanam* and *iṣṭa daivam*, notions well-known in South Indian *bhakti* religiosity.

In Gugudu, visits to sacred sites are of two types: primary visits occur during regular days, including Thursdays and Fridays, and secondary visits occur during the month of Muharram. Daily *ziyārat* helps visitors start their day afresh. For devotees, the pīr is a reliable adviser in every act of life, either materialistic or spiritual. In a way, these worshippers make him a witness to the events of their personal lives, such as when they move into a new house, buy new things, send children to school, setting dates for marriages, name newborn children, and take vows for childbirth. Before beginning anything important, they make a *ziyārat,* or vow, to the *pīru swāmi*, offering sugar while having the *fātehā* recited. Once the vow is accepted, they will come back and perform the ritual *kandūri* meal.

In many ways, the pīr plays the role of *iṣṭa daivam* (chosen deity), in the manner typical of Hindu devotional practice across South India. Though Muslims consider Kullayappa a *walī*,[20] in practice their reverence, too, for him seems similar to what is done for an *iṣṭa daivam.*

Evening Music and Dances

During non-Muharram days, especially Thursday evenings, folk-performance groups from other villages visit the pīr-house to perform, often for the entire night, before returning the next morning.[21] The firepit at the pīr-house is the locus of all these folk performances, and thus it is a center for much of community life in Gugudu. When the performers are dancers, they form a circle around the firepit and join hands in a dance known as *alāvā aḍugulu* in Telugu; the term translates into "the firepit step dance." As with other dances during Muharram, the audience eventually joins hands and also dances around the firepit with the performers.

Major Themes in the Muharram Celebration

In this section, I briefly discuss how the practices of Muharram represent the ritualization of the local pīr tradition, in so far as the pīr is the paradigmatic element in public activities of the holiday. Though devotees stick to a basic ritual framework provided by the events of Karbala from the Shi'a traditions, the actual experience of Muharram varies as various caste groups constantly add to or adjust the basic pattern. In Gugudu's Muharram celebration, the values and themes of local religious life give a new rationale for Muharram, as the portrayal of Kullayappa as a member of the Prophet's family makes clear.

The exemplary personality attributed to the pīr Kullayappa in Muharram reflects the appropriation of values and practices from an uninstitutionalized Sufism and to a lesser extent South Indian *bhakti* tradition.

I use the term "uninstitutionalized Sufism" here to mean that what is practiced and valued in the context cannot be traced to specific Sufi orders (*silsilah*s), and that ritual frameworks are instead defined by local devotional networks.[22]

It is very clear that devotees from both Muslim and non-Muslim caste groups consider the pīr Kullayappa to be a member of the Prophet's family. They also give him a role in their lives similar to the imams typical of Shiism. In the local Muharram narrative, the *ahl-e-bayt* or the family of the Prophet has more than five members. Outside the conventional five (the Prophet, Fatima, 'Ali, Husain, and Hasan), the three brothers of Kullayappa are also added.

Public rituals such as *kandūri, ākhri, ziyāratu,* processions such as *china sarigettu, peda sarigettu,* and the personal ritual *faqīri* constantly emphasize the power and authority of the pīr. At every public ritual, the devotees continuously use the expression *"dīn gōvindā."* As one might expect, the origin of this term is attributed to the pīr himself. When the pīr made his first appearance, he taught his first devotee Tirumala Kondanna to utter this "difficult" phrase that combines the Islamic term *dīn* with the Hindu epithet *Gōvindā*. At first, it was hard for Tirumala Kondanna to utter it, but after he began to try it became natural to him. When I asked the *muzāvar* about such expressions in Gugudu, he explained to me various other terms that combine Islam and Hinduism. He referred to mixed terms like *ziyāratu darśanam, fātehā puja,* and explained them through the impact of the Sufi pīrs. He said:

My father used to tell me about these mixed words. When Sufi pīrs like Penukonda Fakhruddin visited villages, they first tried to get used to the local practices themselves with local devotional terms, and most of these pīrs began to combine these terms with locally popular religions to spread the message of their Sufi *silsilah*. I think the term "Kullayappa" is also of similar usage.

This specific usage of mixed terminology spreads over every aspect of rituals and activities around the house. Though pīr-house is the most common usage, some non-local devotees use *pīr guḍi* or *pīr-makānam gudi,* which means "temple of the pīr-house." As one enters the premises of the pīr-house, he hears more such mixed devotional terms, and they are indispensable in any conversation. *Sarigettu meravaṇi* is one such prominent mixed word, used by devotees during processions. This very broad term not only signifies the procession of the pīrs, but also reflects a heightened devotional attitude.

In Gugudu, Muharram processions are not just occasions for the recollection of the martyrs, but also intense devotional practices in which the pīr is imagined as a guest coming in procession to visit homes in the village. The visit of guests of such importance is considered very rare. Nevertheless, many villagers deliberately claim that these guests are visiting only their house and their family. To make guests feel welcome, and interested in coming again, they work hard to make the premises clean, attractive, and pure. As I observed during my fieldwork in Gugudu and neighboring villages, almost every family in most of these villages kept some hours of the day aside to clean and make the house pure (*pak*) as an open invitation to the pīrs. They start whitewashing their houses at least a month before Muharram, and carefully decorate the lower parts of their walls with red color and small white depictions of the ritual standards, neatly specifying three fingers and an oval shaped image with little moons on it. "If you're not *pak* (pure), the pīr even won't spare a look at you," said one female devotee. As I was watching her standing before her house, she had beautifully drawn a tiny image of the ritual standard on the red-coated lower part of the wall. She said, "This is little *pīr swami*. It's as auspicious as white rice powder design (in Telugu, "muggu") before my house."

When the pīrs walk through the streets in a public procession, it is also a moment in which some devotees say that they have a dialogue with the pīrs. As they consider this walking a visit to their house, they also personalize this public procession. They narrate several stories to demonstrate this aspect of personalization. I have observed a clear pattern in public pīr processions which begin at the pīr-house and continue in the direction of the devotee's house. At first, the pīrs cross the outer space of the pīr-house, which is also called *nadi boddu*. This *nadi boddu* is a clearly defined public space in any village where people meet for social activities and meetings along with public religious performances. However, during Muharram these spaces acquire multiple meanings as the pīrs move about them. As long as the pīrs move around or walk within this public space, they remain public pīrs. As soon as they cross this *nadi boddu* and begin to walk into the streets, they become "personal" pīrs for each group in the village.[23] Many Muharram narratives in Telugu talk particularly about these boundaries and non-Muslim neighborhoods in the village. Some narratives describe in detail the ritual process that Hassan and Husain observed before going into battle at Karbala. While describing this process, many Telugu narratives also provide a route map of the processions on the seventh and tenth days of Muharram. For instance:

They've been to the farmers' neighborhood,
The farmers gave them long grain rice.
They've been to potters' neighborhood,
The potters gave them nice pots for sherbet.
They've been to the vaiśyas' neighborhood,
The vaiśyas gave them incense sticks.
They've been to the mādiga neighborhoods
The mādiga came with drums.

These door-to-door rituals are followed very carefully in almost all villages, and the performance of drumming takes on a significant part of the ritual process. In addition, these rituals specify the patronage system of Muharram in a village. Interestingly, most of these neighborhoods are considered "impure" in traditional Hindu terms. However, in the context of Muharram, as non-Muslims clearly observe purity rituals, these barriers are erased temporarily.

When the pīrs arrive to the neighborhood, women in particular bring several pots of water from their homes and pour them over the feet of the men carrying the standards of the pīrs, as if they were pouring water on the feet of the pīrs themselves. In addition, they bring garlands of flowers or coconuts to honor the pīrs. It is always their personal moment with the pīrs; they pray for their families and they publicly display the signs of their vow (*mannat*). Some even arrange for private drummers to invite the pīrs. Almost every devotee personalizes this experience in such a way that the pīrs are given emotions, too. "The pīrs' eyes were so bright when they came to our house." "For some reason, their faces were saddened." "The color of the pīrs clothing suddenly changed." These are typical comments in such moments. Clearly, other devotees might have a totally different feeling at these moments. But they will record each moment of these public processions and recollect them throughout the year.

The above descriptions and discussion give us a sense of the extent to which the pīrs impact the lives of devotees, both publically and personally. During these processions, some devotees display a total surrender to the pīrs, known as *prapatti* or *imān*. The terms *bhakti* and *prapatti, ibādat,* and *imān* are commonly used. Though *bhakti* and *ibādat* have a similar meaning to the English term "devotion," the other two terms have different meanings. *Prapatti* is a Vaishnavite term to denote "total surrender," while *imān* is an Islamic term meaning "faith." Devotees use these terms with two referents: first, in reference to the body and, second, to the mind, by constant recollection or *japam*. To express *prapatti*, non-Muslim communities perform *porlu daṇḍālu* (rolling the wet bodies), which Muslims consider to be a "bad ritual."[24] Many Muslim women consider this kind of bodily ritual even as "depopularizing" (to use their Urdu phrase, *badnām karnā*) Muharram or "disrespecting the *pīrs*." A sixty-year-old Imam Bibi said, "Muharram is an occasion to recollect memories of the pīrs (*zikr*). Constant recollection, *fātehā,* and fasting are the three means of total devotion. They cover both body and mind rituals, but non-Muslims excessively depend upon bodily rituals like *porlu daṁḍālu and pradakṣiṇa.*"

Pīrs and Persons: Toward *Faqīri*

In this chapter, I have provided a description of various public rituals that occur during Muharram in Gugudu. However, I have not dealt with one very specific ritual, *faqīri,* which typically lasts from the seventh to tenth day, and in some instances is done for forty days. Villagers consider *faqīri* to be a personal ritual that develops their ethical character, and as a spiritual device that infuses their everyday lives with religious values. *Faqīri,* though practiced in a collective way in the context of the thirteen-day public rituals of Muharram, is a strongly individualized practice. The next chapter will focus on this practice, and the diverse interpretations by which this temporary ascetic practice is understood in Gugudu.

CHAPTER 4 | *Faqīri*: Practicing Temporary Asceticism

For us, Kullayappa is the only God. All his stories and all his remembrances and every act we perform in his name are inseparable from our everyday life. We know other gods too, but they're not part of our world; only Kullayappa lives with us and stays with us in our village. He is the only God who came down all this way to reach us. And we pour all our energies to reach him again. He pulls us towards him as the village had pulled him towards it.

—LAKSHMI REDDI (85)[1]

Faqr faqīri—"Poverty is my pride."

—PROPHET MUHAMMAD[2]

Introduction

Born into a non-Muslim farming community, local agriculturalist and Muharram ritual expert Lakshmi Reddi visits the village pīr-house every morning and evening to pay respects to the pīr Kullayappa. Invoking the name of the pīr, Lakshmi Reddi asks the *muzāvar* to recite the first verse of the Quran.[3] But when Reddi visits the pīr-house on the seventh day of Muharram, his actions indicate that this is a special occasion for him. After taking a bath in the holy well, he goes to the pīr-house and hands to the *muzāvar* the red thread that he has made specifically for this occasion. The thread symbolizes the martyrdom of the pīr. For all devotees, wearing the thread means following the path of the pīr. After laying the sacred thread in front of the ritual standard of the pīr, the *muzāvar* recites the first verse of the Quran and returns the thread to Lakshmi Reddi, who then puts it around his neck.

This ritual formally marks the undertaking of *faqīri*, which Reddi and other devotees like him in Gugudu enact during Muharram. Both Hindus and Muslims observe the ritual of *faqīri* in the memory of the Muslim martyrs. When these villagers use the term *faqīri*, however, they mean by it is not only the enactment of three-day ritual vow, but also a specific way of life as ordained by the pīr.

In Gugudu and its neighboring villages, it is customary for every devotee to observe *faqīri* or (as it is called in Telugu) *faqīru dīkṣa*, during Muharram. For three days they observe a fast called *okka poddu* (literally "one meal" in Telugu). They eat what they believe the pīr ate and they follow his example to demonstrate their devotion to him. The observance of *faqīri* reveals their passionate devotion to the pīrs, and also their efforts to refashion their personal lives after the ethical model of the pīr. However, as part of the Muharram tradition, these *faqīri* rituals by extension help to refashion the interaction between a person and the devotional community, in that the pīr Kullayappa will remain their model throughout life, providing guidance for how to eat, sleep, and do work in the fields or cattlesheds. This chapter argues that *faqīri* acquires the status of an alternate and temporary ascetic practice by a blending of Muslim and Hindu ascetic practices, such as the case of Gugudu's own story. The practice of *faqīri* replicates the movement of Gugudu from a wilderness *(araṇyam)* to a village *(ūru)* with a clearly defined community life.

Geographically, Gugudu as a village *(ūru)* is not one village, but a combination of two villages, the old village *(pāta ūru)* and the new village *(kotta ūru)*. Villagers believe that the entry of the pīr brought a "good turn" to the village, in terms of physical surroundings and the well-being of the community in the face of endlessly recurring drought conditions. The act of *faqīri* marks this specific turn in the life of Gugudu. For that reason, in addition to being called "the village of the *pīru swāmi*" or the "village of Muharram," Gugudu is also called the village of the *faqīrs*. The oral history of the village suggests that the practice of *faqīri* began at the same time as did the public ritual of Muharram.

Faqīri is an Arabic term that derives from *faqr,* meaning "poverty." Across the Islamic world, *faqīri* is an act of embracing poverty on the path of purification, but in Gugudu, it also is connected to the journey of devotion to local saints and pīrs.[4] In Gugudu, the village legend narrates that *faqīri* began when Lakshmi Reddi's ancestor Kondanna was personally blessed by the pīr and advised to perform *faqīri* annually during Muharram. Although Reddi feels that he has a special place in the practice of *faqīri* in Gugudu, he is not alone in its practice. However, he also asserts that he was born to perform *faqīri* and claims that it is the pīr himself who chose those who will lead a *faqīri* life. These people, like Reddi, try to continue the lessons they learned from *faqīri* throughout the rest of the year. Thousands of devotees who make a visit to Gugudu enact *faqīri* as temporary asceticism for a few days during the month of Muharram. In this chapter, along with the personal story of Lakshmi Reddi, I will focus on other devotee narratives from Gugudu's Muharram celebration. We shall see that these devotees understand *faqīri* as an alternative system to the more conventional modes of asceticism, particularly as it relocates the location of *tapas* away from the wilderness (*araṇyam*), where it so commonly occurs in the ascetic practices of Hinduism. This chapter will also explore the question of how non-Muslims perform *faqīri* as a local version of asceticism highlighting the significance of community life in the village (*ūru*), rather than as asceticism born out of the wilderness (*araṇyam*). I will also describe lower-caste Muslim practices of *faqīri,* so that we gain a sense of the shape of the ritual in different social groups.

This chapter has three parts: first, it offers a general account of asceticism in South Asia to highlight the shift to temporary ascetic practice as practiced in Gugudu; second, it presents the individual narratives of local ascetics; and third, it offers some specific interpretations of this locally inflected ascetic practice and its place in the tradition of Muharram.

Within Hindu traditions, the practice of asceticism has been conceived of as a means to transcend the social world, and as a "complete abandonment of all social life."[5] Patrick Olivelle notes five defining elements of the traditional Hindu system of asceticism: (1) the cutting of social and kinship ties; (2) an itinerant lifestyle, without a fixed home; (3) mendicancy, associated with the abandonment of socially recognized economic activities and the ownership of property, especially food; (4) abandonment of ritual activities customary within society; and (5) adherence to celibacy. In this system, ascetic life is a fixed path that cannot be taken up by members of all castes and is often limited to Brahmins.

In Islam, the practice of asceticism is also often restricted to particular social groups. Regarding asceticism as conducive to mystical experience, Sufis follow several ascetic practices, many of which are esoteric in their interpretation. The practice of *faqīri* is considered by different Sufi orders to be an exclusive tradition with rigorous rituals. Various studies on Islam understand the practice of *faqīri* as a specific Sufi esoteric act, or a practice at the lower end of the Sufi hierarchy of mystical practices.[6] In many of these studies, *faqīrs* are seen as a distinctive group with special powers and ritual practices. Often, as Richard Eaton observed, the term is applied to a particular person with extraordinary miraculous powers, or persons who choose a specific religious path by joining a *faqīr* order.[7] The classical definition of asceticism in the Islamic tradition has three stages: (1) renunciation of the world; (2) renunciation of the happy feeling of having achieved renunciation; and (3) the stage in which the ascetic regards the world as so unimportant "that he no longer looks at it."[8] For all their differences, both Islam and Hinduism in South Asia both distinguish asceticism as a set of austere practices that transcend the social world and its boundaries, but are appropriate for relatively few people.

The Idea of Temporary Asceticism

Departing from what we might expect based on these standard accounts of asceticism in South Asia, evidence from Gugudu indicates that *faqīri* is undertaken as a temporary practice which in fact ultimately reaffirms the social world rather than transcends it. In a way typical of *vrata* practice, both Hindus and Muslim during Muharram enact *faqīri* for either three or forty days, but devotees claim that the results of *faqīri* stay with them throughout the rest of the year, transformed into an ethical model for ordinary actions. Most of the devotees perceive temporary asceticism as producing an inner state that transcends external acts like visiting the pīr-house, circling around the firepit, and other food rituals. Contrary to the classical understandings of asceticism in Hinduism and Islam, the temporary asceticism found in Gugudu is a largely unrestricted practice whose practitioners retain their places within the social sphere. At the same time, *faqīri* does have some of the social features typical of traditional asceticism. It contests usual hierarchies and social boundaries by allowing the members of all groups into an open ritual arena.

Most importantly, Dalits and women undertake *faqīri* in various forms. While Dalits consider *faqīri* an opportunity to participate in ascetic practice, women consider it a *vrata* (vow) and perform it for themselves or on behalf of men. As opposed to traditional notions of asceticism in both Hinduism and Islam, this practice connects various aspects of social life, including the temple and village deity practices. In the process, the practice of temporary asceticism systematically shifts the ascetic from the wilderness (*araṇyam*) to the center of the village (*ūru*).[9] In Gugudu, this form of ascetic practice enforces social cohesion, as *faqīrs* strictly adhere to various village-centered responsibilities and rituals. Like *vrata* and other Hindu vows, *faqīri* insists upon certain restrictions. However, while *vrata* is aimed at wish fulfillment, the practice of *faqīri* provides a model for an ideal way of life that individuals chose to continue throughout their lives. In addition, within some family traditions, *faqīri* functions as a method for teaching ethics, collective responsibility, and as a path beyond the self (the feeling of *sva* or *svantam* as expressed in Telugu).

In Gugudu and many other villages in Andhra, the practice of *faqīri* during Muharram is understood as a lifestyle rather than a temporary mode of religious practice. In the public festivities of Muharram, non-Brahmin caste groups construct an active ascetic practice that encourages ritual communication and moral understanding between different social and religious groups. This can be considered a "transfer of ritual"—"a shift of a (rite or) ritual into another or changed context"[10]—in so far as the practices of *faqīri* are shifted to the context of Muharram. This transfer of ritual is yet another tool to authenticate the power of the local pīr during Muharram, while not undermining the emphasis on allegiance to the Prophet's family so characteristic of Muharram in the Shi'a world. In addition, the modes and strategies which village devotees use to connect the local pīrs with the Karbala martyrs joins them in the processes of localized Islam, especially when local pīrs are perceived to be part of the family of the Prophet. This expansion of the genealogy of the Prophet's family is a foundational aspect in the embedding of Islam in the public events of Muharram. Performing *faqīri* becomes one of the ways for devotees to express their love for the Prophet's family.

Faqīri is practiced in various ways during the year, and devotees observe *faqīri* practices on non-Muharram days as well. They begin *faqīri* three days before Thursday or Friday, or if they live close to Gugudu village, they begin any Thursday or Friday after a visit to the pīr-house. Such devotees will observe their *faqīri* vows for an entire week. Yet as one non-Muslim devotee, Narayana, explained it, *faqīri* during Muharram is always considered to be "powerful and more efficacious." Fifty-year-old Narayana lives in Narpala, a semiurban place close to Gugudu. He visits Gugudu every Thursday with his family and observes *faqīri* both during Muharram and occasionally on non-Muharram days. Narayana claims that his family began to observe *faqīri* at least ten generations ago, and if one counts each generation as roughly twenty-five years, this meant his family had been observing *faqīri* for more than two centuries.

Narayana is not exceptional; many families go back several generations when they talk about *faqīri*. These families make a concerted effort to impart the practices and ethics of *faqīri* to their children through stories, anecdotes, and personal memories. The key parts of this are the establishment of the pīr as family deity, and *faqīri* as a family practice.

The Triangle of *Faqīri*: *Barkatu*, *Niyyatu*, and *Faqīri* Narratives

Caste groups make a clear distinction between an ordinary person and *faqīri*, even when that person may outwardly only be *faqīr* or "pure" by wearing the sacred thread. Similarly, Gugudu is commonly portrayed as a village with *niyyatu* and *barkatu*, clean and prosperous at both a personal and communal level. Often, villages associated with a particular pīr are seen to possess a collective personality similar to the imagined personality of the village pīr. Thus for many pilgrims and villagers, Gugudu has the personality of Kullayappa. If a person behaves improperly, villagers feel that it is a "blot on the very personality of the pīr," in this case on Kullayappa. This is one direct way in which the local pīr is made into a role model. Examination of a few life stories demonstrates how the ethical process of person building is also village building. The image of Gugudu is so closely tied to the pīr that when I told friends in Ananta Puram that I was going to Gugudu, they immediately said, "Oh, it's Kullayappa village," and followed that up by suggesting that while there I meet the heirs of Tirumala Kondanna and their families.

Lakshmi Reddi: *Faqiri* as a Model

Although for most devotees *faqīri* is a temporary ascetic practice, Lakshmi Reddi has made it his life's purpose, and he abides by the *faqīri* lifestyle throughout the year. Eighty-five-year-old Reddi, the heir of Kondanna, is unmarried. He says he has never owned anything himself and proclaims that poverty is his pride. In December 2006 when I met him for the first time, he was living with his brother's family. It was a very small house with a small verandah, one big room, and one kitchen. One afternoon when I visited, Reddi had eaten lunch and was walking toward the *pīr-house*. As soon as he saw me, he invited me to his brother's home and the first question he asked me was whether I had had lunch. When I declined, he immediately asked his nephew's wife to bring lunch for me. When he saw that I was hesitant, he told me, "Don't hesitate. We will just give you what we eat. I'm very sorry we don't eat white rice. We just eat *rāgi mudda* (a ball made of millets) and *pappu* (lentils). That's all we have, that's all we eat, and that's all that the *pīru swami* has bestowed upon us."

As Reddi had explained in a different context, *faqiri* has taught his family two values: hospitality and the sharing of food. He said, "Even if an enemy visits your place, you have to be friendly and respect him or her as a guest. You need to be very tolerant to do so. So hospitality means tolerance and not being hostile. Secondly, sharing should begin with food. That was the first lesson our ancestor Kondanna learned from the *pīru swāmi*."

"It's the *pīru swāmi*'s *prasādam*," Reddi repeated while I was trying hard to eat the millet ball. I looked into his face questioningly, and he began to explain: "Yes, it's true. The *pīru swāmi* gave us this much, and it was his *order* that we not get more than this food today. That's how our family *faqīri* begins. It begins with food and extends to spirituality (*ātma jñānam*) in search of the *paramatma* (the ultimate soul)."

Popular lore expands on the food story of Lakshmi Reddi's family, since it has now become a part of the ritual of *kandūri* itself. In several villages around Gugudu, villagers repeated the same story about *faqīri*, and connected it to Reddi's. They often said, "*faqīri* is the first boon offered to them for their great devotion. Live with whatever you get today. In their family [there was] no word about tomorrow." Villagers believe that that was how the *faqīri* vow began during Muharram, when the *pīru swāmi* appeared to Tirumala Kondanna, the ancestor of Lakshmi Reddi. As believed by many devotees, the *pīru swāmi* was very particular about rituals related to food. In many pīr stories, the pīr teaches that "food is the direct result of all our actions. Those who get enough food for today, those are good people. To earn the day's food, everyone has to till the land, tend the cattle, and use his or her body as a tool." These stories give us a sense of the formation of peasant community in these villages, and how their life-styles are defined through infusing their personal lives with community spirit, making farming the center of their livelihood.

Lakshmi Reddi's journey as a *faqīr* began at the age of ten, and since then he has never turned away from his life as a *faqīr*. He remembers every small detail from village life, and many times pointed out, "I have seen more than eighty Muharrams in the village. Personally I consider it a great fortune for me." Being the oldest *faqīr* in the village, he commands great respect in Gugudu and the neighboring villages.

He explained that most of the important things in his life "just happened as if they were all predetermined." When his father died, he took responsibility for his family, including the responsibility of carrying the pīrs during Muharram with his younger brother Tirupatayya. Since they have a joint family, additional responsibilities continued to come his way. For him, *faqīri* is foundational for his entire life:

Faqīri made a big impact on me, specifically with regard to family and community. Since I was initiated into this ritual experience at a younger age, it laid a foundation for my life. The *pīru svāmi* might not have told me directly, but I felt as if I were getting a message from him every moment. I feel sometimes like he is an integral part of my every thought and action.

His first sacred thread experience is still fresh in his memory. He explained it as if it had just happened:

It was Thursday morning. I had had my sacred thread prepared the day before. In those days we used to make sacred threads ourselves. It was always fascinating to see that colorful shiny string. In those days they were made so beautifully that I used to feel bad about removing it on the tenth day. But you have to remove it on the tenth day. Otherwise, the vow fails. Nowadays, we don't find that much work in the making of these threads. They're just using two threads and one silky thread. Now they need to make thousands and thousands of threads and it has become a business to make and sell the threads.

I asked: "So now there is an increase in the number of *faqīrs*?!" "Definitely. Now we have more pilgrims too, and every pilgrim performs this ritual. In spite of the increasing numbers, I don't see much difference in the observance of this ritual."

Then, Reddi began to describe his first experience of being a *faqīr.* "Everyone who wants to become a *faqīr* should first purify themselves in every way. I was ten years old and eagerly waiting for that great moment. Actually I wanted to observe *faqīri* much earlier, as I was so anxious to put on the beautiful silky thread. My father never allowed me to do so: 'I know you are anxious but you're not ready yet. Mere anxiety isn't enough. If you're wearing the thread, it's a very strict vow. You can't afford to make mistakes with *niyyatu niṭṭu.*'" For the first time in his life, Reddi heard the term *niyyatu niṭṭu.* When I asked him to explain this term, he told me that "*niyyatu niṭṭu* is pure intention, appropriate action, and pure devotion." I commented that *niyyatu* is an Islamic term and *niṭṭu* is a colloquial usage for *niṣṭha,* which is a very common Hindu term for "strict observance of rituals."

Reddi answered, "I know it's both *turaka* (Muslim) and Hindu. But I always heard them together ever since my childhood. So I can't see them as separate terms now. I used to hear the term almost everyday from my parents. Not only in the context of devotion, but they used to tell me that every act and word should have *niyyatu niṭṭu.*"

Each Muharram is a prominent event in his life. In addition to his role as a bearer of the metal battle standards of the pīrs, he also believes that what happens during Muharram is the foundation of his personal life, or more precisely, as he once said, "Rather than Muharram, I would say the *pīru swāmi*. He remains my guide and he makes me walk through every phase of life." He understands Muharram as an event that legitimizes the *niyyatu niṣṭha* that he learned from the *pīru swami* and tries to maintain throughout the rest of year. For Lakshmi Reddi, *niyyatu niṣṭha is* very personal:

> LR: Everything begins with you and ends with you. Many things that we do such as going to the *pīr-makānam* performing *fāteha*, prostrating before the firepit, and walking along with the public procession are just external acts. Beyond these, you have your own self *(ātma).* How are you going to face it? That remains the source of all thoughts and actions around Muharram and the *pīru swāmi.* First, I see it as an opportunity to look inside. That's what we learn from the *pīru swāmi.* When he first appeared to our ancestor, the *pīru swāmi* made him to think about his "self." The journey into *niyyatu* begins there.
>
> AM: If you think *niyyatu* is personal, what happens when you walk in a public procession carrying the pīr?
>
> LR: I know thousands of devotees strain to touch me when walking in a procession. Yet I always know that it's not actually me that they're trying to approach, but the *pīru swāmi.* If you think it's because of you, your ego gets bloated and all your *niyyatu* goes bad. I never forget that I'm a poor peasant and I've been given this great fortune to carry the pīr. While the procession moves forward, I remain within myself constantly uttering the name of the *pīru swami.*

These conversations indicate that Lakshmi Reddi has a clear sense of the boundaries between the private and public. Reddi says that the continual enactment of *faqīri* has made him perceive these boundaries clearly. For him, as he explained from his life events and experiences, the *faqīri* vow has infused his personality with enough moral strength and uprightness to face his hard life. In the process, he has also learned to restrain himself from bodily desires. Since Lakshmi Reddi began observing *faqīri* at age ten, he had become accustomed to most *faqīri* basics, including abstinence from sexual pleasure, by the time he had reached his youth.

Although careful not to make easy generalizations, Reddi seemed to believe that these *faqīri* rituals can bring similar changes in the life of any person who takes *ziyāratu darśanam* of the pīr. He explained, "It also depends on how deep you're into the *faqīri*, but most people who take this vow stick with it. At least in my experience I have seen that clearly. You are supposed to follow this for three days only, but it also depends on the person. Some observe for ten days, and some for forty days, and some, though very few, observe for a lifetime."

Obulesu: An Untouchable's Path to Purity

A common theme in *niyyatu, barkatu,* and *faqīri* is that they are never defined by the boundaries of caste hierarchies or by distinctions of pure and impure. Rather, they contest the usual constraints of caste hierarchy. Members of lower-caste communities that are often considered polluted castes enter into a space of purity through the practice of *faqīri* and the attainment of *niyyatu* and *barkatu*. Devotees consider *faqīri* to be an opportunity to travel a path of purification, and they vehemently claim this path as their own way of communicating with the deity.

Born into an untouchable caste, Obulesu considers this path of *faqīri* a wide door opened to fulfill his desire for devotion. Unlike Lakshmi Reddi, Obulesu has not made a lifetime commitment to *faqīri*. The twenty year old observes *faqīri* for only ten days a year, yet the ethics of *faqīri* shape his lifestyle just as they do Reddi's. Obulesu has been observing *faqīri* for five years. He usually begins fasting on the first day of Muharram, observing the local practice of *vokka poddu* (one meal a day). He begins his fast early in the morning and eats just an evening meal after the *fātehā* at the *pīr-house* [Figure 4.1].

The night before the first *ziyāratu darśanam* of the pīr during the month of Muharram, Obulesu prepares himself for the *faqīri* ritual. He prepares his own sacred thread out of red, green, and silky threads. In the early morning, he bathes fully and then goes to the pīr-house for *darśanam* of the *pīru swāmi*. The *muzāvar* recites the *fateha* over his sacred thread and returns it to him. Obulesu puts on the sacred thread, while "the *pīru swāmi* watches him."

Obulesu is not allowed entry into the pīr-house for any part of this ritual. Instead, he must remain by the steps between the firepit and the front entrance of the *pīr-house*; his social identity as an untouchable forbids him from entering the house. He considers himself as "pure" as other devotees,

FIGURE 4.1 For Obulesu's family, visiting Gugudu is an annual pilgrimage ritual.

and assertively contests this established notion of purity as something that could only be held by upper-caste people. During several conversations with me, he also argued that the castes that are now being treated as upper castes were actually lower castes at a certain point in history, referring to the rise of the Reddi caste from a low agrarian caste called *kāpu*. Dalits like Obulesu are very aware of these changes in caste status over time. Due to their consistent agricultural activity and land ownership, they became wealthy and were able to move to the next level of the upper middle class in the local social hierarchy. However, in everyday life they are still called a "farming" caste in most of the villages though their new last name is Reddi.[11]

Yet Obulesu silently accepts the local hierarchy when it comes to practice. He would never himself venture to step into the house or touch the metal battle standard. He said: "There should be some good reason to do so. I remember many instances when two or three *mādiga* devotees tried touching the steps at the house: the next moment they fell into the firepit and got injured severely. Even if you do something wrong unknowingly, the fire will soon punish you. However, if you have sacred thread, it will protect you. *Pīru swami* has never denied my right to worship, and when it comes to devotion everyone is pure in body and heart, too."

Fakkeerappa: The Return of the *Faqīr*

Some personal *faqīri* narratives explain the connection with land and reveal the interactions between people, land, and community. The story of Fakkeerappa, for instance, and his vow as a *faqīr* tells the story of the village lands and the formation of the new village *ūru*.[12]

After a certain land dispute with his brother, Fakkeerappa made a secret vow that he would become a wandering *faqīr* after the next Muharram if the two could reach an agreement. The very next month he and his brother came to an amicable agreement, thus settling the long-standing dispute. One night he decided to leave everything and begin his life as a wandering *faqīr*. After several hours of walking, he stopped at a *dargāh* on the way and rested there for the night. When he woke up the next morning, though, he turned back toward his village. When I asked him, "What made you change your mind? And what about your *faqīri*?" he answered:

F: The *pīru swāmi* appeared in my dream and wanted me to go back. He told me that leaving family and land is a greater sin than not keeping a vow. Instead, he suggested an alternate *faqīri* ritual that would allow me to continue my domestic duties. He made it clear that his rituals and vows are only to make one pure in his intentions, not be irresponsible.

AM: Were you satisfied with this way out?

F: Not actually. For a long time, I feared that this dream would destroy my *niyyatu.* But somehow I became convinced that the *pīru swāmi* wanted me to do so. Even before deciding whether it was right or wrong, my feet turned back as if pulled by some *śakti* (power).

AM: From your experience, what do you think are the most important aspects of *faqīri*?

F: I became more particular about *niyyatu* and *nēki* (acts of faith). I received those aspects earlier in my life, since my parents gave me the name Fakkeerappa out of respect for the Muharram pīrs. Yet, after this great event in my life, I'm now more open to *faqīri* and I have begun to develop a dialogue with my "self." I realized that *faqīri* is something connected to your inner self rather than an external display like wearing a sacred thread and just observing three or four days of fasting. *Niyyatu* is a very big word. It covers every aspect of *faqīri,* and *nēki* fills the remaining part. If you've just got *niyyatu* and no *nēki,* it's of no use.

AM: What do you mean by *nēki*?

F: Merit followed by the act of giving. The condition of being ready to give whatever you have. That's what Muharram pīrs showed in their lives. They sacrificed even the last drop of their blood. In our village, Muslims always say that if you don't do *nēki*, there will be no *barkatu* (blessing). If you give water to someone who is thirsty, you get ten *nēki* for every glass of water. If you give food to a hungry person, you get fifty *nēki*. Count your *nēki* all through life. *Niyyatu* follows you then.

As we can see in this conversation, Fakkeerappa found a way to stay with his family and village, but with certain conditions that involved the performance of temporary asceticism. When Fakkeerappa returned to his village and family, he made a new vow to observe *faqīri* for forty days, rather than for the customary three days. With added gratitude for being released from his original vow, Fakkeerappa began to extend his *faqīri* more elaborately into everyday life. Fakkeerappa perceives the impact of the Muharram pīrs in an ethical triangle of *niyyatu, faqīri,* and *barkatu.* For him, these three are the most important aspects of the Muharram pīr tradition, each one following the other.

Faqīri as a Caste Practice

For lower-caste Muslims, locally called *dudēkula* (cotton carders), the *faqīri* ritual also provides an opportunity for a family reunion. In such an instance, the pīrs acquire the status of family or caste deity, known as *kula daivam.* Madar Wali is a businessman who runs a small bedding or cotton mattress store in Karnataka. For his family, going to Gugudu is like a "little *hajj.*" In addition, it is an occasion just like any marriage or big festival that brings all his brothers and sisters together. While his father was still alive, the family was a joint one, but then all his brothers and sisters, to use Madar Wali's words, "left the nest and went their separate ways to eke out a life." They now produce mattresses and pillows out of cotton. They work hard throughout the year, and save their money to visit Gugudu with their families. They make it a point that wherever they are on their journey through life, on the seventh day of Muharram they should be in Gugudu. For them the real Muharram begins on this day, because it is the day when Qasim the great grandson of the Prophet, was martyred in Karbala. They

FIGURE 4.2 Lower-caste Muslim groups (*dudēkula*) visit Gugudu with food and drink for the hungry pirs.

rent a house for a week and all their families meet and share the experience [Figure 4.2].

Madar Wali said, "Now we feel like homeless birds. But when we come to Gugudu, we feel like having our own nest, (*gūḍu*), and just like birds we come back to the nest trying to return to our good old days of being a joint family." Being an older brother in the family, Madar Wali represents his family's tradition, too. During their stay in Gugudu, one afternoon when the place was bustling with activity, with kids playing and shouting, the whole family was busy working and talking joyously with each other while they prepared the *kandūri* food.

They had arrived in Gugudu the day before the seventh, and prepared everything for the next morning's *faqīri* ritual. Madar Wali's family does not believe much in miracles; even their women strongly argue that there is no notion of miracle in Islam.

"Then what makes you come all the way to Gugudu?" I asked them.

"Muharram means *faqīri* and the pīrs for us. We don't see anything beyond it," they replied.

For Madar's family *faqīri* is the ultimate ritual, reminding them of the value and purpose of life. The family begins to observe *faqīri* rituals on the seventh day of Muharram, and they continue until *ākhri* or the final (tenth) day.

> MW: We observe *faqīri* only for three days, that's what our elders told us. The ritual has a close connection to the Karbala events: it begins on the seventh day, since that was the day the enemy cut off the water and food supply to the martyrs, and Qasim was martyred on the battlefield. Recollecting their martyrdom, we empathize with them by fasting.
>
> AM: Fasting is common in both religions, but what does *faqīri* mean to you?
>
> MW: Practically we observe *faqīri* for three days only. Along with fasting, we abstain from bodily pleasures to maintain purity by all possible means. On the seventh of Muharram we wear the *nakhi* thread after reciting *fātehā* in the *pīr-makānam*. On the tenth day of Muharram (the day of *shahādat*), we remove it and leave it in the holy well when the final rites are done. Again, three days before the fortieth day we observe *faqīri* but without the red thread. The red thread is specifically for Muharram *faqīri*.
>
> AM: How does the *faqīri* ritual affect you personally?
>
> MW: Since we have been doing *faqīri* for several generations, it's seeped deep into our lifestyle, as water into the soil. Now I cannot separate it from my personality. My grandfather used to say, "*Nafs kō mārō.*" (Kill the lower self.) The "lower self" is something like *şaitān* (evil) always trying to take you over. It interrupts your *zikr;* it won't allow you to remain pure; it allures you with all its staggering appearances and emotions. My grandfather's and my father's generation had relatively more time and patience to constantly keep itself pure. Nowadays, it's not possible. I see this as an age of commercialization. People tend more toward business rather than piety. We need an immediate model to follow and we can't wait for it. *Faqīri* serves both purposes equally. In a *faqīri* ritual, you have an immediate model in the form of the pīr that guides you and warns you constantly. Three days of *faqīri* provides you a model for how to observe various acts of purity in everyday life.

As we can see from this narrative of Madar Wali, the practice of *faqīri* has deeper implications for particular groups, as in this case when one section of the Muslim subcaste considers it a caste tradition. It is not surprising that the *faqīri* thread is almost a symbol of pride of this Muslim subcaste.

Kullayamma: Gender and *Faqīri*

Born into an untouchable caste, Kullayamma was given the name of the *pīru swāmi*. Now forty years old, Kullayamma observes *faqīri* in the same manner that male devotees do. Wearing the sacred thread, Kullayamma observes fasting and *zikr* for the entire ten days. But she is aware that it is not common for women to observe *faqīri* in this way, as fewer and fewer women perform *faqīri* rituals. I had the following conversation with Kullayamma:

AM: I hear that women are now no longer observing *faqīri*

K: Several things interrupt their practice. As all male members in a family usually observe *faqīri,* it has been an automatic additional burden upon female members in that family. Secondly, most of the women, rather than observing *faqīri,* observe a "three-nights stay" in the *pīr-makānam*.

AM: But, you're not allowed into the *pīr-makānam*?

K: Yes, we do this in the Lord Hanuman temple. We generally avoid doing these night stays during the seventh to tenth days of Muharram.

AM: Is there any specific reason?

K: It's because we don't find space in the temple to do night stays during Muharram. So we prefer to do it outside of Muharram, starting any Thursday and continuing till the third day.

AM: That means you made some adjustments with the ritual, yes?

K: We have to. Since Muharram is important for everyone in the family, we have to make this adjustment. Moreover, we have three Kullayappas (three people with the same name) in the family. My husband is called Kullayappa, my fifteen-year-old son is called Kullayappa, and so am I. Our parents from both sides also observe *faqīri*. Since I'm the youngest in the family, I usually prefer adjustments in order to make arrangements for their *faqīri* rituals.

AM: Arrangements means . . . ?

K: They eat only one meal every day, before sunrise. So I get up earlier and prepare their meal. Serving the *faqīrs* is also an act of merit (*puṇyam savābu*). Instead, I will observe *faqīri* even before Muharram.

AM: Is it considered *faqīri* if you're doing it outside of Muharram?

K: It has been traditional in our family for several generations. Even some male members observe it outside the festival. My mother always preferred to do it outside Muharram.

AM: Do you observe as everyone else does during Muharram?

K: Except the *faqīri* ritual we do everything. Moreover, we visit Gugudu very often, after every *faqīri* ritual. But we never miss observing this ritual.

AM: Why is your family very particular about this ritual?

K: Everyone has his own story. The common story is that most of the devotees observe *faqīri* for two reasons: wish fulfillment and secondly, even without any practical reason.

AM: People also do it without any specific purpose?

K: Without reason means with no practical purpose in mind, like seeking relief from ailments or being able to bear children. My family has no particular reason to observe *faqīri* except that it has been a practice for several generations in our family. Long ago we were told that one of our predecessors stopped doing it and their family met with all kinds of terrible consequences.

AM: So you do have a purpose, don't you?

K: Yes, we do. But it's not an immediate practical reason. Anyways, we never even thought of not doing this.

While we were talking about this, Kullayamma's mother, Pedda Kullayamma (Kullayamma Senior), intervened and began to narrate a story of

FIGURE 4.3 The seventh day of Muharram is basically a women's ritual.

one person who not only failed to perform *faqīri*, but also made ridiculous comments about the village *faqīrs*. The story seems significant in communicating the ritual efficacy of the pīrs, and reveals a narrative strategy for empowering the pīr and the *faqīri* tradition. I recorded similar versions of the same story in many villages around Gugudu [Figure 4.3].

Teaching *Faqīri*: Story of a Fierce Pīr and an Arrogant *Faqīr*

Devotees draw on various methods to teach the practice of *faqīri* to their children. Though the actual practice of *faqīri* itself remains an important method for imparting the practices and values of *faqīri* to younger generations, devotees also make conscious efforts to inculcate ethics verbally. Obviously, the oral narrative traditions associated with Muharram powerfully suggest an alternative model for leading a good life, and play a crucial role in the community. Devotees tell stories about the family of the Prophet and particularly emphasize the sacrifices made by the Prophet's grandsons, thus establishing a clear role model of someone with a perfect *niyyatu* and collective spirit that can bring *barkatu* to the village. Though villagers do not have direct knowledge of classical Islamic texts, these pīr narratives do give them knowledge of a particular ethical code [Figure 4.4.].

Devotees tell many stories about the pīr's modes of teachings. As Kullayamma explained to me, "The pīr teaches you in many ways. He talks to us by various modes such as dreams, experiences, and signs. When you're in constant *yaadi* (remembrance), he never fails to communicate with you." Generally, the pīr's teachings take on a final form in stories. Many of these stories revolve around the specific morals that the villagers value and try to observe in their lives together. Here is one story that I heard in several villages:

> This is a real story. Not a fiction or fabricated one. It just happened in our village, Gūḷa Pāleṁ. You know we call the *pīru svāmi* "Lālū pīr swāmi" (in Urdu "*lāl*" means red) in our village since his body is all red with blood after the great battle of Karbala. While Kullayappa is compassionate, Lālū swāmi is ferocious and everyone call him "fierce pīr." There is a popular saying in the village that for those who perform *faqiri* he is like an umbrella, for those who do not perform *faqiri* he is like red ferocious fire. You remember what happened to those goldsmith brothers when they couldn't hold the pīr and threw him into the well? The very next day the whole village was punished by a ferocious fire. Same in this story. It all happened during Muharram. The *pīr swami* was walking around the village with thirty-three

FIGURE 4.4 *Faqīrs* go around the village telling the stories of the pīr.

torches showing him the path. When the procession was coming down the hill, he reached a street called Konakandla veedhi. One arrogant Nagappa was in the procession too. Earlier he used to observe *faqiri* as it was his family tradition. This Muharram, some worm crept into his brain and spoiled it, and he stopped observing *faqiri*. While the procession was going through the street, the arrogant Nagappa stopped the procession and shot straight to the pīr. He yelled at the pīr arrogantly and challenged him to show him some miracle. Everyone was mad, but the person carrying the pīr was quiet and smiling peacefully, as if nothing had happened. As Nagappa continued yelling, after a while the ritual standard-bearer said, "Nagappa, you're in a bad mood. Just go home."

So, see what was happening at his place: his wife so healthy and so beautiful unexpectedly fell ill. When he got home, all the women who were so worried surrounded him and began weeping. "Nagappa, it's good you came at the right moment. Look at your wife . . . the doctor said that there is no hope. It's just a matter of one or two days. No cure. Nothing can save her life." And his servant came and told him that all his cattle had been behaving crazily, not even touching water or fodder.

This had never happened before in his lifetime. What was going on? He ran back to see the pīr. The procession was still in street. It hadn't even inched forward. The pīr was in the same place and the carrier was smiling as if he had been waiting for Nagappa for at least an hour. Nagappa began to weep like a child. Immediately he asked someone to bring one *faqīri* thread and sugar. Someone gave him the red thread and some sugar. The *muzavar* recited the Quranic verse over the *faqīri* thread and gave it back to him.

As he was about to head back to his place, the standard-bearer stopped him and said, "Nagappa, don't leave until the procession ends. Leave after my *ākhri*. Your wife is now doing fine and everything will be all right."

Since then, Nagappa has never missed even a single *faqiri*. He visits Gugudu during Muharram, yet he also took complete responsibility for Muharram practices in his own village.

This story has several variations in this region, as village narrators continue to add more details to evoke the village spaces. Nevertheless, the theme of the story remains the same: the legitimization of *faqīri* rituals during Muharram. When Kullayamma told me this story, she did not stop with just narrating it, but also began to interpret it. She interpreted this story on the basis of two sources, namely her own life experience and what she knew of the experience of the village itself. Her narratives about not performing *faqīri* focused mostly on the trouble that occurred as a result. On a broader level, she extended the similar fear of failure to the community level. Her stories and interpretations clearly establish *faqīri* as a model based on the oral hagiographies of the pīrs as exemplary models.

She said, "What we know about devotion is all from these pīr stories. This has continued for several generations. I learnt it from my parents, and my daughters learnt it from me. I never tried to say anything explicitly to them, they just learnt it from my ritual activities (*ācāram maryādalu*), and when they listened to my stories they were all impressed by the *niyyatu* of the pīr." As we have observed from the above *faqīri* narratives, it is understandable that these village devotees consider the local pīr to be an exemplary model, but they also narrate stories about him in a manner that establishes their close connections to the pīrs.

Faqīri as Temporary Asceticism

As we can see from the above *faqīri* narratives, different village communities have developed parallel temporary ascetic practices premised on a distinctive journey from the wilderness to the center of the *ūru*. Most of the pīr narratives portray this theme as a central idea of Muharram, and the pīr-house is therefore strategically located at the center of the village. Kullayappa in his two positions as pīr and deity, establishes the connections between various communities, while emphasizing the social accountability of devotional practices. Thus Muharram becomes a central stage to perform these practices in different ways. Similarly, Kullayappa's hagiography redefines the ritual contours of ascetic practice in *faqīri* as a combination of Hindu and Muslim rituals, and also householder and renunciatory practices. Village devotees, however, also imbue the vow of *faqīri* with ethical foundations drawn from Sufism and the story of Muharram.

Faqīri and Muharram Practices

Schubel defines Shi'ism "as the school of thought in Islam which stresses personal allegiance and devotion to the Prophet and his family as the most crucial element and sign of one's submission to the will of God."[13] Various caste groups in Gugudu reformulate this definition of Shi'i Islamic practice by extending the boundaries of each Muharram ritual, and by providing alternate meanings to each Muharram practice. In the village context, these caste groups modify the notion of personal allegiance by centering most of their rituals on a local pīr, thus clearly highlighting the significance of local Muharram traditions. Close observation of the *faqīri* rituals in a village Muharram context would show that the very concept of the exemplary model as explained in normative Islam also undergoes deep changes. While in urban and normative Shi'a practice, the prominence of the *faqīri* rituals is always secondary in Muharram, it becomes not only central but also transformative in villages, so far as *faqīri* is connected to the worship of local pīrs, who are treated as if they are deities [Figure 4.5].

During the 2007 Muharram in Gugudu I observed that almost every pilgrim who made a visit to the *pīru swāmi* observed some degree of *faqīri*. It was estimated that 300,000 pilgrims visited and stayed in Gugudu for three days, but this is not the total number of people who observed *faqīri*. I observed that the inhabitants of several villages observe these rituals en masse. When I asked one non-Muslim pilgrim who came from Kadapa district about this, he told me that "many people won't be able to come, yet they observe *faqīri* and remove the sacred threads on the tenth day and throw them into the local wells or rivers, where the final rites would be performed for the martyrs."

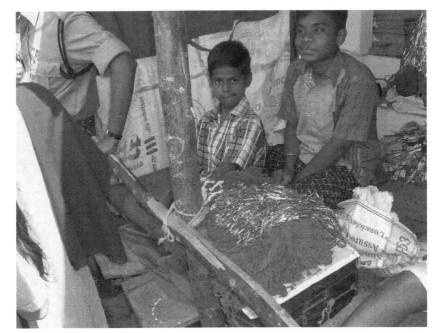

FIGURE 4.5 *Faqīri* threads for sale during Muharram.

AM: What is this thread for? Is it for the Karbala martyrs?

PILGRIM: Not actually. Our first prayer goes to the local pīr. However, we believe that all pīrs are from Karbala and that Karbala is everywhere."

AM: You know about the battle of Karbala?

P: I have known these stories from my parents and local people since my childhood. Everybody knows the story of Karbala. Even non-*turakas*[14] give the names of Hassan and Husain to their children.

AM: What is this *faqīri* for?

P: The pīrs were martyred for us. They sacrificed everything and lived for the people. *Faqīri* is their memory. By observing *faqīri*, we remember them and follow and respect their path.

AM: So Kullayappa was also martyred with Hasan and Husain?

P: Kullayappa was their brother. Not only one Kullayappa but three Kullayappas were there. They were all brothers. They fought with the enemy on behalf of the poor people.

AM: You observe *faqīri* only during Muharram days?

P: Wearing the thread, we observe it for three days. Thread is just a symbol for memory, *yādi gurtu*. (Here he used a mixed Urdu-Telugu term for memory.) Even if we remove the symbol the memory remains. The symbol is only to reinforce the memory. As long as the memory is alive, *faqīri* becomes a habit of our body.

Primarily, *faqīri* rituals encourage devotees to go beyond just offering sugar *fateha* and *kandūri* and embrace a process of self-transformation that is lifelong. This is so important that *faqīri* has come to define Muharram in Gugudu for many.

Lakshmi Reddi said, "Without *faqīri* there is no Muharram. If you're not observing *faqīri* you're not even supposed to come to Gugudu. *Faqīri* comes first, then other practices. Once you begin to observe *faqīri*, you don't have to observe other rituals. It covers every aspect of Muharram and that's all you can do for the pīrs." At first I thought that Reddi's support for the *faqīri* rituals was just his subjective opinion. But when I began to meet and converse with many devotees, local and pilgrims, I saw that most of them also consider *faqīri* to be the primary requirement for performing or participating in other Muharram rituals as an interface between yogi and Sufi practices.

As Obulesu observed, "When you're observing *faqīri*, you are *pāk* (pure). This *pāk* is not just physical, but mental, too. You're focusing on the pīr both physically and mentally. So *faqīri* opens a door and then you enter into the *pīr-makānam*. As an untouchable I'm never allowed to enter the *makānam*. Still, in my inner heart I feel as if I'm always closer to the pīr and his sacred space." During several conversations Obulesu became emotional about this, and when he spoke about this notion of purity he always asserted that "not even Muslims could compete with me in my purity." Observing *faqīri* puts Obulesu in a very strong position psychologically, lifting him from his low status as an untouchable to a higher subjective status, from which he believes he can communicate directly with the pīr.

People clearly have their own reasons for observing *faqīri,* and the meanings of the practice may vary according to their personal background, family history, and social status. Nevertheless, most devotees emphasize one basic fact: *faqīri* is primarily an embodiment of purity. Moreover, bodily purity has a prominent role in *faqīri*, but ultimately it is secondary to the inner purity, the *niyyatu*, that is realized by *faqīri*.

As Obulesu and Kullayamma put it in their own ways, their bodies have always been considered 'impure' by others, as if having no real ability to perform any ritual. But through *faqīri* there is a space for them to claim both ritual authority and devotional power. In claiming ritual authority they even go to the extent of asserting that their purity is stronger than that of someone who is upper caste or Muslim.

One early morning at a tea shop in front of the pīr-house, I had a lengthy conversation with Obulesu over a cup of tea. He told me:

Once we put on the red thread, our *īmānu* (the Telugu equivalent of the Islamic term *īmān,* or "faith") reaches its height. Since our *īmānu* is stronger, even if we walk through the fire we won't feel its heat. You do not see anyone complaining of simple bruises. *Niyyatu* is important. *Faqīri* actually prepares you for everything, including the final fire-walk. So the fire-walk is an ultimate test for our purity in performing rituals. Sometimes even Muslims wonder how this could happen! Purity has no caste. If you have true *niyyatu,* even pīrs will approach you and embrace you. Only pīrs have those open arms. All remaining gods and yogis won't even touch us, and some are even scared of touching our shadows. They always say, "Keep your distance!" while pīrs say, "Come closer." We move closer with our *īmānu* and purity.[15]

Wearing the red thread is clearly not just a ritual. In the way that Obulesu describes it, one has to be completely clean before wearing the thread. It is a common practice that after removing hair from the private parts of the body, one has to take a complete bath before being given the thread. Kullayappa said, "A simple bath won't work. You have to clean everything; bodily cleanliness is the primary requirement of *faqīri*. The very early morning after the first prayer in the mosque, we go to the holy well and take a bath there. After the bath, we go to the *makānam* and the *muzāvar* recites *fātehā* over the thread. Then, while the pīrs watch us, we wear the red thread."

In some cases, as with Lakshmi Reddi, this ritual purity reaches its height in the choice to remain permanently unmarried, in order to abstain from sexual impurities. During my fieldwork in and around Gugudu, I observed at least five people who remained unmarried as a part of their vow to be *faqīrs* forever. Fakkeerappa told me: "It's like you are wedded to the *faqīri* way of life. Personally, this state of mind and body gives me a lot of psychological relief. I strongly feel that I have attained victory over this body, and transcended its limits."

Even when *faqīri* is considered a personal ritual, the presence of *faqīrs* with sacred threads functions like a charismatic presence in the community that directly appeals to others. When devotees wear the sacred thread after the formal initiation (*dīkṣa*) ritual of *faqīri*, the thread becomes a point of discussion. While relatives and friends continually ask the *faqīr* the details of his *faqīri* practice, even new persons with a familiar knowledge of *faqīri* practice begin to converse with the *faqīrs*. The conversations begin with questions about when someone started the *faqīri dīkṣa* and how the practice is going; eventually they explore issues such as *faqīri* ethics and their impact on the ascetic.

Several of these personal experiences related to the body resonate with the pīr narrative traditions, as well as with folk genres and proverbs used in everyday life. In all these, various aspects of the body become metaphors, and the severed bodies of the Karbala martyrs become a recurring theme in the pīr narratives. The ritual standard of the pīr itself represents the body of the pīr. Various caste groups have a clear knowledge of this bodily representation of the pīrs, and they interpret these representations on different levels. Very often the red sacred thread is understood as the "hungry and thirsty innards of the martyrs." In my conversations with *faqīri* practitioners, they often talked about the impact of the thread on their bodies.

"When you have a thread on your body, it's a constant reminder that you're a *faqīr,* as if it's saying repeatedly, 'You are a *faqīr.* A pure and clean *faqīr.* It doesn't mean that we behave differently without a thread. But when there is a thread on the body, it constantly reminds you that you are a *faqīr.* The thread still dictates our inner life even when it's not there. But when it's there it's like a direct command from the pīr," said Obulesu. However, he accepted that people would take extra care in the matters of food and purity when they were wearing the thread during the ten days of Muharram. And Fakkeerappa commented, "Now I see some people observing the Swami Ayyappa vow for forty days. They wear black clothes and observe all the purity rituals. This is a new *bhakti* trend. But see, we have been doing *faqīri* for many years, indeed many centuries since it came to us from our ancestors."

Although local Muslims are generally not particularly careful about *faqīri*, they ritually observe fasting and abstinence from bodily pleasures for three or ten days during Muharram. However, many of them continue to wear the red thread during Muharram even if they are not engaged in the stricter forms of *faqīri*. Khaja Husain, a Muslim pilgrim, said,

> For me it's just a symbol of Karbala martyrdom. It reminds me of all those tragic events and moments and all their suffering. When you remember them, you cannot avoid fasting. As a Muslim, I never forget those tragic moments in the Prophet's family. They are all etched into my memory forever. For a Muslim, *zikr* is itself a reminder. Though I never use the rosary, I would never forget *zikr*. For us Muslims, *zikr* is an integral part of everyday life. When you observe *tahāra*, when you go to the mosque and when you recite *fateha*, you do *zikr* every time. But Muharram is different. Muharram is a very important celebration for Hindus too. Hindus need objects and material sources to do *zikr*. Wearing the red thread has a kind of symbolic significance for them.[16]

During our conversations, Husain made distinctions like this between Hindu and Muslim observances of Muharram, doing so through recourse to the practices of localized Islam. He told me, "They need symbols; they need objects to keep their mind focused. But for us, *hussēniyat* (allegiance to Husain) stays inside forever. Nothing erases it and you don't need some external force or object to remind you about it."

As we have repeatedly seen in the *faqīri* narratives from Gugudu, the pīr-house plays a central role in grounding the alternative ascetic practice of *faqīri*. My observations in this chapter point out significant Muslim influences, both Sufi and Shi'ism, on these ascetic practices. The various *faqīri* narratives described in this chapter all portray an alternative ascetic life that continually draws on the practices of Sufism but transfers them to the context of Muharram, where they are connected to other religious practices in the public rituals of Gugudu's Muharram.

| Debating Rituals: The Politics of "True" Islam

The Idea of *Imān* and *'Amal*: Purifying the Faith

In the previous chapters, I described and analyzed a few concepts and terms that have become popular in the realm of local Islam. In this chapter, I will focus on the politics of "true" Islam as they have become manifest in recent reformist activity in Gugudu, although it must be noted that such an activity is not confined to Gugudu. During my stay in the village, I attended Friday sermons and prayers at the local mosque. One of the most intriguing and enjoyable experiences was to meet the mosque's imam Jaffer and converse with him for hours and hours in the early morning or at the evening *namāz*. We shared ideas about religious affairs as well as family matters. Jaffer, like many Islamic preachers, vehemently and assertively emphasizes the importance of the Quran and the traditions of the Prophet (*sunnah*). But he is also sympathetic to the needs of the villagers and spends lot of time talking to them about their personal problems, irrespective of whether he approves of the way that they are religious.

Helpful and kind as he was, Jaffer finished every talk with a line such as, "Everything will be alright, but you should at least perform one *namāz* a day." Even ordinary non-Muslims in the village respect Jaffer for his religious knowledge, perhaps even more so than for his good nature. Jaffer is a compassionate man and shows considerable empathy toward the villagers, but he also knows that when it comes to *namāz*, very few of them care about his words. Most importantly, he is never one to mince words, as when he discusses local pīr practices. One evening before the night prayer during the month of Muharram, Jaffer said, "This is not Islam and this is not true Muharram. And this pīr is false. It's all made-up now. Enjoyment replaces mourning. Festivity replaces tragedy. The question is, then: why are these people so persistent about following every ritual of Karbala? I still believe that their faith (*īmān*)[1] is unwavering and remains the driving force in their everyday lives. This is what they've learnt from Islam. They truly submit in their devotion to the martyrs, but where has this pīr come from? I never understand."

Jaffer's comments reflect the viewpoint of many reformist groups across South Asia who have set out to "purify" Islamic life. In the case of Gugudu, most of the debates and the purification efforts of reformists are centered on the authority of the local pīrs and on local interpretations of Muharram. In several conversations Jaffer touched upon a number of more general issues which have increasingly become points of tension in Islamic communities in South Asia. He discussed three of these key issues: first, the relevance of local rituals which he called *bid'a* (rejected or innovative practice); second, the character and significance of true practice (*'amal*); and third, faith (*īmān*) as expressed and articulated by Muharram devotees. During my fieldwork, I observed that the terms that Jaffer used—*bid'a*, *'amal,* and *īmān*—had in many ways become contentious in the community. In many places, particularly during the month of Muharram, young reformist Muslims are actively involved in teaching and circulating the idea of "true Islam," or *asli islām* as they call it.

Rejecting local practices of Islam as *bid'a*, a sentiment Jaffer and several other young Muslims in Gugudu articulated, is not a new idea. The history of Islamic revivalism in India took a new turn in the late nineteenth century in north India when, as Barbara Metcalf has observed, "a group of men, scholarly and pious, set out to argue by any means of propaganda they could lay their hands on, that Islam as practiced in their society was misguided."[2] Metcalf has studied the use of scriptural sources that began to play a significant role in the critique of existing local religious practices. In this chapter, I will focus on a similar but smaller scale revivalist process in Gugudu. This incarnation of Islamic revivalism, however, has taken a new turn, by challenging the practices of local Islam in which many Muslims participate, in the growing shadow of Hindu nationalism.

These challenges to local devotion are often voiced in a sarcastic manner. As Jaffer commented: "I never understand how if the pīr is so powerful and has immense *karāmat* (miraculous powers), why he couldn't walk by himself? Village people are so blind that they can't see that it's just a long stick with some metal on its head that has no life at all." Whenever Jaffer refers to the pīr, whom he calls "*stick ṣaitān*," he follows his sarcasm with talk about *asli islām*. Jaffer's words echo what many contemporary imams and Islamic preachers now say. These religious figures have the aim of "reforming" or "purifying" local Muslim practices, and are bent on the removal of what they describe as "erratic" and "inappropriate innovative rituals" (*bid'a*) in their villages. While their focus is on critiquing the Islamic parts of local devotion, what is called *dēhāti islām* (village level or folk Islam) practices, they also give themselves new authority in the community on the basis of their command of the textual sources of global Islam. As Jaffer explained, "Our only effort is to purify the lower self (*nafs*) that inhabits these places in the form of incorrect practices and a lot of *shirk* ('forbidden') activities." However, devotees including Muslims assert that the pīr has brought prosperity to them, and performing rituals to him increases the merit they receive. In addition, the ever-increasing number of pilgrims strengthens the confidence of the devotees that their local Islamic practices are recognized in the wider world [Figure 5.1].

Though it is not unusual to criticize the veneration of the pīrs in Islam,[3] the controversy over the proper practices by groups committed to reformist Islam has been on the rise, and is now familiar in Telugu-speaking Muslim communities. Currently, young imams trained in reciting the Quran but familiar with Telugu as well as Urdu and Arabic are actively involved in suppressing local Islamic practices on the grounds that they are

FIGURE 5.1 Despite various controversies, the number of Muslim pilgrims has been growing since a decade.

"un-Islamic." Fluency in Telugu, together with an ability to read and interpret Quranic materials in Telugu, has now become the most important criteria for these trained imams. It is significant just how prominent the use of Telugu has become in this reformist movement. In many village mosques, these imams recite from the Telugu translations of the Quran rather than the Arabic text. Commentarial literature and other secondary texts are also found in Telugu.

Groups of young Muslims have begun to interfere in a variety of local ritual activities. Most of the pīr-houses or Muslim shrines have their own structure of authority, with a fixed administrative group that takes care of financial and institutional matters and custodians who act as authorities on ritual activities and other religious matters. There is a growing expectation that the local mosque should be the center of Muslim life because it is a center of *asli* Islamic practices. While pīr-house activities continue to draw thousands of devotees and pilgrims regardless of background and allow them to participate in a shared realm of religion, the mosque-centered activities construct a discrete "Muslim" identity. Tensions between local Islam and reformist Islam are now visible in community life, as middle-class and young Muslims are gradually moving away from the pīr-house that has been their family tradition toward the mosque. Something analogous is also occurring among non-Muslims, with more people gaining a sense of themselves as "Hindus," as this is defined by a global Hinduism.

When I met Jaffer for the first time in Gugudu, he was in his thirties. He had come to this village determined, to use his words, "to remove the evil that has engulfed this village for several centuries and obstructed the path of pure faith (*īmān*)." For him, most of the ritual activities that center on the *pīr-makānam* are "just acts of evil that constantly work against the straight path of Islam." As he phrased it, "They are troubles created by Satan on the path of devotion. These people in their eagerness to reach Allah lost their way by indulging in demonic acts." However, Jaffer acknowledges that "Whatever they are doing, they are doing it with great faith (*īmān*). One cannot be a skeptic about their immense faith in Islam. The only thing is that they don't know what true Islam is. And being ignorant about the Quran and the significance of prayer makes these people follow these blind practices. Since they're illiterate, uneducated, and ignorant, they blindly believe that these local pīrs are gods or messengers. So we need to reform their minds and turn them to the straight path."

Statements such as Jaffer's raise questions about the future of Muharram in Gugudu, questions that are already being answered in the present. This chapter presents "Hindu" and "Muslim" perceptions of the future of the Muharram festival, and the pīr practices in Gugudu. To discuss these patterns of change at a broader level, I will also use evidence from other villages in Andhra. But my discussion is mostly based on my work in Gugudu and its surrounding villages. This chapter has three sections: (1) tensions around conducting a public holiday such as Muharram; (2) the theme of pīr practices and ritual sites in the current religious environment; and (3) tensions between actual practices and reformist efforts to "purify" these practices.

These three issues are interconnected to each other as they relate to notions of pure and impure religion—a "pure" Islam locally known as *asli* (true) Islam, and a "pure" Hinduism locally known as *dharma hindū matam* (*dharma* Hinduism),[4] both opposed to Gugudu's shared devotional practices. In cities, where urban ritual spaces are more exposed to recent ideological activities, and in many small towns where the polarized Hindu and Muslim groups have become significant, non-Muslim participation in the rituals of the pīrs and in the Muharram festivities has decreased significantly over the past decade, with Muslims increasingly wanting to close such activities to non-Muslims.

Contesting Muharram as a Public Ritual

As we have seen, Muharram in Gugudu has been a legacy handed down through several generations, most predominantly as a set of public rituals. For previous generations in the village, the local theologies that justified this holiday were as informal as they were ingenious. For example, it was believed by Asanna, one avid participant in Muharram practices, that there was an, "an agreement for common good between the deities and the pīrs. Whatever you do for the pīrs, it is not actually for the pīrs, but for the village, the well-being of the entire locality."[5] What constitutes public, and what is meant by the common good, have both become sources of disagreement between members of the new generation of "Hindus" and "Muslims." Both groups have developed an ambivalent relationship with the public nature of Muharram and the pīr-focused rituals. I use the word "ambivalent" since some Hindu groups, particularly those who are lower caste or older, still stick to the tradition, and consider Muharram to be for everyone, while some younger Hindus and Muslims reject entirely the tradition of Muharram, Hindus because of the "Muslim" identity of Muharram and Muslims in the name of *bid'a*. For many younger Muslims, Muharram in Gugudu is just a "Hindu Muharram," whereas for many younger Hindus, Muharram has no relevance to a "Hindu" way of life. They define Muharram as *paradharmam* 'other religions', emphasizing *para-*, or "other." However, older villagers like Asanna still believe that "this rejection of Muharram is temporary. Most of the villagers know how important Muharram is for their everyday life and for local community life. If we stop doing Muharram that would signify the end of the village." Nevertheless, these younger voices are determined to continue expressing their dissent against Muharram practices and local forms of religion focused on the pīrs, such as Kullayappa.

Changes in Ritual Perceptions

"In those days Muharram was everything in a village. What you see now is just a little trace of it!" said Adellu, a low-caste man who performs Muharram rituals in a non-Muslim neighborhood in Bodhan, a small town in the district of Adilabad. Though this town has a long history of celebrating Muharram, since 1990 a clear division between Hindus and Muslims has been established in lieu of the rise of religious nationalism and Islamic reformism. Now a shared Muharram has become just a memory for most in this town. Still, in some small pockets of this town, some devotees continue to perform Muharram in small ways. The neighborhood where Adellu lives has built a small house of pīrs and has been continuing the tradition of venerating them so that the divine blessing (*barkatu*) does not vanish from this place. Even now the residents of this neighborhood believe that it is "only because of this public ritual [that] our place is peaceful and prosperous. Whatever the conditions, however the times change, we are not going to stop celebrating Muharram. Failure to do so would result in utter poverty, diseases, and death. Once a place loses its *barkatu*, it is impossible to regain it." It is locally believed that on the tenth day of Muharram Adellu becomes possessed by Hassan and Husain, who speak through him. Devotees who travel to listen to his words call Adellu *"turaka dēvuḍu"* (Muslim God) when he is possessed by the martyr pīrs. However, the most important aspect of Muharram in this neighborhood is the construction of an alternate space for the public events of the holiday. Against all odds, these devotees have built a house for pīrs, at which each year they perform small-size processions without the support of authorities or patrons.

Though the public rituals of Muharram have a history of several centuries in many South Indian villages, they have not remained static over those years. In Andhra, these practices have evolved in connection with changes in political circumstances. In the Deccan, the tradition of

Muharram has an interconnected history with Sufism, which eventually paved the way for the expansion of Islam even into remote corners of the region. Muharram provided a public space for many Sufi practices, and the religious history of these places, as recorded in various folk songs, martyr-saint rituals, and public religious performances, is also a history of this composite cultural space. However, this shared space has now increasingly become a politicized space, in which Hindus and Muslims are strictly differentiated, and particularly so after the recent upsurge of religious nationalism. These changes are now erasing the history of shared devotion and are inscribing new religious identities in these places.

The most significant impact of these changes is the gradual vanishing of "the houses of the pīrs," called locally *pīr-makaanam* or *pīrla cāviḍi*. Since at least the rule of the Qutub Shahis (1512–1681), these pīr-houses have been the meeting place for various caste groups of Hindus and Muslims. The Qutub Shahi rulers had successfully introduced and integrated Persian arts and literature into the local life of the Deccan. The landscape today is still dotted with pīr-houses, even in remote villages in Andhra, a testament to the legacy of this dynasty. Though the history of Shiism in the Deccan goes back to the Bahmanis,[6] it was during the reign of the Qutub Shahis, who funded the construction of the pīr-houses in many villages, that Shii beliefs and practices became diffused throughout the region. In a way, by constructing these pīr-houses, the Qutub Shahis both provided a public space for shared devotional practices and facilitated their political rule as well. This locally adapted and flexible religious policy remained a trait of the State of Hyderabad for a long time.

As Furuqi Munis has observed, "Hyderabad's religious policies were undoubtedly tempered by the knowledge that the vast majority of the Nizam's subjects were not Muslims."[7] Though these traces of the past are clearly visible in the landscape of Hyderabad, we also find a coherent picture of this impact of Shi'i Islam in remote villages of Andhra. Various religious rituals and devotional practices at village-level Andhra explain this legacy of the Qutub Shahi dynasty, as well as reveal contemporary tensions as well.[8]

Ritual Changes and Hindu-Muslim Debates

"These days the new generation has gotten into many strange ideas. For several centuries, Muharram has been our tradition and our practice. Now this new generation has gotten this sudden idea that Muharram is a

'Muslim' festival and they question why we Hindus should do this. Let us see how long these sudden ideas last!" said Fakkeerappa, a seventy-five-year-old low-caste Hindu from Gugudu. For Fakkeerappa, the shift that has been taking place since the 1990s is a "sudden idea." However, this idea has a much longer history than Fakkeerappa may have realized. When saying this, Fakkeerappa was referring to the changes in the way younger Hindus and Muslims have thought about Muharram and pīr practices since the demolition of the Babri Mosque in Ayodhya on December 6, 1992.[9] After this incident, the line between Hindus and Muslims in the village began to harden, and Muharram began to be seen as a "Muslim" ritual in some villages.

Though riots and violence have not been uncommon during Muharram in urban areas such as Bombay, Calcutta, Delhi, Lucknow, and Hyderabad, the holiday remains relatively peaceful at the village level. Now this shared religious culture is being challenged by developments in the wake of the Babri Mosque destruction. As Peter Gottschalk observed in Arampur:

> Local residents describe the contemporary erosion of common identities overlapping religious identities when they reflect that in earlier decades both Hindus and Muslims participated in the Durga Puja and Muharram processions. Some residents express regret that such cross-participation seldom occurs nowadays and blame the current environment of communalist politics for the change. Undoubtedly and not without connection, contemporary Islamic revivalist ideas have influenced many local Muslims to avoid "un-Islamic" activities, including Muharram processions, while groups like the RSS [Rashtriya Swayamsevak Sangh] revile "non-Indian" (read: Muslim) celebrations.[10]

The post-Babri Mosque unrest has clearly affected Muharram for both Hindus and Muslims in Gugudu. However, these developments have impacted these local communities in different ways. In his study on saint worship in Gujarat, Edward Simpson made similar observations about Muharram. According to him, the political turmoil and subsequent violence have fostered unity among Muslims, and those previously dismissive of the festivities have begun to support the public rituals and saint worship "as a way of manufacturing unity among Muslims or between Hindus and Muslims."[11] In the case of Andhra, the impact of this political violence has had a different impact on ritual culture, as some non-Muslim caste groups have begun to see Muharram as an Islamic event rather than a source of shared devotion, while Muslim revivalist groups have begun to see it as "un-Islamic." Just as Gottschalk observed in Arampur, these shifting attitudes have impacted equally the public rituals of Muharram and the pīr practices.

As we saw in the statement of Fakkeerappa quoted above, we have two very different viewpoints about the observance of Muharram. Hindu caste groups in several villages go so far as to claim Muharram as solely their event. However, in Gugudu and nearby villages, many villagers still observe Muharram as a shared devotional practice, in spite of the activities of Hindu and Muslim reformist groups. As Fakkeerappa put it above, these villagers believe that efforts in the name of "purifiying" religion will not last long.

On my visits to several villages around Gugudu, I found that the religious life and devotional practices of many of these villages are still centered on the shared practices of Muharram. Many of these villages have a strong Sufi background, and are dotted by several Sufi shrines. In a way, what Nasr has observed in the case of Sunni societies is true in these villages, too: "The influence of Sufism on Muslim life and thought has generated tolerance for Shi'ism in many Sunni societies. Where Sufism defines Islamic piety, Shi'a have found greater acceptance."[12] Yet various local forms of Sufism are not confined to the aspects as described in different institutionalized *silsilahs*. Very clearly, locally specific forms of Sufism are present in these villages, which contest the boundaries of institutionalized Sufi practices.

Pīrs and Ritual Sites

The very idea of a pīr is a manifestation of the shared devotional realm of Shiism and Sufism in the local religions of Andhra. Richard Eaton has observed that Sufis in spite of their mystical backgrounds played an important social role in the making of medieval communities.[13] Making a clear distinction in the perceptions of Sufism, Imtiaz Ahmed explains, "Most orthodox Muslims see any form of Sufism or close interchange with other religions as a danger to true Islam. For them, the Sufis lacked the appropriate moral rigour, other however particularly non-Muslims venerated the Sufi saints for their moral superiority."[14]

Three prominent Sufi shrines are invoked repeatedly in several oral narratives in Gugudu, and those who visit Gugudu generally make a pilgrimage to these sites, which are popular for their Sufi elements and mystical powers. The shrines—Baba Fakhruddin *dargāh* in Penukoṇḍa,[15] Mastan *dargāh* in Guntakal, and Ameenuddin *dargāh* in Kaḍapa—represent three distinctive Sufi schools, and are also popular for their Muharram traditions. Though both Hindu and Muslim devotees visit these places, in many ways these sites have predominantly Islamic histories, unlike the shared history found in Gugudu. The public rituals of Muharram at these places do, however, provide a devotional space for non-Muslim devotees, who travel to them on their way to Gugudu. Even as the number of pilgrims and devotees has been on the rise, there has been a consistent effort to differentiate between "pure" and "impure" practices even within this Sufi tradition, in a manner similar to the tensions between local Islam and localized Islam in Gugudu. Reformist groups explain that there is a hierarchy of sites and traditions that places Kadapa and Sufi traditions on the top, *dargāh* practices at Guntakal in the middle, and practices such as those in Gugudu on a lower level. While Penukonda and Kadapa Sufi practices are marked as more "Islamic" in a way, or "high Islamic" by local Muslims, Gugudu is denigrated as *dēhāti islām,* or "village Islam."[16] Though these sites have certain common features, such as large numbers of visiting pilgrims, local Karbala narratives, and Muharram observances, the three Sufi shrines, unlike Gugudu, have a strict administrative system which tries to promote Islamic devotional practices by all means. As Gugudu has no such Islamic administrative arrangement, there is no central means for promoting localized Islam in Gugudu. Due to the increase in revenue each year from pilgrims, Gugudu is now under the control of the Department of Temple Endowments, but these authorities rarely interfere in any ritual activities around the shrines, and restrict themselves to law and order and the financial management of the shrine.

The shrine of the pīr in Gugudu continues to attract thousands of pilgrims each year, but tensions over the nature of the shrine and its pīr also continue. Saleem a reformist activist, who was traveling in and around Gugudu during Muharram, told me, "The problem occurs when you equate the pīr with God." Many non-Muslim pilgrims continue to accept the authority of the pīr as absolute, to the point that they consider the pīr to be divine. For Muslims, however, the pīr's nature is more tenuous. For some, the pīr is a mediator between god and devotee, but other Muslims perceive the devotional practices of such people otherwise. Saleem argued that "Those who visit the pīr-house, they make the *muzāvar* recite the *al-fateha,* which is nothing but another manifestation of the *ṣahādā* that unhesitatingly pronounces that 'there is no God but God.' But actually in action, these devotees contradict the *shahādāt* and consider the pīr as God." When discussing this aspect, reformists use the term *shirk,* an Arabic term for perceiving someone or something as being on par with Allah, one of the worst offenses one can commit in Islam. As Jaffer told me during one Friday sermon in the month of Muharram:

> Equating some thing or person with God is nothing but violating the very foundation of the Islamic notion of unity (*tawhīd*). Though these devotees have immense faith in God, their "Hindu" ideas make that faith impure, and their ritual of reciting *fātehā* contradicts their other actions. Once you begin to read or listen to the Quran, that reading or listening itself purifies all your impure beliefs and practices. We have to accept the divine hierarchy as defined by our religious thinkers. The Prophet's movement itself was against all sorts of idolatry or magical powers, and the entire history of the arrival of Islam, and the journeys taken up by the Prophet, were to end those wrongdoings and false devotional practices. If you have faith in Islam and still believe in magical powers and idolatry, that's of no use.

What local imams such as Jaffer have been trying to do, in promoting a localized Islam in Gugudu, is to replace the idea of Muharram in local religion with a predominantly Sunni version of Karbala. Like any Sunni Muslim, Jaffer's perception of Muharram is as something confined to "history." This, of course, also contrasts with the Shi'a understandings of Muharram, which is, as Nasr puts it, "the beginning, the motif around which faith has been shaped." This critique of Muharram extends to practices connected with shrines, too, which again are a place where local religion and the larger Shi'a tradition overlap. Shrines in Shi'a Islam are, Nasr says, "locations of spiritual grace (*baraka*), where God is present in a special way and most likely to answer cries for help. [Devotees] seek blessings from these shrines and pray to saints to heal them and grant them their wishes. They believe that the shrines will imbue them with divine blessings and cleanse their souls."[17]

Friday sermons at mosques are key in the critique of the practices and values of local religion. Many now are focused on the three terms *bid'a*, *'amal*, and *īmān*, which we noted above. In the next section, I will discuss the role of these key terms in the current debate in Gugudu about "*asli islām*," and the various strategies that reformist groups have used to promote localized Islam. It is important to keep in mind that this is a local movement, even if what is happening in Gugudu is similar to what is happening across the Islamic world. Locally produced religious materials in Telugu play a crucial role in the activity of the reformists, and I will discuss this textual activity in order to locate its significance in localized Islam.

"Islamic" Texts and Muharram Rituals

In his study on the Trinidadian tradition of Muharram called *Hosay*, Frank Korom discusses the controversy "that focuses on the way that Hosay is practiced in Trinidad, or even whether it should be practiced at all."[18] Presenting different viewpoints of Shi'a and Sunnis, Korom tries to capture the different shades of conflict that surround these ritual practices. That there is local variation in ritual practices is well-known, and textual sources of the tradition can be used to justify such variations. This is obvious with the Shi'a observances of Muharram, and some scholars have been able to show that textual materials have been altered to justify what appear otherwise to be innovations. As David Thurfjell has observed in his study of changes in ritual practice among Islamic men in contemporary Iran, "canonical understandings can be seen as a tool box from which the informants may pick whatever ideas they need in their own personal situation."[19] But this toolbox approach to texts has itself become a magnet for tension in debates centered on the propriety of the values and practices of local religion in Islam. A search for "true" religion is not confined to reformist Muslim groups, and local "Hindus" under the impact of nationalist forces have begun their own debates over whether Gugudu's religion is "Hindu."

The intractability of these debates has encouraged recourse among young Muslims to various secondary-level religious texts which circulate in translation. I use the term "secondary texts" here to acknowledge that many in these reformist groups consider the Quran to be the exclusive primary text and central source for all aspects of Islam. These young Muslim groups see themselves as cleansing Islam of impurities. Their members are mostly between the ages of eighteen and thirty-five, and they are now very active in many villages, even though their numbers are still relatively small. These groups use various media, including books, audio and sermons, to spread their idea of "proper" Islamic ethics, and through these media they have made a significant impact on young Muslims across Andhra since the 1990s. These new media have replaced many modes of traditional learning, and, as the anthropologist Bowen observed in Gayo religion in Indonesia, those who use them have "sought to create students who were socially modern as well as religiously literate."[20] When I asked Jaffer about the use of Telugu in as a language to disseminate Islamic ideas, he explained, "These days very few people read Arabic or Urdu in villages. Earlier, there was a lot of emphasis placed on Arabic or Urdu education, and parents used to take great care that their children receive an

Islamic education (he used the term *dīni mālumāt* for religious knowledge) by their teenage years. Now things are quickly changing. There is no emphasis on Arabic or even Urdu. Even Urdu speaking is fading out. But the interest in Islamic knowledge is endlessly increasing."[21] When I asked him about "Islamic knowledge," he mentioned not only the Five Pillars of Islam, but also tried to explain the notion of *ibādat* (devotion) in terms of *asli islām.*

The public festivities and rituals of Muharram have become a stage for tensions between *local* Islam and *localized* Islam. Reformist groups typically portray the events of Muharram and the pīr practices as an "impure and fake version" of Islam. Their efforts are matched by those of non-Muslim youth groups, who are now bent on discouraging their own community from participating in the daily rituals and Muharram devotional practices in local Islam.

Asserting their identity as "Muslims," as an identity that overrides all others, reformist groups present what they see as "the actual message of the Quran."[22] It is not uncommon in many village mosques to find at least two copies of the Quran carefully placed on the small built-in or wooden shelves. But it is also largely the case that these Qurans are not used, but instead gather dust on the shelves, untouched by anyone for years. The rare exception might be when the imam of the mosque opens the Quran as a display in the festival sermons called *khutba*. Things are now changing in many ways, and middle- and upper-middle-class Muslim youth now expect to read the Quran themselves. To use Jaffer's words, "Village Muslims are slowly on the path of reform and reeducation." This "reeducation" involves four textual tools: (1) the Quran; (2) Islamic literature translated into Telugu; (3) sermons on Fridays as well as those during the ten days of Muharram, and (4) a new text entitled *Faza'il-e-'Amal* (*The Merits of Practice*), originally written in Urdu but transliterated into Telugu, which is being used extensively now. This last text is very clearly aimed at reaching Telugu literate and Urdu-speaking Muslims. The use of *Faza'il-e-'Amal* (*The Merits of Practice*) and other texts is crucial in the development of a localized Islam in the context of Muharram.

Islamic Literature in Telugu

The increase of Islamic publications in Telugu not only reflects the increasing number of Muslims who are speaking Telugu in Andhra Pradesh, but also the growing awareness of the necessity to have proper knowledge about Islam, with the idea of "proper knowledge" connected to what is found in books. This connection is so basic that it is possible to say that localized Islam is a *textualized religion*, whereas local Islam in Gugudu is structured by rituals and oral narratives. The publications of the Telugu Islamic Publications, known for its paperback editions of Islamic books in Telugu, are now found even in the most remote villages in Andhra. As the readership for such literature has grown, the publishing house has also started a weekly magazine focused on more general social and political issues, with accompanying Islamic interpretations. This publishing house was established at the end of the 1980s, and its publications became popular in the 1990s, at the same time the activities of Hindu nationalists began to occupy a significant place in public consciousness. Telugu Islamic Publications, popularly known as TIP in Andhra, has employed new marketing methods to great success, including using mobile book vans to reach remote villages, and setting up reader's clubs to attract students and youth in distributing its books. The publisher has now published more than two hundred titles, all in Telugu. In fact, its rise has been so phenomenal that recently other Telugu-medium Islamic publication groups have been formed, further increasing the number of Islamic texts being published every year in Telugu. These publishing houses have drawn on a group of Islamic scholars, whose published works have given them a new eminence in the Muslim public sphere. In 2006, there were at least fifty scholars whose work on various Islamic texts in Telugu was routinely published. Hameedullah Sheriff, the translator of the Quran into modern Telugu prose, set a model for how to translate and interpret Islamic texts, once read only in Arabic. Sheriff's translation of the Quran is now found in almost every local mosque in Andhra. It has been published in several editions. Commentaries on Islamic texts and practices have also been in circulation in Andhra. In addition, the gradual decrease of the usage of Urdu script, even among Muslims, has added to the spread of these Telugu texts. For a new generation of Urdu-speaking but Telugu-reading Muslims, these texts are the only sources with which to improve their understanding of Islam. But what these texts give them is a version of localized Islam.

The increasing accessibility of Islamic literature has made it possible for reformist groups and literate Muslims to refer to textual sources with authoritative interpretations even in ordinary discussions. For instance, when I asked the *muzāvar* in Gugudu about the origin of the name Kullayappa, he opened the Telugu translation of the Quran and read the *Khul* verse from it. Other Muslims in Gugudu also give a similar explanation for the name of the pīr Kullayappa.

Though Islamic literature in Telugu is not a completely new phenomenon, the recent rise of Telugu writings on Islam has encouraged a shift toward the devotional practices (*ibādat*) of localized Islam, which are self-consciously presented as part of an effort to reform local Islam (*dēhāti islām*). Closer analysis of these Telugu 'Islamic' texts reveals that they fall into five broad genres: (1) those which translate and interpret foundational texts like the Quran; (2) those which apply Quranic interpretations to local social issues; (3) literature on the basic tenets of Islamic law; (4) narratives of the life of Prophet and his family, including stories of women which address recent women's issues; and, (5) magazines which connect current issues and analyze them under the lens of Islam.

The Role of the Quran

Imam Bi is from a remote village in Karnataka. She has been visiting the pīr-house in Gugudu during the month of Muharram for at least forty years. During one of our conversations in Gugudu, she commented that "There is no conflict between the idea of the *rasūl* (messenger) and the *walī*. *Rasūl* is *Rasūl* and *walī* is *walī*. I believe in the idea that there are intimate persons who are close to the rank of Allah. The Quran is all about those intimate persons." Imam Bi's comments, indeed, directed me toward another key aspect of Muharram pīr rituals: the role of the Quran and the "Islamic" rituals in Muslim understanding of their participation in local religion. Though she did not mention or refer to any Quranic verses to talk about "bad" and "good" rituals, like other Muslims she presumably has a sense that there is a clear distinction between what is "Islamic" and what is "un-Islamic." For Imam Bi, as for many Muslim women, reading the Quran has become the primary ritual during Muharram. This is possible because the Quran is now accessible to her thanks to the work of reformers who promote localized Islam.[23]

However, this practice of reading the Quran during Muharram has very little impact on other local practices done during Muharram. The tradition of Muharram in local Islam persists. The Karbala memories and the sacrifice of Husain still hold great importance for many village Muslims, although interestingly some rituals seem to be observed even more fervently by non-Muslims rather than Muslims. In particular, non-Muslim communities are very specific about the *faqīri* rituals they observe, fasting for ten days, as opposed to Muslims, who do them only three. As one Muslim religious leader put it, "Actually, Hindus' power of *īmān* is greater. Once they believe it, they keep it strong. That makes Muharram a stronger tradition, too."[24]

Texts as Tools in the Process of "Islamic Reeducation"

The wide dissemination of the new text *Faza'il-e-'Amal* (The Merits of Practice) has occurred through two means in particular: imams in mosques read certain chapters during the sermon on Fridays, and parents read stories from this text to their children at home. As a secondary text, *Fazail* is actually not a new text, but the increasing use of this text in recent times raises many questions in relation to recent efforts to bring *asli islām* to villages. As far as reformist Muslim groups are concerned, these two means of dissemination are crucial in constructing a new "Islamic" identity, and *'amal* (ritual or practice) remains the key term throughout this textual discourse. Either at the mosque or at home, the main objective of reading this text is to develop awareness of a "true" Islamic practice. The text was initially popularized by the Islamic organization Tablighi Jamāt.[25] It was written in Urdu by Shaikhul Hadith Maulana Muhammad Zakariyya Kaandhlawi, and first appeared in two volumes with twelve chapters in each volume. My focus in this section is on the dissemination of Telugu versions of this text in Gugudu and other villages in Andhra Pradesh. Most interestingly, among the local Muslim community these editions are transliterated from Urdu into Telugu script, making it accessible to local Muslims who speak Urdu but cannot read it. As the back cover of this book states:

> This book is a vast treasure of fundamental Islamic teachings put together with great efforts by Maulana Muhammad Zakariyya (Rah.), one of the most tireless crusaders of the Tabhligi Mission. It consistis of chapters like stories of Sahabah, virtues of Salaat, the Holy Quran, Tabligh, Dhikr, Ramadhan, and Islamic degeneration and its remedy; and is armed with immense persuasive power. The book arouses in the reader the fear of Allah and a fervent desire to mold one's life according to Islamic teachings.

As is clear from these words, the ultimate objective of this text is first to arouse fear of Allah (*qauf* in local Urdu usage), and second, to mold an individual's life according to Islamic ethics. Here I will focus on its relevance in the context of current Muslim practices in Gugudu.

In the villages of Andhra, local mosques and Muslim families use a transliterated version of this text. In other words, they are reading Urdu in Telugu script. During my visits to several towns, I observed that most of the towns now have at least one Islamic book stall, which sells Telugu versions of Islamic literature published by various publishers, along with paraphernalia such as Islamic calendars, rosaries, audio cassettes and compact discs of Islamic sermons. As many store owners explained to me, *Faza'il-e-'Amal* is the most popular text sold in almost every store. One vendor told me, "Not just town Muslims but every Muslim family now has begun to own at least one copy of this book. Sometimes I'll order twenty copies in a week and by the next Friday they're all sold out. Now even village Muslims are interested in learning about *asli islām*." As many of the store owners put it, "This text has become a source book for Islamic practices in the current turbulent times of 'un-Islamic' practices." The increasing circulation of this text even into remote villages, and the devotional patterns centered on the ideas as communicated in this text, reveals a new mode of Islamic discourse. As explained in the foreword of the text, its intended audience is primarily women and children. Using the faith and practices of women and children from the Prophet's time as a model, the text aims to "create in them an Islamic spirit of love and esteem for Sahabah, and thereby improve their *īmān*."[26]

However, in actual practice the text plays a different role. In many local mosques it is customary to read certain chapters from the Quran after the prayers on Fridays or on other special days. Usually, the imam will read a few verses from the Quran, and then situate them in a relation to contemporary local issues. This ritual reading of the Quran has now been replaced by readings from *Faza'il-e-'Amal*. Since the text is in simple Urdu, most of the imams at local mosques prefer to use it as a kind of sermon, too. The Tablighi Jamāt, an Islamic organization which has been offering training to many religious preachers and sending them to village mosques, started making this text required reading, and most of the new generation of preachers come directly from this new learning tradition. Jaffer, who performs daily prayers in the mosque in Gugudu, told me that he actually was trained in reading and explaining this text, though reading and reciting the Quran was a prerequisite for receiving training from the Tablighi Jamāt. During my visits to the local mosques and in conversations with village imams, I observed that many imams prefer to use *Faza'il-e-'Amal* over the Quran. One imam said:

> Reciting from the Quran and interpreting the verses might lead to interpolations, and in the process we might be making our own interpretations. Many times local imams run into problems, as their comments create some unwanted discussion in the village. As you know, the Muslim situation is really sensitive at this point. We really don't want to create any kind of controversy, and our purpose is to spread a good word about Islamic practices, and improve people's *īmān*. *Fazai'l* has solved such local

problems, since it is written by an Indian scholar and intended mostly for Indian Muslims. When we started using this text, many theoretical and interpretive issues are harmoniously settled.

In a way, this text serves to mediate between the Quran and the local Muslim community by providing a possible framework for understanding "proper" Islamic belief and ritual. Having explained the significant role of this new text, let me elaborate on how this text finds its place in religious sermons inside and outside the mosque.

Politics of Sermons: Inside and Outside the Mosque

Along similar lines, the nature of sermons on Fridays and special days (*khutba*) in local mosques has undergone significant changes through an emphasis on reeducation.[27] Rather than focusing on general virtues and universal topics such as the Five Pillars of Islam, the imams trained by Tablighi now address specific local issues in their sermons. As concerns about the status of Indian Muslims as minorities have increased with the intensification of communal politics in the 1990s, hardened communal boundaries have helped make the mosque not only a center for religious learning but also a key part of efforts by Muslim community (*ummah*) to regain its prominence.

Sermons in village mosques offer us an opportunity to gain a deeper understanding of these concerns about "minority" status, and one process by which divisions between Muslims and non-Muslims have hardened. Since 1992, when the disputed Babri Mosque was demolished in Ayodhya, village sermons have begun to focus more on "Islamic" identity, often by defining "true" Islam "real" Muslims. Islamic sermons can be publically given both inside and outside the mosque. Inside the mosque, there has been a heavy usage of texts like the Quran and the *Fazai'l*, aimed at regular participants in the prayers. In such cases, sermons deal more with religious issues, and tend to motivate the participants toward activities like reading and reciting the Quran. Outside sermons focus on broader issues and are intended to reach larger audiences. The most important sources for building a heightened sense of community among Muslims have been audio cassettes and CDs of Islamic sermons, which often also include lectures and recitations of Karbala verses.

These Friday sermons often follow a structural pattern that contains three parts: first, condemnation of current misconceptions about Islam; second, a careful selection of local social issues; and third, reinforcement of a specific "Islamic" religiosity through careful citations from the Quran and *hadith*. Apart from responding to political questions, the most important feature of this reinforcement of Islamic identity has been to define the boundaries of "Islamic" rituals and practices, especially regarding pīr practices and Muharram rituals. During the ten days of Muharram in Gugudu, I made it a point to attend morning and evening prayers at the mosque. Every morning after prayer, Jaffer read specific parts from the *Fazai'l* and then condemning local Muharram practices.

In such sermons, Jaffer unhesitatingly rejected some of the rituals that were going on at the pīr-house. During the ten days of Muharram, Jaffer focused in his sermons on the three key concepts of *bid'a*, *'amal,* and *īmān*, and most days he never failed to address the day's rituals at the pīr-house, offering a sharp critique using passages from the texts. On the sixth day of Muharram, when most of the devotees at the pīr-house in Gugudu were busy preparing the firepit for the seventh-day fire-walk, Saleem, a Muslim imam from the neighboring town, gathered a few Muslims before the mosque and gave a lecture focusing on the term *bid'a,* which he defined as "improper and inappropriate innovation," emphasizing "improper" and "inappropriate." He expanded on these two adjectives, saying,

> In Islam we have two categories of devotional practices (*'amal*): the physical and the spiritual. Again, the physical is of two types: performing body rituals and giving away your money or whatever you have. Whatever you do, you should do it with right intention (*niyyat*). The value of any action depends on the intention. And again, the value of intention depends on the appropriate and proper practice as defined by the Quran. All other practices, such as fire-walks, walking around the firepit, worshipping objects, making vows, etc., are just *bid'a*, improper innovations. There is no space for such improper, inappropriate practices in *asli islām*.

In a way, Saleem's approach to sermons was different from most imams and Islamic speakers, as he invited questions and discussion after each sermon. Saleem's entire focus was on local Muharram practices in Gugudu, and his audience was one segment of devotees who came to Gugudu to worship the local pīr. In addition, Saleem met many of these Muslim devotees before the sermon. He convinced them to come to the mosque and to his special sermons, enjoining them to "behave like true Muslim[s] and worship the one and only Allah." Thirty-year-old Saleem is one of the young reformists who has been trained in Islam by reading Telugu Islamic books. He has attended Islamic theological training camps to learn Arabic and Urdu. He is very particular about the practice of the Five Pillars of Islam, and his ultimate personal goal is to make a pilgrimage to Mecca. Though he has a small business in a nearby town, most of his activities are dedicated to religious teaching in various villages and urban places across Andhra. During one of our meetings, he explained his life's mission in the following way:

> My entire focus is on teenagers and those under twenty-five years of age. I consider that age to be a very significant time to turn your life toward Islam. After twenty-five, your ideas get somehow settled and you never pay attention to what others are saying. This is what exactly Hindu groups are also doing.

During much of our conversation, Saleem mentioned Hindu activism in villages, but he never explicitly said that his actions were reactions to the Hindu activism. His anger and passion, however, reveal negative perceptions about various aspects of Hindu activism. Though he does also does not mention Hindu activism in his formal sermons, during our informal conversations, Saleem never tired of referring to various aspects of Hindu activism, which he said was "rampant and violent" in many local places. He specifically mentioned the bodily practices of Hindus, which he saw as being preparation for "waging a war against the Muslims."

> Bodily practices, in the Islamic sense, are different from these Hindu activist perceptions. For these people, bodily practice means building muscles. Islam never defines the body in that way. Ask those Hindus who perform *faqīri* during Muharram what they mean by body practice.

Saleem's invoking of the practice of *faqīri* is strategic here, and he explained that "even the Hindus respect Islamic bodily practices, which really aim for spiritual goals." Though Saleem rejects many of the devotional practices in Gugudu, he tries to draw on some of practices, such as reciting *fātehā*, *faqīri,* and *ziyārat* rituals such as visiting graves, to explain more about the impact of the ethics of Islam. On most occasions when he gives sermons, he begins with one such practice and then tries to explain what is *bid'a* about it, contrasting it with proper Islamic practice by closely analyzing each ritual.

Conclusion: Tensions between Bid'a and 'Amal

From the various strategies that religious reformists use in their sermons, meetings and debates, we get a clear sense of what these groups hope to cultivate in local religion. Three key terms—*bid'a, 'amal,* and *īmān*—are repeatedly used in reformist discourse, and very frequently these debates over practice revolve around fixing the contours of *bid'a* and *īmān* in various ways. *Bid'a* is often considered the "conceptual battleground where issues of concepts of authenticity and authority are contested by modern Muslims."[28] As Sabah Mahmood has explained, "*Bid'a* is a term in Islamic doctrine that refers to unwanted innovations, beliefs, or practices for which there was no precedent at the time of the Prophet, and which are therefore best avoided."[29] However, as Mahmood has also observed in her study, this term is ambiguous when it comes to practice, and as her informants expressed, "Remember that it is our right to select from any of the opinions available in the four schools, even if the opinion happens to be noncanonical or anomalous."[30] Though there are strict cautions, such as "every innovation is 'misguidance' and every misguidance leads to the Fire (i.e., hell),"[31] when it comes to practice, what makes a practice either *bid'a* or acceptable is always a contested issue. Several times even during daily prayers in mosques, it is not uncommon to see those who have come for *namāz* arguing about appropriate practice and *bid'a*. When it comes to large public rituals this controversy is even more visible. The appropriate way of performing Muharram rituals has been debated for many years now, with most of the practices followed by Shi'a being considered *bid'a*. As Hyder has observed, "A handful of non-Shi'i groups, including some segments of the Saudi-backed Wahabbis or Salafis, label Muharram commemorations as *bid'a*, unlawful accretions to Islam condemned by the Prophet; to these groups *'alams* reflect polytheism (*shirk*)."[32] This perception of polytheism in local religion is not uncommon, but in practice even Muslims in Gugudu who point this out as *shirk* never fail to observe *ziyārat*, and keep the images of metal standards in their homes.

When I started my field research in Andhra, many local Muslim informants and Islamic scholars at first questioned me: "Why Muharram? Why not Ramadan if you're interested in studying the "real" Muslim community?" Later, they explained, "There is no Muharram now in any village except in Hyderabad. Now Muharram is totally a rejected innovation, *bid'a*." These two statements show their clear rejection of Muharram practices, but more importantly they show that the contents of urban debates over Islamic practice now reach even remote villages in Andhra. So ubiquitous are these discussions on *bid'a* and *'amal* that Ramadan is routinely mentioned whenever someone starts talking about Muharram. During many Friday sermons, I have also heard local imams and Islamic speakers emphasizing the importance of Ramadan practices, which are considered *sahī āmāl* ("true" or "pure" practices), while consistently labeling Mu-harram *bid'a*.

When I met several local imams and local-level Islamic speakers over the course of my fieldwork, they strategically tried their best to steer my questions toward the subject of Ramadan. Whenever I asked a question about Muharram specifically, they turned that question toward the Five Pillars of Islam, and explained to me that "Ramadan is the embodiment of all Islamic ethics, particularly, the Five Pillars. Ramadan is the *sahī āmāl* (pure practice)." During our conversations, Saleem read some passages from *Fazai'l-e-'Amal* that explain and emphasize the importance of Rama-dan. Referring to the text, he said:

> It is stated in the Hadith: "If my *Ummah* realized what Ramadan really is, they would wish that the whole year would just be Ramadan." In another Hadith, we are told that "the fasting of Ramadan and fasting three days of every month keep evil away from the heart." What these villagers are doing during Muharram is nothing but that kind of fasting. But fasting has no use until you perform a prayer and express your right intention. If you don't have that religious knowledge, you should go to the nearby mosque and join the *ummah* that performs the prayer.

As clear from references to joining the *ummah* in the above quotation, most of these sermons, arguments and teachings are a part of a larger effort to encourage a localized Islam that will connect places like Gugudu to the larger Islamic community. But they are equally clear that this vision of *ummah* has no place for many of the values and practices of Gugudu's local Islam.

| Conclusion

To learn about the pīr is to learn about the village, and to worship the
pīr is to worship the land.

—OBULESU, A DALIT FROM GUGUDU

MUMTAZ HUSAIN, A LOCAL tea-stall operator, had always been eager to hear
about my real intention in writing about Gugudu. "What are you ultimately
going to say about our village?" was his question after every cup of tea and
each conversation we had during my nine-month stay in Gugudu. Not only
Mumtaz, but also several other people from various backgrounds asked me
this question, albeit each with different connotations, various shades of
meaning, and different ways of expression. Pressed, I too answered in multiple ways. The question was intriguing for them, but it was for me as well.
Each day when I lingered at the pīr-house in the early mornings, having a
cup of tea with villagers and pilgrims or reading a newspaper there, I would
spend a lot engaging in conversation and discussion about the pīr, as well as
routine matters in the village. At night before going to bed, as I read my field
notes, and gathered my thoughts and wrote, I would ask myself, "What ex-
actly am I going to say about this village and its Muharram celebration?"

My focus was on more than just this village when I started my fieldwork
in 2006. And though my purpose in coming to this village may have been
to study the public rituals of Muharram, what I found took me on different
paths than I expected. But when I now consider the real intention of that
question, "What are you going to say finally about our village?" I begin to
understand that their emphasis was not simply on the village, but also on
their pride in the tradition of the local pīr, Kullayappa, or their worries that
what I write might bring disrepute on the village. Some even went to the
extent of making these latter sentiments explicit, warning me about

commonly held misconceptions about the pīr. "Urban and educated people never are able to understand the pīr. They always say that this is somewhat of a wrong or inferior level of belief, and consider the pīr a lesser deity, which is not true. If it was true, why do even many urban and educated people also come and pray to the pīr. People say different and do different," said low-caste devotee Obulesu during one evening conversation over tea. Mumtaz, serving us another round of tea, continued, "Yes, urban Muslims are also like that. They consider themselves true Muslims and disregard our pīrs and our practices. I don't say that the pīr is God. But the pīr is the one who has almost reached that point. The pīr connects us with God, and most importantly, the pīr connects us to each other, as the *ummah*, the community of believers." Khaja, another pilgrim, added, "If Muharram is about the protection of the *ummah*, then the pīrs stood and shed their blood for it."

I began to realize that these informants were gradually pushing me toward their understanding of the practices of the pīr tradition, which they saw as the focus of Muharram. For them, to understand Muharram in Gugudu I needed to understand the functionality of this local figure in Gugudu. Particularly, in a village which has no Shii Muslims and very few Muslim families, what is the function of Muharram and the pīrs, which themselves come from the Shii tradition? In terms of "community" (*ummah*), as Mumtaz and Khaja tried to explain it, what causes this community to develop a system of beliefs around the pīr? What I found in Gugudu was not only different than what I expected, it was both more tense and intense. There were not only "age-old" devotional practices and "traditional" narratives. These devotees and pilgrims, the men and women who lived in Gugudu or came to it as pilgrims, were not living in a static world of beliefs and practices, waiting for me observe them. Their world was constantly changing, and part of these changes was how it they were connected to the world beyond Gugudu.

The contours of devotion were not confined to the geographical space of the pīr-house, mosque, or even physical boundaries of Gugudu. Not only the villagers, but the three hundred thousand pilgrims as well all claimed Gugudu as *their* place, the abode of their family and caste pīr, Kullayappa. Theirs was a religious world much more complex than I could bound within any single category. Thus I have found conceptually useful what I have called local and localized Islam. The category of local Islam includes much of what is often called "village religion," or "popular Islam." But with this term I have tried to develop a category which emphasizes that every version of local Islam constructs its own vision of Islam within a set of locally defined practices appropriated from global

Islam. In addition, this feature of local Islam is in tension with another way of engaging global Islam, which is localized Islam. Thus, this book has had two key concerns: local Islam and localized Islam.

I was raised a Muslim myself, and Karbala has had a significant place in my life, just as it had a significant place in the life of my childhood village. The entire village used to eagerly await Muharram. I grew up watching the dynamic ritual standards of the local pīrs like Hasan and Husain. The metal battle standards which symbolized these martyrs used to walk and play around us just like any other child. Local pīr-houses were our theaters of childhood, where we used to imagine alternate stories of the pīr, and stage them for fun. The firepits that glowed with red burning eyes used to haunt our childhood dreams.

As a poet and short-story writer, I regularly develop images and metaphors borrowed from my childhood memories of Karbala.[1] Among them, the most fascinating experience was the storytelling evenings with my mother and grandmother, who never tired of telling us stories about the battle of Karbala, particularly those of Imam Husain and his mother Fatima.[2] Most of those stories were in Urdu. From her dog-eared notebook of Karbala songs, my mother used to recite many songs, gathering all the children together in one place beforehand. Here is how I remember one of those oral verses:

> Mother Fatima was in my dream last night,
> Washing the battlefield of Karbala with her endless tears,
> Sweeping the battlefield of Karbala with her long tresses.
> And when I asked her why you are doing this on this night,
> "Hello, Fatima, here is the earth that's going to take my son into its lap."
> "Hello, Fatima, I want to keep it clean and fresh before he falls down into her lap."[3]

Dreams are a typical setting for these songs and narratives. In this instance, Fatima meets Fatima, Fatima asks Fatima, Fatima responds to Fatima. The setting itself often felt dreamlike. It was difficult for us to hold back our tears, and usually every storytelling session came to an end with sobs. As I grew up, I began to understand that this was not a private memory, but part of a collective memory, rekindled every year at Muharram when large numbers of Muslims join together on the tenth day and bid farewell to the martyrs, weeping and wailing. Why do people tell martyr stories? Why do people remember only some characters from the Battle of Karbala? What makes their death so prominent in public memory? Such were the questions I asked then. Now, after encountering a different set of narratives and rituals in Gugudu, I ask instead: why is what I remember from my childhood village different from the public memory of Gugudu? Various moments in my fieldwork in Gugudu often made me move back and forth from my childhood days, which in retrospect seem uncomplicated compared to contemporary times with their political tensions.

The days I have spent in Gugudu have unsettled most of my knowledge about the Muslim-centered stories of the martyrs of Karbala. This has come most strongly from the distinctions between my domestic knowledge of Muharram in my childhood home and the dominance of the public realm of Karbala. It does not mean that I was unfamiliar with this extended realm of Muharram or the pīr practices, but it never occurred to me that I had been participating in a world that had larger implications than what I had learned from my family. In this way, the journey to Gugudu in part has to do with my own subjective narratives as well. This journey gave me new insight into my own familiar world of Muharram through the lens of local Islam and also localized Islam.

Muharram: Domestic and Public

I have tried to argue, in focusing on a wide range rituals in Gugudu, that the boundaries of domestic and public overlap, as observed in the food ritual of *kandūri* and the temporary ascetic practice of *faqīri*. Much like the domestic space of my childhood, where my Sunni mother and grandmother used to narrate Karbala stories, blurring religious boundaries, for several non-Muslim families in and around Gugudu, Muharram began at home, in the local language of Telugu. As the repository of local public memory, connecting and preserving various strands of religion into one singular narrative and set of rituals, Muharram plays a central role in the making of local Islam. Most of these local Muharram narratives are sprinkled with Shi'a terms and ideas. Most of these terms describe sacred spaces within the confines of the village, and transform it into the homeland and battlefield of the Karbala martyrs.

The story of Karbala is told in a local idiom, and the martyrs including the Holy Five here speak Telugu and lead an ordinary life like any village peasant or artisan.[4] Most importantly, the family of the Prophet becomes the family of all, and their stories become everyone's family stories. This network of stories and social relations is what eventually constructs a community (*ummah*) and defines the religious life of the village. The basic structure of the Karbala narratives of Karbala in Telugu differs from that of the narratives told in Urdu, as it encompasses multiple communities, languages, and religious vocabularies. In such a distinctive journey, Telugu narratives move out of their limited, domestic boundaries of *ummah* as defined by Islamic theology. When my mother used the term *ummah* it had only one meaning, which was Islamic in nature. But in Gugudu the conceptual contours of *ummah* and the Telugu alternate *ummaḍi* (collectivity) embrace multiple meanings. For instance, Fatima in my mother's narrative is always a family person and an embodiment of feminine sensibilities. Contrary to this, Fatima in many Telugu narratives in Gugudu, while still an epitome of feminine sensibilities, becomes a "public" person as one who performs final rites for her sons. Thus, their heads are made everlasting symbols of martyrdom and community. The imagined Fatima as ideal mother of great warriors and her display of their heads in the public space, demonstrates one instance of appropriation of the Karbala narrative into a regional idiom.

In essence, the memory of my mother and the memories of those in Gugudu have similar origins, but they are directed at very different horizons of understanding. Just how different are they? What makes Muharram so public in Gugudu's devotion? These two questions have been central to my depiction of Gugudu (Chapter 1) and description of the narratives of the local pīr Kullayappa (Chapter 2). Chapter 1 describes the village of Gugudu, focusing particularly on the sacred sites associated with the Kullayappa tradition. Like many South Indian villages, Gugudu has both Hindu and Muslim sacred spaces, but unlike other villages, the pīr-house has become the center of the village and the center of local Islam, the Muharram tradition of which highlights shared practices. The local form of Islam draws on many traditions, including Vaishnavism, the temporary yogic practice of asceticism, village deity worship, and an "unbound" Sufism. Moreover, "Islam" comes to encompass all of these in the public rituals of Muharram. As in many villages in Andhra, in Gugudu, Muharram has become the most visible expression of local Islam. Throughout this work, I have shown how Muharram offers us a fascinating window into this shared religious life that has been ordained by the intervention of regional exemplars and holy persons appearing in Islamic guise.

The Pīr and Local Ethics

In Chapter 2, I presented various stories as told and interpreted by different castes in Gugudu. In the Shii tradition, the centrality of the family of the Prophet, particularly 'Ali and his son Imam Husain, is crucial and takes on political significance for Shi'as. In both Hinduism and Islam, holy person-ages play a prominent role in imparting religious learning, and demonstrate a distinctive form of religious teaching. Though each religion has its own traditions and practices, as I have argued in Chapter 1, local pīrs reveal a divergent and open system of ritual life and devotional practices which seemingly combines the practices of various religions.

Chapter 2 mapped the journey of the local pīr Kullayappa into personal and public lives in Gugudu. Besides worshipping the family of the Prophet, local villagers extend the family tree of the Prophet by imagining local pīrs in the context of Muharram. Complicating current scholarship on Shi'a-centered narratives and ritual performances during Muharram, the idea of local pīrs further extends the realm of Karbala. This notion of Karbala has further roots in the collective identity of the local community and the construction of an alternate *ummah* that aims to establish a village with "pure intention" (*niyyatu*) and passionate love for a particular place. In a way, this is similar to many Sufi traditions popular in South India. However, most studies of Sufism in South India focus more on mystical traditions and ignore the aspect of public Islam[5] that is so prominent in the Muharram tradition of Gugudu. One of the larger arguments of this book is that the Muharram tradition is supplemented locally by various understandings of local pīrs, whose religious teachings have the potential for tension and change in the devotional practices of Muharram. This claim has implications for many of the religiously plural communities in South Asia.

Public Event: Beginnings and Endings

In Chapter 3, I continued to elaborate on the spread of these pīr-centered ideas as they are performed in the public devotional practices of Muharram, by analyzing narrative evidence from the oral stories of villagers in Gugudu. South Indian villages commonly have a tradition of public religious events that includes *jātara*[6] or *tirunāḷḷa* and pilgrimages, locally called *tīrtham*. Numerous studies have explored this aspect of public religion, but village Muharram traditions, like the one found in Gugudu, have thus far been largely absent from scholarly discussions. Arguing that the pīr-houses and their related public rituals have been crucial in the making of the notion of "village" (*ūru*) for at least several centuries, I have suggested that Muharram is more than a public aspect of global Islam.

Though I stayed in Gugudu for much of my research, I also managed to visit neighboring villages and places, and to follow an imagined itinerary of the pīrs as given in the stories told by devotees. As I began to visit these villages and meet more people from more caste groups, I realized that each place had its own storehouse of narrative and ritual knowledge about the pīrs, and this encouraged me to dig deeper into the specifics of religious life in each place. In many places and place legends, the pīrs play a central role in the performances of Muharram, but what Muharram was now about was the question that kept coming up.

It is commonplace in many studies of Shi'ism to understand Muharram as an instrument of redemptive suffering for all believers, and to portray the tenth day as always a public display of mourning and solidarity for the martyrs of Karbala.[7] Muharram performers in Gugudu, however, revise this idea of redemptive suffering, though they continue to give importance to the final rites of the tenth day as well. As Tirupatayya explained to me, "Muharram is not just about the ending, but about the beginning as well." Though we have enough scholarship to understand the significance of the ending of Karbala, we until now do not understand why the beginning should be celebrated, or why there should be a form of celebration at all. "Don't you think the lives of martyrs are as important as their deaths?" questioned Mumtaz Husain one day as we discussed the "merriment" present in local Muharram festivities.[8]

In Gugudu, each day in the thirteen-day Muharram represents a phase in the life of the martyrs, and thus the first day is as important as the tenth day. The first day marks the beginning of a new village. As Tirupatayya recalled the words of the pīr, "The day I entered into your village would be the beginning of a life of purity and prosperity." Thus when the villagers view the moon on the first day of Muharram, that is their "new" year, and their "beginning" of a life with *niyyatu* of "pure intention." So the public festivities begin with a reenactment of the entire history of the village, focusing on the sustainability of that *niyyatu* through the rest of the holiday and beyond. Close examination of these thirteen days of rituals reveals that various alternative meanings can be produced in a single local Muharram. Many Telugu narratives performed during the holiday narrate the entire life stories of the martyrs and local pīrs, that include joyous days when they shared food, ambivalent moments when they struggled between liminal spaces, and finally the definitive moments of their martyrdom. To provide a detailed picture of this extended realm of Muharram rituals, I have also described some of the rituals enacted during non-Muharram days in Gugudu. In addition, I have shown the range of interpretations offered by different caste groups in order to demonstrate the breadth of significance perceived in Muharram. Even though many devotees enact the vow of *faqīri* at a personal level, their practice also reflects the public nature of devotion in the village. While describing the significance of *faqīri* at a personal level in Chapter 4, I have focused especially on the public aspect of the *faqīri*.

The Politics of Muharram: A Textual Turn

The wide popularity of various Karbala rituals and their ramifications for public spaces in Gugudu have inevitably made Muharram a site of contestation. Many of the rituals associated with Muharram in local Islam are now challenged by reformist Muslims on behalf of a localized Islam. This process of localizing Islam, in the sense of establishing a "true Islam" locally through the reforming of the Islam that is already there, might be seen primarily as a textual turn, as I have illustrated in Chapter 5.

In Gugudu, like in many places in Andhra, Muslims are increasingly accessing texts that interpret *hadith*[9] and the Quran.[10] The arrival of these texts has had a significant impact on the religious and social life of Muslims, even in small villages like Gugudu. As a result of the dissemination of their contents through reading, sermons, and discussion, some young Muslims in Gugudu now forcefully reject the tradition of Muharram. Under the notion of *asli islām*,[11] the activity of these men has had two effects on local Islam. First, it has solidified local Muslims' sense of belonging to a global religious community, and has thus undermined the possibility of a shared and inclusive religious culture. Second, it has served to distinguish certain local devotional practices as "Islamic" but in need of reform, and others as "un-Islamic" and perhaps even "Hindu" and in need of being rejected. This has made it increasingly difficult to perceive local Islam in the village. Reformist Muslims have made it an objective of theirs to transform how local devotion is perceived, and to do so have come to rely increasingly on textual sources, sermons inside and outside the mosque, and new media such as audio cassettes. It is worth emphasizing that in spite of all this emphasis on strengthening an exclusive Muslim identity, all of these textual materials are available in Telugu, with the sole aim to reach Telugu-literate, yet Urdu-speaking Muslims. Multiple translations of the Quran, various *hadith*-based commentarial texts, and booklets that introduce key Islamic terms, including *īmān, namāz,* and *jihād,* frequently run into several Telugu editions every year.

In general, these texts purport to provide a "true" Islamic perspective on various current issues, alongside relevant passages from the Quran. The dissemination of these texts, and the reading practices and reception associated with them, has already impacted the practices within local Islam itself. In their sermons and discussions, local imams or preachers speak often with reference to these texts about local practices connected with Muharram and the pīr tradition. As one Islamic scholar explained to me, "For a long time, we made a mistake by not focusing on village-level Muslim practices. But over a decade we have seen a gradual decay in the ethics of Muslims. Since they do not have access to Islamic learning and knowledge, they're more exposed to Hindu practices. Now we feel the need to rectify these practices and reform this process. We have a multi-pronged strategy to achieve this goal. First, we have to provide basic learning materials that give a basic understanding of *dīni mālumāt* (religious knowledge). The focus on producing these textual materials has nothing to do with fundamentalism. We are secular and democratic in our outlook. We are just trying to reform impure practices."

As I have explained in Chapter 5, these phenomena of production and reception of reformist Islamic materials has been most successful among younger Muslims.[12] My focus in regards to such textual politics has been limited to the scope of their relation to Muharram in local devotion, but this issue deserves more focused and detailed ethnographic research. As this textual activity continues to increase, the impact of reformism on local Islam might be the separation of the community to the point that Muslim participation in Gugudu's Muharram festivities would cease.

Appropriating Karbala and Local Islam

"Whatever you do in my name, you do it in your own way." Devotees of Kullayappa frequently refer in their narratives to this saying as the words of the pīr himself. By using this phrase, devotees legitimate their right to alter, appropriate, and authenticate blended rituals. The success of Muharram as a public ritual in Gugudu lies in this openness and malleability. For many devotees, Muharram has shown them the possibility of shared devotion, which in turn shapes their idea of devotion and allows them to refashion their everyday lives in its sensibilities.

As demonstrated in this book, the tradition of Muharram in local religious life has never been static. A picture of the appropriation and reinterpretation of Karbala can be seen in one of earliest short stories written in Telugu. In 1910, when colonial British officers were collecting for the first time census statistics, and categorically defining the religious boundaries between "Hindus" and "Muslims,"[13] Gurajaḍa Appa Rao, the pioneer of modern Telugu literature,[14] wrote a short story entitled, "Gods, What's

Your Name?," about Muharram and devotional life generally in a village.[15] Against colonial efforts to fix a "Hindu" identity, Gurajaḍa's story highlights the heterogeneity of various castes and sects among Hindus, and offers a complicated picture of local devotion. This in turn also suggests an alternative way of writing the history of Hinduism.

Gurajaḍa's story depicts the dimensions of multiplicity and interpracticality in local devotion in many ways. The story primarily raises the question of real faith (*īmān*) in devotion. In turn, it defines the practical contours of devotion. The story refers to various themes of Islam, including submission to God and faith (*īmān*), as defined not by scripture but by the local practices of devotees. Here is one scene from the story:

> Nancharamma looked around and asked everyone, "Is that pīr saheb here?" Soon, the Pīr Saheb walked to her and said, folding his hands, "Right here. I submit to you." This Pīr Saheb originally belonged to the cotton-carders caste (*Dudēkula*). Yet he is a great devotee of Rama and sings hymns to him. He practices complex yoga and has a monastery on the roadside that attracts many disciples.
>
> "Hi, Saheb, can you walk over the burning coals?"
>
> "If you order me so, I can do it easily."[16]

Another scene emphasizes the significance of faith, and points out the lack of faith among Hindus gathered there, who fight each other in the name of Shiva and Vishnu.

> "Don't you know about Vaishnavas? They're nothing but Muslims. Do you know what the pīr is? It's nothing but the three symbolic lines which appear on the brow of Viṣṇu. You know that pīrs are worshipped in our town and Hindus do the fire-walk all the time. Look there, we worship that pīr every year and we are not Saivas or Vaiṣṇavas when we go there. Even Saivas go so far as to say that the pīr is nothing but Siva's trident.
>
> Then, the Brahmin said sighing, "Wow, not only human beings, even gods are hybrid in these modern times."

The story ends by suggesting that real faith is "total surrender" (*prapatti*), as described in Vaishnava *bhakti*, but that this surrender is to local pīrs rather than to Viṣhnu. While presenting the history of the arrival of pīrs to local devotion, the story emphasizes various themes such as the public rituals of Muharram, and locates their significance in the formation of a local Islam which borrows extensively from Sufi and Shi'i practices.

Ninety-four years after the first appearance of Gurajaḍa' story, the Telugu short-story writer Nisar wrote *Mulki,* which shows the great shift in the ways that Muharram is perceived and performed in many villages today.[17] The story begins with a description of the fire-walk on the ninth day of Muharram, and proceeds to offer a vivid portrayal of the entire ritual process of the public event. At its heart, it tells a story of a person who in life never compromised his right and proper intention (*niyyatu*), which in turn has attracted the entire village to the public rituals of Muharram. Yet the most important theme of the story is intense passion for the "motherland" (*vatan* or *mulki* in Urdu). For the protagonist Abbas and his family, the public rituals of Muharram have roots in this passion for motherland. Positioning itself against the Hindu nationalist argument that Muslims do not belong in India, the story focuses on the strong sense of place in the celebration of Muharram. At one particularly crucial point in the story, the villagers collectively support Abbas:

> "Abbas should stay in the village. We are never going to let him go."
>
> "Yes, Abbas should not leave the village. A village with no Muslim has no *barakat* (divine blessing)."
>
> "Yes, Abbas should not leave the village. He is always there for good and for *niyyatu*. He is always there when we want to do *kandūri*. He is always there when we want to do the festival of pīrs."

The main reason for allowing Abbas to stay in the village was his role in public rituals, and his personal *niyyatu*, which eventually leads to the *barakatu* of the entire village. While highlighting the importance of Muharram as a public ritual, the story also laments the non-participation of some "Hindu" castes in present-day Muharram celebrations. However, the story ends with many of these caste groups realizing that this holiday is crucial to their village, in spite of the differences among its inhabitants.

> "This is the only public festival we perform irrespective of caste, high and low. This is everyone's festival."
>
> "It's good that these Muslim brothers came back and are doing this again. We suffered a lot in their absence."
>
> "Here is your motherland. Don't leave it, and don't make this village an orphan, without a pīr to bless us."

Nisar's story suggests what a village may be like without a Muharram celebration, and highlights the moment when the villagers realize just what an unfortunate fate this would be. The story portrays the Muharram through various stages of history in local devotion in Andhra. Moreover, these literary representations of Muharram document various appropriations of Muharram in local devotion. The question that remains central throughout this holiday's evolution is this: how do communities perceive and pursue the idea of Muharram through the course of time? Focusing on Gugudu, my response has centered on the argument that Muharram is an alternative devotional practice for many villages. It is an alternative to a dominant religion that dictates fixed identities and rejects the multiplicity and dynamism of local devotion. More importantly, the public events of Muharram are a central manifestation of a dynamic and lively ritual culture.

As always, the most fascinating moment in the events of Muharram is the tenth-day procession. Whenever I think of Muharram in Gugudu, this image of the final procession comes to mind. In this ritual, the local pīr Kullayappa and his brothers, including Hasan and Husain, are taken out for the nightlong procession. Thousands of devotees and *faqīrs* have waited for that great moment when they will take final *darśanam* of the pīrs. After reciting the *fātehā*, the *muzāvar* hands over the pīr to Tirupatayya's family, who receive him, saying "*Dīn Gōvindā.*" After briefly walking around the firepit, the procession moves through each lane in the village. This walk is always very slow and ambivalent, an endless series of steps forward and then backward, and then forward again. At one point, Tirupatayya told me,

> The pīr actually doesn't want to leave. He wants to stay in his 'real and complete form' (*nija rūpam*) in the village. But this is the tradition, that he is supposed to be seen only during Muharram, and not on other days. I can see tears in his eyes. Ritually, we are required to perform his final rites. But the pīrs never die. It's always symbolic. Death is just one moment in the story of their lives. They die to make us realize the reality of the death. And, you know, it's my dream to die in the local Karbala, close to the place where we perform their final rites.

The final procession was never a happy time for the thousands of devotees, each one experiencing personally this last viewing of the pīrs for the year. Each devotee engages with the pīrs in her own way, and performs rituals in order to make this final meeting possible in a distinctive mode. The meaning of Karbala and the message of the pīr are her own, as they bear uniquely on her own life. I hope to have captured in this book at least some of the intensity of this shared devotion to the pīrs, as it appears and is contested through the twin lenses of local and localized Islam.

NOTES

Introduction

1. Flueckiger, (2004):723–25; (2006):2.

2. Dale Eickelman, "The Study of Islam in Local Contexts," in Richard Martin, ed., *Contributions to Asian Studies*, 17 (1982):1.

3. For more on "resolute localism," see Engseng Ho, 2010, 67 and 188.

4. Yasmin Saikia's recent book *Women, War, and the Making of Bangladesh* shows how we can analyze Islamic values without returning to the Islamic legal system of *sharia*; 101.

5. Veer, 1994; Kamrava, 2011.

6. See Tony Stewart's essay in *Beyond Turk and Hindu*, 2000.

7. Cohen, 2007; Stewart, 2007.

8. Young, 1995.

9. Karbala is within the geographical boundaries of present-day Iraq. Nevertheless, Karbala is more than a place, as it symbolically refers to the entire history of Shi'ism, and the gradual development of Muharram events. Karbala represents, as David Pinault has put it, "an overriding paradigm of persecution, exclusion and suffering." Michael Fischer, in *Iran: From Religious Dispute to Revolution*, used the key term "Karbala paradigm" to comprehend the interactions between Karbala and the modern Islamic world. Since the 1980s, in particular, traditional mourning of the Karbala martyrdom has been replaced "with active witnessing through political demonstration" in Iran and to a certain extent, in Lebanon. In turn, this has led to the revival of Shi'a Islam as a theological force rather than as a political tool. These studies demonstrate the breadth of the idea of Karbala as it has manifested in various political and religious ways. This makes possible the envisioning of many Karbalas. Korom has rightly pointed out that "the Karbala paradigm is a force as vital and potent today as it was during the first few centuries after the original event; it is one without parallel in human history." For more on the theme of Karbala, see David Pinault, *The Shiites: Rituals and Popular Piety in a Muslim Community* (New York: Palgrave, 2001); Michael Fischer, *Iran: From Religious Dispute to Revolution* (Cambridge: Harvard University Press, 1980); for a detailed discussion of these aspects,

see Michael Fischer and Mehdi Abedi, *Debating Muslims: Cultural Dialogues in Post-modernity and Tradition* (Madison: University of Wisconsin Press, 1990), xxviii; for more on the revival of Shia Islam in the post-Iranian Revolution period, see Seyyed Vali Reja Nasr, *The Shia Revival: How Conflicts within Islam Shape the Future* (New York: Norton, 2006); Frank J. Korom, *Hosay Trinidad*, 16.

10. For more on this dramatic aspect of Muharram performances in Iran, Trinidad, and South India, see Peter Chelkowski, J., ed., *Tazi'yeh—Ritual and Drama in Iran* (New York: New York University, 1979), 4–6; Frank J. Korom, *Hosay Trinidad: Muharram Performances in an Indo-Caribbean Diaspora* (Philadelphia: University of Pennsylvania Press, 2003), 128–94; Ja'far Sharif, *Islam in India or the Qanun-i- Islam*, G. A. Herklots, trans., (Oxford University Press, 1921; reprint ed., London: Curzon, 1975), 182.

11. For an understanding of Islam in a pluralist society, see David Pinault, *Notes from the Fortune-telling Parrot: Islam and the Struggle for Religious Pluralism in Pakistan* (*London*: Equinox Publishing, 2008); for a clear delineation of this distinction, see Are Knudsen, "Islam in Local Contexts: Localised Islam in Northern Pakistan," in Gerald Jackson, ed., *NIASnytt: Asia Insights*, 3, (2008):25.

12. Mines discusses how festivals "redraw" village boundaries and reconfigure social organization. For more on this aspect of *Ur*, see E. Valentine Daniel, *Fluid Signs: Being a Person the Tamil Way* (Berkeley: University of California Press, 1984); Diane P. Mines, *Fierce Gods: Inequality, Ritual, and the Politics of Dignity in a South Indian Village* (Bloomington: Indiana University Press, 2005).

13. For more on religious nationalism in India, see Peter Van der Veer, *Religious Nationalism: Hindus and Muslims in India*, (Berkeley: University of California Press, 1994).

14. See Richard K. Wolf, "Embodiment and Ambivalence: Emotion in South Asian Muharram Drumming," *The Yearbook for Traditional Music* 32 (2000):81–116.

15. Abdul Qadir Jilani (d. 1166) was the founder of the Qadiri Silsila and was well-known as a patron of the South Asian Sufi tradition. For an understanding of Nizamuddin Awliya, see Desiderio Pinto, *Pir-Muridi Relationship: A Study of the Nizamuddin Dargah* (New Delhi: Manohar Publications, 1995). For a detailed study of Khaja Mohinuddin Chisti, see P. M. Currie, *The shrine and cult of Mu'īn al-Dīn Chishtī of Ajmer* (Delhi: Oxford University Press, 2006); for Deccani sources on this tradition see H. K. Sherwani and P. M. Joshi, eds., *A History of Medieval Deccan (1295–1724)* (Hyderabad: Government of Andhra Pradesh, 1974), 22; For a better understanding of Sufi saints in South Asia, see Robert Rozehnal, *Islamic Sufism Unbound: Politics and Piety in Twenty-first Century Pakistan* (New York: Palgrave Macmillan, 2007); Pnina Werbner, *Pilgrims of Love : The Anthropology of a Global Sufi Cult* (Bloomington: Indiana University Press, 2003); Carl W. Ernst and Bruce B. Lawrence, *Sufi Martyrs of Love: The Chisti Order in South Asia and Beyond* (New York: Palgrave Macmillan, 2002); Katherine Ewing, *Arguing Sainthood: Modernity, Psychoanalysis, and Islam* (Durham: Duke University Press, 1997); P. M. Currie, *The Shrine and Cult of Mu'in al Din Chisti of Ajmer* (Delhi: Oxford University Press, 1989); Richard M. Eaton, *The Sufis of Bijapur* (Princeton, NJ: Princeton University Press, 1978). For a history of the Sufi Movement in the Deccan, see K. A. Nizami, "Sufi Movement in the Deccan," in H. K. Sherwani and P. M. Joshi., eds., *History of Medieval Deccan (1295–1724)*, (Hyderabad: Government of Andhra Pradesh),175–99; Baba Fakhruddin: As the hagiography of this saint narrates, Babayya was a Hindu prince

who turned into a *faqīr* and went to Mecca, where his preceptor Nathar Vali, the Saint of Trichinnopoly, gave him a sapling and asked him to settle down at the place where it blossomed. This occurred at the Iswara Temple at Penukonda. The temple later turned into a mosque and a *dargāh* after the death of Baba Fakruddin. Both Haider and Tippu granted endowments to this sacred shrine. For more on Baba Fakhruddin, see Bayly, *Saints, Goddesses and Kings*, 122–23,125–28.

16. Ernst and Lawrence, *The Sufi Martyrs of Love*, 2.

17. For a relevant discussion on the role of imams in Shi'a theology, see Korom, *Hosay*, 27–30; Takim, *Heirs of the Prophet*, 37.

18. For a detailed description of Gugudu and its sacred spaces, see Chapter 1. It is generally held that Anantapur is known for its big tank, Anantasagaram (boundless ocean), which stands near the western and eastern sluices upon which the villages of Anantasagaram and Bukkaraya Samudram were constructed by Chikkavodeya, the minister of Bukka-I, (1344–1377 C.E.), the Vijayanagar ruler. For a discussion on Bukkaraya and "an ideological extension of the process of borrowing" between Bukka and the sultan, see Phillip B. Wagoner, "Harihara, Bukka, and the Sultan: The Delhi Sultanate in the Political Imagination of Vijayanagara," in David Gilmartin and Bruce Lawrence, eds., *Beyond Turk and Hindu* (Gainesville, FL: University Press of Florida, 2000), 300–26.

19. In both the normative telling and the many retellings of the Ramayana, Guha's character and story have little importance. His story is only mentioned to demonstrate intense devotion to Rama. Contrary to this, in the Ramayana of Gugudu, Guha becomes the central character. For a discussion on multiple retellings of the Ramayana, see Paula Richman, ed., *Many Ramayanas: The Diversity of a Narrative Tradition in South Asia* (Berkeley: University of California Press, 1991); for a general understanding of the Ramayana as an epic, see Robert P. Goldman, *The Ramayana of Valmiki: An Epic of Ancient India* (Princeton, NJ: Princeton University Press, 1990); for a Muslim interpretation of the Ramayana tradition, see Vasudha Narayanan, "The Ramayana and its Muslim Interpreters," in Paula Richman, ed., *Questioning Ramayanas: A South Asian Tradition* (Berkeley: University of California Press, 2001), 265; for a discussion on the localization of the Ramayana narrative, see Leela Prasad, *Poetics of Conduct: Oral Narrative and Moral Being in a South Indian Town* (New York: Columbia University Press, 2007), 25–26.

20. For more on this term, see Philip B. Wagoner, "Sultan among Hindu Kings" *Journal of Asian Studies*, vol. 55, and (Nov. 1996):853 and 861. According to Verghese, the *kullayi* came into use at some point around the middle of the fifteenth century; Anila Verghese, "Court Attire of Vijayanagara Empire (From a Study of Monuments)," *Quarterly Journal of the Mythic Society* (Bangalore), vol. 82, no. 1–2: 43–61.

21. As defined by Newby, the term *niyyah* "strikes a balance between extremes of orthodoxy or orthopraxy"; Gordon D. Newby, *A Concise Encyclopedia of Islam* (Oxford: One World, 2002), 166.

22. For a general understanding of the term *barakat* in Islamic terms, see Oliver Leaman, "*Baraka*" Oliver Leaman, ed., *The Quran: an Encyclopedia* (London and New York: Routledge, 2006), 109–14. However, a definition given by Gordon D. Newby in *A Concise Encyclopedia of Islam* is relevant. As defined by Newby, "*Baraka* in the Sufi tradition is the blessings and supernatural powers brought from God through the mediation of a *wali* or saint. In popular belief, *Baraka* is associated with places as well as people," 41–42.

23. For historical details on the Qutub Shahis, see Shervani, *A History of Deccan,* 413–490.

24. A recently published Telugu version of the hagiography of Baba Fakruddin explains that this Sufi pīr sent out four *faqīrs* in four different directions to disseminate the ideas of Sufism. The most important aspect of this book is its emphasis on the Persian origins of Baba Fakhruddin's ideas, Khaja Ruknoddin Ahmed Hussaini, *Hazarat Sayyed Baba Fakhruddin Hussaini Vaari Jeevita Charitra,* (Dargah Publications: Penukonda, 2006).

25. For a discussion about these tensions between local and localized Islams, see Chapter 5.

26. Interview with Khaja Ruknoddin Ahmed Hussaini, the local custodian of the shrine at Penukonda, November 16, 2006.

27. Tirupatayya, one of the storytellers of Muharram in Gugudu, actually referred to the rule of the Mughals in his narrative. He explained to me how hard local pīrs struggled to unshackle the chains of Mughal Islam, and returned to Gugudu to remain there permanently. For more on interactions between Mughals and Hyder Ali of Mysore, see Irfan Habib, ed., *Confronting Colonialism: Resistance and Modernization under Haider Ali and Tippu Sultan* (New Delhi: Tulika, 1999). For an understanding of villages under the rule of Tippu Sultan, see A. R. Kulkarni, *Explorations in the Deccan History* (Delhi: Pragati Publications, 2002), 68–78.

28. More than just a physical place, the old well is a recurring spatial metaphor in many Muharram narratives in Telugu. In an effort to save their lives from the enemy Yazid, the martyrs of Karbala are said to have hid in an old well on the battlefield of Karbala.

29. I have collected and recorded several versions of this story of the final battle in and around Gugudu. The story has similar versions everywhere. However, the historicity of this story is unclear. Still, the idea of martyrdom as understood and narrated in local Islam is worth exploring. This idea of martyrdom coincides with the local oral narratives of other martyrs.

30. For an explanation of the term *tarikh* and its relevance for South India, see Velcheru Narayana Rao, David Shulman, and Sanjay Subrahmanyam, *Textures of Time: Writing History in South India, 1600–1800* (New York: Other Press, 2003), 184–251.

31. Conversation with Khaja Husain, January 20, 2007.

Chapter 1

1. Tirupatayya and the *Mujāvar* Hussainappa used the same sentence in Telugu to describe the formation of the new village: "*Voka vooru chani poyindi, inko vooriki punar janma vacchindi.*" Conversations with Tirupatayya and Hussainappa, October 10, 2006.

2. The first gazetteer prepared on Anantapur in 1905 describes Gugudu as below:

"Gugudu is best known for its Mohurrum. As in other cases in this district, this strange to relate, is entirely managed by the Hindus of the village, the Muhammadans taking but a small part in it. Hindus to the number of several thousands also come in for the ceremony from the adjoining villages. The heads of the villages sit at the '*Mohurrum chavidi*' and collect contributions from the visitors in locked tin-money boxes. These receipts are most carefully set aside for the necessary expenses and any surplus is lent out at interest or invested in land to form a permanent endowment for the annual upkeep of the Mohurrum. Most curious of all, the principal attraction of the feast is a fire-walking ceremony, which takes place twice during its course, on the ninth and eleventh days. First the musicians, who are *Mangalas* by caste, walk through the fire and then follow all sorts and conditions of others, both Hindus and Muhammadans. The same thing on a smaller scale is done at the Mohurrum at Malyavantam. The Muhammadan Pirs at Gugudu are held in great veneration and all castes, even Brahmans it is said, make their vows to them and distribute sugar to the poor if they are successful in obtaining their object of their desires." W. Francis, *Madras District Gazeteer: Anantapur* (Madras: Addison and Co., 1905), 47–48.

3. To understand the importance of *baraka* as a term which legitimated political authority, see Richard Eaton, "Temple Desecration and Indo-Muslim states" in David Gilmartin and Bruce Lawrence, *Beyond Turk and Hindu*, 246–271.

4.

TABLE 1.1 Population of Gūgūḍu
Total Population: 2620; Men: 1332, Women: 1288

CATEGORIES OF CASTES	CASTE GROUPS	HOUSEHOLDS	TOTAL NUMBER	OCCUPATIONS
Scheduled Castes	Mala/madiga	151	727	leather and agricultural workers
Backward Castes	Bōya/vadde	289	1400	agricultural workers, stone masons
Upper castes	Reddy	73	311	Agriculture
Muslims	Dudekula	38	182	small businesses, welding, van drivers and cotton

5. *Bōya*: Gugudu and in particular the district of Anantapur has the biggest population of the *Bōya* caste group. This particular caste takes pride in its caste history, which they trace back to Valmiki, the poet who "authored" the Indian epic Ramayana. This caste group is also called *Valmiki* caste now in this district. Recently, this caste group has built a temple to Valmiki in the town of Anantapur. In Gugudu, the *Bōya* caste actively participates in the public events during Muharram, as they consider Kullayappa as the avataram of Guha, the boatman who ferried Lord Rama during his forest life. It is said that Guha also belongs to *Bōya* caste. More details about this story are in Chapter 2.

6. Local newspapers and media continually publish stories of migration from these villages, and lament the diminishing population at the village level. During my stay in Gugudu, I used to read at least one story a day in local newspapers about the migrations, and criticism of the negligence of government departments in dealing with this. For a detailed analysis of drought conditions in the district of Anantapur, see Palagummi Sainath, *Everybody Loves a Good Drought: Stories from India's Poorest Districts* (New York: Penguin Books, 1996).

7. Interview with Madar Sahib (75), January 19, 2007.

8. *Pīr-makaanam*: the Telugu form of the Urdu word *Makaan,* which means "house."

9. As Stuart Blackburn has observed, "More than a story with endless variation, the story of Rama is an ocean of stories and a moral code. Although it is largely a Hindu tradition, the story of Rama so pervades the cultures of South Asia that it is known by many

Muslims, Christians, Jains, and Buddhists as well." Stuart Blackburn, "Ramayana," in *South Asian Folklore: An Encyclopedia*, Margaret Mills et al., eds. (New York: Routledge, 2003) 509.

10. Diana Mines, *Fierce Gods*, 31.

11. He used a Telugu phrase for "the union with the God" (*bhaktitō paramātmalō līnaṁ kāvaḍaṁ* . . . which translates into "with devotion, immersing into the great soul").

12. Kaandhlawi. *Faza'il-e-A'maal*, 1993.

13. *dīn Gōvindā*: a shared devotional term used in the context of the public rituals in the month of Muharram. This term is discussed further in Chapter 2.

14. Narsimhulu's words in Telugu were *"adi bhaktiki haddu anna māṭa."*

15. Narsimhulu's words in Telugu were *"guṁḍaṁ kāḍa modalu ī karbalā bāyi dākā rakarakāla kaḷalū anipistayi."*

16. Tikkaya Swamy lived to the age of 120 years. Stories about his last rites are now part of local folklore in this region. Biruduraju Ramaraju, *Andhra Yogulu*, vol. 5, 37–43.

17. For more on Tikkaya Swamy, see Biruduraju Ramaraju, *Andhra Yogulu*, vol. 5, 37–43.

18. This devotion to Siva is described further in Chapter 3.

19. For more on Baba Fakhruddin and Penukonda, see Susan Bayly, *Saints, Goddesses, and Kings,* 122–26.

Chapter 2

1. The history of the pīr is vague. No records are available except the oral narratives which talk about the arrival of Islam and Muharram. Tirupatayya himself was never sure of any specific time period. But the sixteenth century seems to be the approximate period, as this region was under the rule of Hyder Ali and Tippu Sultan. For more details about the history of this area, see Gurajada Appa Rao, ed., *The Annals of Hande Anantapuram Charitra* (Madras: V. Ramaswamy Sastrulu, 1920).

2. Conversation with Quddus, ninety-year-old Muslim (Jangama, Karimnagar District, November14–15, 2006). Quddus was among the group of pīr storytellers for many years in his village. However, his stories were in Urdu. He said, "Though we have both Urdu and Telugu stories, as we began to have more of a Telugu-speaking audience, we too began to tell more stories in Telugu than in Urdu. Moreover, as time went on, we began to have more Telugu-speaking performers too." In many villages, Muslim storytellers are now rare. Many come from non-Muslim castes. In the villages close to Jan agama, I have recorded several versions of pīr stories. Most of these storytellers are either washermen or lower-caste artisans. When asked about this change, Quddus said, "It's just because they're blessed, and the aspect of *niyyatu* in their personality is increasing. *Ibādat* (devotion) for the pīr has no caste or high-low level variations. To put it simply, pīrs are pīrs for us (Muslims), and pīrs are gods for them. That makes a huge difference."

3. The cults of Ramdev and Satya pir are popular for their shared Hindu-Muslim practices. Tony Stewart and Dominique-Sila Khan have studied these aspects of Ramdev and Satya Pīr. See Dominique-Sila Khan, **Conversions and Shifting Identities: Ramdev Pīr and the Ismailis in Rajasthan (New Delhi: Manohar Publications, 1997), and for the study of Satya pīr, see** Tony K. Stewart, *Fabulous Females and Peerless Pirs: Tales of Mad Adventure in Old Bengal* (New York: Oxford University Press, 2004).

As explained by Anne Murphy, Ram Dev is a folk hero/deity widely revered in Rajasthan, Madhya Pradesh, Gujarat, Punjab and other parts of Western India, mainly by Meghvals and other members of the scheduled castes. He is generally depicted on a horse, mounted as a warrior. Ram Dev has traditionally been revered by Muslims and Hindus alike, and is accepted by Hindu adherents as an incarnation of Krishna. See Anne Murphy"Ram Dev" in South *Asian Folklore: An Encyclopaedia*, Margaret Mills, Peter J. Claus and Sarah Diamonds, eds., (New York: Routledge, 2003), 513–14.

4. In Telugu, "the man who carries the god" (*devunni yetthukune vaadu*).

5. For a detailed discussion of the shifting role of Brahman temple priests, see Chris J. Fuller, *The Renewal of the Priesthood: Modernity and Traditionalism in a South Indian Temple* (Princeton, NJ: Princeton University Press, 2003), 49–71. However, focusing only on Hindu practices in the village would help us little in understanding local practices. The argument here covers both Hindu and Muslim religious elements as a way to document the subversion of the Brahmin priesthood. Isabelle Clark-Deces also discusses the aspect of the "demise of the Brahmins" in a village in Tamil Nadu. See Clark-Deces, *The Encounter Never Ends: A Return to the Field of Tamil Rituals* (Albany: State University of New York Press, 2007),101.

6. The straight translation of his idiomatic expression in Telugu, "*burralo yedo purugu tolichinattu . . .* " would be "as if some insect began to scratch my brain."

7. We will discuss this aspect of pīr and God separately. Though the devotional practices and rituals are similar, the naming pattern itself differs.

8. For a detailed study of the rise of Islam and agrarian order in the East, see Richard M. Eaton, *The Rise of Islam and the Bengal Frontier, 1204–1760* (Berkeley: University of California Press, 1993).

9. Obyeysekere, *The Fire-walkers of Kataragama*, 466–67.

10. Such an interaction of Vaishanavism and Islamic narratives is not uncommon in local religious practice. For instance, see Tony K. Stewart, "Alternate Structures of Authority: Satya Pir on the Frontiers of Bengal", in Gilmartin and Lawrence, eds., *Beyond Turk and Hindu*, 24.

"Despite certain similarities, stories of Satya pīr fall into clearly differentiated groups, reflecting differing vocabularies, narrative styles, and orientations toward divine and worldly power. As we shall see, some stories (which we might loosely label as "Hindu") see Satya Pīr as yet another incarnation of Vishnu, especially suited to the disintegrating terms of the Kali Age wherein dharma is at extreme risk. Another group (which we might loosely label "Muslim") portray him as but a pīr, albeit a special one who resides in an ethereal Mecca and who can be conjured with heartfelt call of his name; . . ."

Though there are Vaishnava narratives about Kullayappa, the narrative world of Kullayappa is not limited to those Vaishnava narratives alone. Those who visit Kullayappa belong to several castes, and those who directly perform various pīr rituals at the pīr-house, belong according to the narratives to sixteen different castes, which include Hindus and Muslims. These sixteen caste groups, as well as the pilgrims, narrate the life of Kullayappa differently.

11. Victor Turner, *The Ritual Process: Structure and Anti-structure* (Chicago: Aldine Publications, 1969), 95.

12. The list of eighteen castes referred to in local pīr stories includes *Kummari* (potters), *Kammari* (goldsmith), Muslims, *Mala*, *Mādiga* (scheduled castes), *Dudēkula* (lower caste Muslims), Reddy, *Bōya* (hunters), *Mangali* (barbers), *Komati* (vysya),

Brahmins, *Chaakali* (washermen), *Vaddera* (stonemasons), *Daasari*, *Besta* (fishermen), *Goundla* (toddy workers), *Golla* (shepherds), and *Sri Vaishnava*.

13. Indeed, this aspect of the new caste structures, and the manipulation of Muharram pīr stories to construct new caste hierarchies, would be a useful study for any sociologist. Since we will be focusing more on devotional and ritual aspects, we will not deal at length with this aspect here. Recently, Tirumali's research on the villages of Telangana has been a good start in this direction. However, he did not connect it to Muharram. If these studies are connected to Muharram, they will reveal the strategies for creating new caste hierarchies in premodern and early modern Andhra villages. Inukonda Tirumali, *Against Dora and Nizam: People's Movement* in *Telangana, 1939–1948* (New Delhi: Kanishka Publishers, 2003).

14. *"Sab bhoot aur taboot Wali se baaraa haath door"* is a popular Deccani Urdu saying in Telugu villages. It means "all idols and temples are twelve hands away from the pīr". This saying clearly critiques Hindu idol worship and temple practices. Even those Muslims who visit the pīr-house every day use this saying.

15. Michael Sells, *Approaching the Qur'an: The Early Revelations* (Ashland, OR: White Cloud Press, 1999), 136. For more on the importance of the theme of "God" in the Quran, see Fazlur Rahman, *Major Approaches to the Quran* (Chicago: Bibliotheca Islamica, 1980), 1–16.

16. Several Interviews with Hameedullah Sheriff, a translator of the Quran into modern spoken Telugu, helped me to understand these particular Quranic connections. The Telugu translation of the Quran is very popular among Telugu-speaking Muslims in Andhra. Along with the publication of the entire Quran, there were also booklets of each *sura* in Telugu with a brief commentary (*Meaning of the Holy Qur'an*, 2004), 849. Including these translations, several of the Telugu Islamic Publications played a significant role in the making of new Muslim identities in the context of Andhra. Specifically, they made an impact on young Muslims who know very little Urdu and Arabic. Recent reform efforts in the local Islamic community gained new momentum after these publications. Mosque-centered Islamic activities in particular took a new turn. These aspects and their impact on village Muharram and pīr rituals will be discussed in the concluding chapter. For more details about these translations, see Shaik Hameedullah Sheriff, trans., *Divya Quran* (Hyderabad: Telugu Islamic Publications, 2004), 849.

17. During this conversation, Sattar Saheb was using three different names interchangeably "Topi Walī Saheb," "Kullayappa" and "Pīr." Yet when he said Kullayappa, he always very clearly used the Urdu pronunciation, saying "Khullayappa."

18. *Fana*: According to S. H. Nasr, "Sufism uses the quintessential form of prayer, the *dhikr* or invocation, in which all otherness and separation from the Divine is removed and man achieves *tawhid*. Though this process of transforming man's psyche appears gradual at first, the *dhikr* finishes by becoming man's real nature and the reality with which he identifies himself. With the help of the *dhikr*, as combined with appropriate forms of meditation of *fikr*, man first gains an integrated soul, pure and whole like gold, and then in the *dhikr* he offers this soul to God in the supreme form of sacrifice. Finally in annihilation (*fana*) and subsistence (*baqa*) he realizes that he never was separated from God even from the outset." Nasr, *Sufi Essays*, 49–50.

19. A popular devotional hymn sung by Chalapati Rayalu. "I've been singing this hymn since my childhood. My father taught me this hymn, and local elders say that my

grandfather composed this hymn. Even now the tradition is that we begin our *japam* with this hymn every night in Muharram." Interview with Chalapati Rayalu, January 10, 2007.

20. For the Narsimha cult in Andhra, see Madabhushi Narasimhacharya, *History of the Cult of Narasimha in Telangana, Andhra Pradesh, from Ancient Period to the Modern Period* (Hyderabad, 1989). For a general understanding of the Narsimha in the Hindu tradition, see Deborah A. Soifer, *The Myths of Narasimha and Vamana: Two Avatars in Cosmological Perspective* (Albany: State University of New York Press, 1991).

21. Recently, under a scheme to renovate the old temples *(devalaya jeernodharana),* this temple was also renovated. Yet its renovation has had no apparent impact, in that not even a single devotee visits the temple anymore.

22. For a better understanding of the term *prapatti* in the Sri Vaishnavite context, see Srilata Raman, *Self-surrender (prapatti) to God in Srivaishnavishnavism: Tamil Cats or Sanskrit Monkeys?* (Hoboken: Taylor and Francis, 2006), 24–51.

23. Telugu hymn: "Paadamulu patti patti /chethulu chutti chutti/patti mokkuduru ninnu kullayappaa!"

24. Wolf, *The Embodiment of Emotion*, 2000.

25. Contemporary Muslim poets in Telugu also use this as a symbolic connection when assertively arguing for continuous interactions between Muslims and Dalits in various social and political movements gaining momentum in Andhra since the 1980s. Most of the Dalit and Muslim poets and writers have begun to use these images connected with *Mādiga* life in their poems. The image of the drum likewise serves many purposes for them. When I observed drumming performances in Gugudu Muharram, I could see a continuum between these literary manifestations and Muharram ritual drumming. For more on Muslim Telugu poetry, see Velcheru Narayana Rao, trans. and ed., *Twentieth Century Telugu Poetry*, New Delhi: Oxford University Press, 2002) and Shaik Yusuf Baba and Panduranga Reddy, eds., *Zalzalah: Anthology of Muslim Telugu Poetry* (Nalgonda: Nasl Ghar Prachuranalu, 2002).

26. Korom, *Hosay*, 164.

27. For an ethnographic profile of the Dudekula caste in Andhra Pradesh, see S. A. A. Saheb, "Dudekula Muslims of Andhra Pradesh," *Economic and Political Weekly*, 38(2003): 4908–12.

28. Yet there are many exceptions too. Although many pīr-houses are open, they do not function throughout the year: we do not find a regular *muzāvar* attending to the devotees. Rather, these devotees come and put flowers and sweets themselves in front of the ritual standards.

29. Matthewson, *Introduction to Islam*, 405.

30. *Imān*: I will discuss this term in detail in my conclusion, where I argue that while the Five Pillars of Islam certainly work in village Islam, the village version of Islam is not limited to the Five Pillars, as both Muslims and Hindus often cross the boundaries of their specific prescriptive religions and enter into a broad, shared world of devotion.

31. W. Francis, *Madras District Gazeteers: Anantapur* (Madras: Addison and Co., 1905), 147–48.

32. For a detailed study of drought and migration in Ananta Puram, see Palagummi Sainath, *Everybody Loves a Good Drought*, 1996. According to the gazetteer of Anantapur published in 1908, "The district has suffered constantly from famines, owing to the lightness of the rainfall . . . in the famine of 1876–77, 137, 347 persons were at one time

in receipt of relief—more than 18 per cent of the total population." *The Imperial Gazetteer of India: Madras* (Calcutta: Superintendent of Government Printing, 1908), 480.

33. Women are often considered passive ritual performers in traditional Muharram public events. However, in the Andhra village context, women are active ritual performers, and I intend to work in the future on the role of Fatima in Muharram festivities, and to discuss more extensively this public aspect of gender in Muharram. Focusing on a public village event called *Fatima Pandaga*, I wish to further this study by focusing particularly on the active role of Muslim women and the ritual aspects of lower-caste Hindu women in the devotional tradition of Muharram.

34. *Fatima Pandaga*: Each year during the month of Muharram, in some parts of Andhra, devotees perform rituals for Fatima, the mother of the Karbala martyrs. They name this celebration *Fatima Pandaga* (Fatima Festival). They tell stories about Fatima, but more importantly, they carry the metal battle standards that symbolize Fatima.

35. Locally known as *"Hussainu vaari Devasthaanam,"* this temple is in the center of the village, and every day Hussain as village deity appears well-dressed in red and green silk clothes, much like other Hindu deities. The villagers believe that Hussain is the savior of the village, and they consult him for every need. Villagers enter or leave the village only after his *darśanam*.

36. Interview with Gorati Venkanna, folk singer, and Allam Rajayya, noted writer in Telugu, October 12, 2006.

37. For the hagiography of Tajuddin Baba, see Ekkirala Bharadwaja, *Sree Hazarat Tajuddin Baba Divya Charitra* (Ongole: Sree Guru Paadukaa Publications, 2003).

38. In every village-level Muharram, firepit stories are almost like a distinct genre, and every villager has some story connected to this firepit. Though Muslims do not speak so particularly about the firepit, for many Hindu devotees, the firepit is a kind of root metaphor. They weave countless stories and memories around this site. And all these stories are connected to the Muharram pīr tradition. They reveal a narrative strategy of identity formation and community development.

Chapter 3

1. I use the word "alive" to mimic the language devotees use to talk about Muharram. As one devotee, Fakkira Reddy, described: "Nowadays, this tradition is dying. Pīrs are no longer considered to be alive. The public celebration is almost dead. More than money, it's a question of *iman* (faith), not having enough faith in the pīrs." Interview with Fakkira Reddy, Gugudu, October 22, 2006. Fakkira Reddy's comments are important in light of the post-1990s developments in Hindu nationalist discourse. I will discuss this aspect in detail in Chapter 5.

2. The metaphors of fire, water, blood, and grave have several functions in local rituals. For more on this aspect, see Schubel, *Religious Performance*, 151–54; and Pinault, *The Horses of Karbala*, 33–36. Recent studies on public performances focus more on religious behavior and sacred meanings. For an understanding of this, see Zain Abdullah, "Sufis on Parade: The Performance of Black, African, and Muslim Identities," in *Journal of the American Academy of Religion*, vol. 77, no. 2, June 2009, 199–237. For an understanding of the role of religious processions in South Asia, see Knut A. Jacobson, ed., *South Asian Religions on Display: Religious Processions in South Asia and in the Diaspora* (London: Routledge, 2008).

3. News report in the *Eenaadu*, the most widely circulated Telugu newspaper, January, 31, 2007.

4. Along similar lines to the Muharram ritual called *langar* in an Islamic way, local devotees made arrangements for this free meal. During the time I was in Gugudu there was a huge response from rich and upper-middle-class devotees for this ritual, as many families came forward to offer free meals during Muharram. For more on *langar*, see Werbner, *The Anthropology of Sufi Pīr*, 101–21.

5. The booklet details the festival rituals as below:

DATE	WEEK DAYS	FESTIVAL RITUALS
21-1-2007	Sunday	Swamy's *pradhama darsanam* (First Darsana)
22-1-2007	Tuesday	Firepit digging ritual
23-1-2007	Wednesday	Installing the Swamy
24-1-2007	Thursday	*Nitya pooja*
25-1-2007	Friday	Fifth *sarigettu*
26-1-2007	Saturday	*Nitya pooja*
27-1-2007	Sunday	*china sarigettu*, Night meravani, and brief fire-walk
28-1-2007	Monday	*Nitya pooja*
29-1-2007	Tuesday	*Peda sarigettu*, Night meravani, and fire-walk
30-1-2007	Wednesday	Swamy's Fire ritual and Evening at 4 *Jaladhi*
31-1-2007	Thursday	*chivari* (Final) *darsanam*

6. For a clear understanding of *jatara*, see Handelman, "The Guises of the Goddess and the Transformation of the Male: Gangamma's Visit to Tirupati and the Continuum of Gender," in David Shulman, ed., *Syllables of Sky* (Delhi: Oxford University Press, 1995), 283–337; Flueckiger, "Wandering from 'Hills to Valleys' with the Goddess: Protection and Freedom in the Matamma Tradition of Andhra," in Tracy Pintchman, ed., *Women's Lives, Women's Rituals in the Hindu Tradition* (New York: Oxford University Press, 2007), 35–54.

7. For an explanation of regularly scheduled *nitya puja*, see Rohan Bastin, *The Domain of Constant Excess: Plural Worship at the Munneswaram Temples in Sri Lanka* (New York: Berghahn Books, 2002), 117–20.

8. For more on the ritual of self-flagellation and *matam*, see Schubel, *Religious Performance*, 145–55.

9. Hyder, *Reliving Karbala*, 55.

10. Ibid.

11. This is similar to what Korom observed in the ritual standard building activity in Trinidad: "In heterogeneous polyethnic cultures such as Trinidad, where many ethnic and religious communities coexist, if not always peacefully, each representative group brings its own preconceived notions to bear on the events being performed and observed. Interpretations and understandings therefore may not always correspond to a prototypical set of historically derived assumptions about the phenomenon performed, and meanings may often vary to such a degree that they become contested and mutually exclusive," Korom, *Hosay Trinidad*, 129.

However, unlike in Trinidad, permanent ritual standards are used in Gugudu. The permanent ritual standards acquire both magical and historical significance in the context of Gugudu and in many places in Andhra. More importantly, like Trinidadians, the devotees of Gugudu do not have to construct these structures; instead, fire-walking, reciting fātehā, and the thirteen days of other dynamic ritual activities replace the major activity of building the structure.

12. For this aspect of Muharram in Hyderabad, see Hyder, *Reliving Karbala,* 9.

13. For more information on Hyderabadi Muharram, see Vedantam and Khaja Moinuddin, *The Muharram in Hyderabad*, 74.

14. These interviews and conversations with pilgrims, devotees and local people were both structured and unstructured, mostly depending on the context. Most important were devotees both within Gugudu and outside Gugudu, with whom I would begin my conversation with very informal questions, and move to more structured interviews if informants were interested.

15. Bastin, *The Domain of Excess*, 94.

16. Like many middle-aged local Muslims, Husēnappa makes a clear-cut distinction between the rituals of mosque and *makānam*. For a new generation of Muslim youth, they are totally separate domains, and they are now tending more toward mosque-centered practices. Middle-aged Muslims accept the veneration of pīrs as a symbolic gesture for recollecting the Karbala martyrs and consider it an essential part of their personal and community life too. By contrast, these young reformist Muslims consider this act of venerating saints a totally un-Islamic and backward practice. I will discuss these tensions between local religion and reformist Muslims in Chapter 5.

17. Like many Urdu words, this is also Telugized as *mannatu.*

18. In this context, the figure of horse is significant, as it reminds people of the story of Karbala and the story of one specific horse called Hurr. It is a dominant symbol of repentance that encompasses many food and water rituals in Muharram. For more on the symbolic importance of horses in Shi'a Islam, see Pinault, *The Horses of Karbala.*

19. Donappa, *Janapada Kalaa Sampada*, 167.

20. For a discussion on the usage of the term *walī*, see Cornell, *The Realms of the Saint,* xvii–xix.

21. During my research, I met one performance group, Subbaraya Peta, and visited their village twenty-five miles from Gugudu. Visiting this village helped me to comprehend the length and breadth of the pīr tradition in the collective memory of local life. Known as a folk-arts village, there I came to know about a great variety of folk-performances that celebrate and commemorate the Karbala martyrs. There is a conscious effort in the village to keep this tradition continuing.

22. For an idea of 'institutional Sufism' see Lawrence, *Notes from a Distant Flute*, 20; Green, *Saints of the Deccan*, Rozehnal, *Islamic Sufism Unbound*, 2007. Lawrence has raised the question, why did institutional Sufism express itself through *silsilahs*? He explores historical evidence to try and understand the works of major Sufi authors in relation to the *silsilahs*. Green, in his study on the saints of the Deccan, has pointed out the importance of studying Sufi shrines and the variety of activities surrounding them (xiv). Rozehnal's study also focuses on the form of Sufism which I speak of here, for which I use the term "uninstitutionalized Sufism."

23. In local Muharram traditions, it's very common that individual families donate money to make the ritual standards used during the holiday. On such occasions, various

local saints acquire the status of Martyr of Karbala too. However, the aspect of personal pīr dominates local practices. Each family or each person identifies himself with a single pīr, who remains his personal pīr forever. Along with regular rituals for the pīrs of Muharram, these people and families also perform rituals for these pīrs.

24. Interview with Imam Bi (60), Gugudu, January 27, 2007.

Chapter 4

1. Conversation with Lakshmi Reddi.

2. For a detailed explanation of the term *faqiri* in the Sufi context, see Annemarie Schimmel, *Mystical Dimensions of Islam*, 12–24. Schimmel discusses at length the notion of poverty (*faqr*) in performing *faqiri,* and also suggests that "*faqr* is almost equated with *fana*, 'annihilation in God.'"

3. The local Telugu usage is *mujaavaru pujari*, a combination of both Muslim and Hindu terms. *Mujaavaru* is the trustee of any Muslim sacred site, and *pujari* is the temple priest.

4. Schimmel, *The Mystical Dimensions of Islam*, 120–24.

5. Patrick Olivelle, *Rules and Regulations of Brahmanical Asceticism*: *Yatidharmasamuccaya of Yadava Prakasa* (Albany: State University of New York Press, 1995), 12.

6. Helene Basu in her study on Sidhis in Gujarat observed that *faqiri* is at the lower end of the Sufi hierarchy (Basu, *Sidhis in Gujarat*), 117. Though she suggests this, and also that those who observe *faqiri* are "threshold people" with liminal identity, we should note that her study focuses on a Muslim community. In their studies of vernacular Islam in South India, Jackie Assayag and Joyce Flueckiger observed that *faqirs* are an identifiable community who are usually invited by the local religious groups to take part in the gatherings. (Assayag, *At the Confluence of Two Rivers*, 133; Flueckiger, *In Amma's Healing Room,* 184). Recently, Akbar Hyder, in his book *Reliving Karbala,* provides an ethnographic account of *faqiri* in the urban context of Hyderabad, where Muharram is also specifically Islamic in nature (Hyder, *Reliving Karbala*), 15.

7. Eaton, *The Sufis of Bijapur*, 317.

8. Schimmel, *Mystical Dimensions*, 37.

9. For a detailed study of the dichotomy between wilderness and village, see Olivelle, *Ascetics and Brahmins*, 43–62.

10. Robert Langer *et al.*, "Transfer of Ritual," *Journal of Ritual Studies* 20 (2006), 1–10.

11. Presently, the upper-caste Reddis have multiple social roles in any village, as they are at different points on the economic map in Andhra. Started as agrarian community, this caste slowly reached the level of village headmen, and then as their economical conditions improved, their social status also increased to upper caste. However they still remain a strong force in challenging Brahminical Hinduism.

12. At first, sixty-five-year-old Fakkirappa's story reminded me of the life story of the eminent Oriya novelist Fakir Mohan Senapati:

For the eight days of Muharram each year . . . I had to dress up as a fakir in knee-breeches, a high-necked, multi-colored coat, and a Muslim cap, with a variegated bag hung on my shoulder and a red lacquered cane held in my hand. Thus attired and my face smeared in pure chalk I would roam through the village morning and afternoon begging from house to house, and in the evening I sold whatever rice I had collected and sent the money to the saints for their offerings." Senapati, *My Times*, 6.

13. Schubel, *Religious Performance*, p. 17.

14. *Turaka*: Muslims are called "*turaka*s" in the villages. To refer to Hindus, villagers usually use "non-Turakas" (*turakalu kaani vaallu*).

15. Interview with Obulesu, October 14, 2006, Gugudu.

16. Interview with Khaja Hussain, businessman, January 26, 2007. He visits Gugudu not only for Kullayappa but also to sell his sweets. For Hussain, pilgrimage is a passionate way of expressing devotion too. Using all his savings, he visits Azmeer and Kadapa Sufi dargahs once a year.

Chapter 5

1. *Imān*: Though *imān* is considered to be the most important pillar of Islam, the interpretations of *imān* differ for Sunnis and Shi'as. For Sunnis, faith is total belief in God, whereas for Shi'as, faith is also toward the family of the Prophet. However, in local religion, as I have observed in Gugudu, faith is as much for God as for the family of the Prophet. Many devotee narratives and interpretations combine both of these aspects in defining the contours of the faith.

2. Barbara Metcalf, "Islam and Custom in Nineteenth Century India," in Richard Martin, ed., *Contributions to Asian Studies*, vol. xvii, (Leiden: E. J. Brill), 62.

3. In his study on Iraqi Shiites, Yitzhak Nakash observed that the cult of saints is an indication of the strong Arab tribal character of Shi'a society in Iraq. According to Nakash, "visits to the shrines of imams and the tombs of local saints played an important social-political role in Iraq. It was believed that, through the visit and the prayers and the votive offerings by the tomb, supplicants could obtain the help and intercession of the saints with God on their behalf." For more on the veneration of saints during the month of Muharram, see Yitzhak Nakash, "The Muharram Rituals and the Cult of the Saints among Iraqi Shiites," in Alessandro Monsutti, Silvia Naef and Farian Sabahi, eds., *The Other Shiites: From the Mediterranean to Central Asia* (Berlin: Peter Lang, 2007), 115–36.

4. During my fieldwork, I also observed an active campaign asserting "*dharma* Hinduism" in small towns where the Muharram tradition is strong. During the month of Muharram, many 'Hindu" organizations distribute pamphlets, organize meetings, and circulate the idea of *dharma*, using terms such as *Hindu dharma rakshana* (the protection of the Hindu *dharma*). One popular banner in Telugu, which appeared at many of the places, read, "*mana dharmam ganga neerul para dharmam yemdamaavi*." (Our dharma is the water of Ganges and the other dharma is a mirage).

5. Interview with Asanna, Adilabad, October 15, 2006.

6. On the political and cultural history of the Deccan, see C. W. Ernst, "Deccan", in *Encyclopaedia Iranica,* and for a detailed history of Bahmanis, see Shervani and Joshi, *History of Medieval Deccan*, 143–222; Shervani, *The Bahmanis of Deccan* (Delhi: Munshiram, 1985), 133–34, 152–55.

7. Munis Furuqui, "At Empīre's End: The Nizam, Hyderabad and Eighteenth Century India," *Modern Asian Studies* (UK: Cambridge University Press, 2009), 43, 1, 5–43.

8. This entire process of introducing Shi'a forms of devotion began with the literary translations of the narratives of Karbala, particularly under the patronage of 'Ali 'Adil Shah of Bijapur and Muhammad Quli Qutb Shah of Golconda. As Karen Ruffle has observed, "In order to make the recitation of the Karbala narrative understandable to those who only knew the local languages of Dakhni and Telugu, the Persian writings of

Mohtasham and Kashefi were simultaneously translated and rendered to reflect the trag-edy of Karbala through a distinctively Indic idiom and worldview. . . . In the seventeenth century, a number of translations of *Rowzat al-Shohada* into the Dakhni dialect were completed. Rama Rao, whose pen name (*takhallus*) was 'Saiva,' was the first Hindu writer of *marsiya* in the Deccan. He received the patronage of 'Ali 'Adil Shah of Bijapur. In addition to writing *marsiya,* in 1681, Rama Rao completed a Dakhni translation of *Rowzat al-Shohada*." Karen Ruffle, "Writing Muharram: The Influence of Mulla Hus-sain," in Rao V. Kishan and A. Satyanarayana, eds., *A Thousand Laurels: Dr. Sadiq Naqvi* (Hyderabad: Osmania University, 2005), 339.

9. For a clear account of the impact of this incident, see David Ludden, "Introduc-tion: Ayodhya, A Window on the world," in David Ludden, ed., *Making India Hindu: Religion, Community, and the Politics of Democracy in India* (New Delhi: Oxford Uni-versity Press, 2005), 1–23.

10. Gottschalk, *Beyond Hindu and Muslim*, 51.

11. Edward Simpson, "The Changing Perspectives of Three Muslim Men on the the Question of Saint Worship over a 10-year Period in Gujarat, Western India," *Modern Asian Studies* 42, 2/3, March/May 2008, 391.

12. Nasr, 60.

13. For an analysis of the role of Sufism in Deccan see Eaton, *Sufis of Bijapur*, 1978.

14. Ahmed, xxii.

15. For more on Baba Fakhruddin, see Bayly, *Saints, Goddesses, and Kings,* 122–23, 201.

16. For more on *dehati Islam,* see Marsden, *The Living Islam*, 2005.

17. Nasr, The Shia Revival, 55.

18. Korom, *Hosay*, 201.

19. Thurfjell, *Living Shi'ism*, 239.

20. Bowen, *Muslims Through the Discourse*, 64.

21. The Disappearance of Urdu is an important aspect of local Muslim life in this context. However, this element requires further investigation. Recently, there has been an effort to reconstruct the idea of Urdu as a language and cultural imagery in the modern writings of Telugu Muslims.

22. Several translations of the Quran and books of interpretation are widely in circu-lation in Andhra.

23. The purpose of the usage of this text is similar to Maulana Thanawi's *Bihisti zewar. Fazail-e-'Amal* is used to make Muslims adhere to the prophetic tradition. How-ever, this text is more popular since the text is also being used extensively in local mosques. In a way, the text has more authority in localized Islam. As Eaton observed about *Bihisti Zewar*: "In the nineteenth century, reformist movements such as that ex-pressed by Maulana Thanawi's *Bihisti Zewar* vigorously opposed the entire culture of saints and shrines, the colorful pageantry they displayed, and above all the claims they possessed an intermediate status between Man and God. Accordingly, supporters of these reformist movements sought to replace the shrine as the source of Islamic moral authority with a reassertion of the Book as the only legitimate source. Theatre, in a word, was to be replaced by Scripture." Richard Eaton, "The Political and Religious Authority of the Shrine of Baba Farid," in Richard Eaton, ed., *India's Islamic Traditions, 711–1750* (New Delhi: Oxford University Press, 2003), 264.

24. Interview with Shaik Jaffer, local imam of the village mosque, January 27, 2007.

25. For more on the activities of the Tabligi Jamaat, see Metcalf, "'Traditionalist' Islamic Activism: Deoband, Tablighis, and Talibs," in Metcalf, ed., *Islamic Contestations*, 265–84.

26. *Fazail-e- 'Amal*, 14.

27. Interview with Jaffer, January 20, 2007. Jaffer himself repeatedly uses the terms *ilm* and *deeni* to refer to this aspect.

28. Ali and Leaman *Islam: Key Concepts*, 55.

29. Mahmood, *The Politics of Piety*, 87.

30. Ibid, 88.

31. Ali and Leaman, *Islam: Key Concepts*, 55.

32. Hyder, *Reliving Karbala*, 69.

Conclusion

1. Literary representations of Muharram have become commonplace in Muslim writing in Telugu. Writers and poets borrow extensively from the images and motifs of Muharram to articulate a Muslim identity in these writings.

2. In one of my short stories, "Gorima," I describe this childhood experience. See Afsar, *Gorimaa*, in Naveen Vasireddy and Papineni Sivasankar, eds., *Katha 2002*, (Hyderabad: Katha Saahiti, 2003), 183–98.

3. During my fieldwork, I recorded numerous Muharram narratives in Urdu from local Muslim communities. Since my aim in this work is to focus on Telugu materials, I haven't used these materials. But as I have observed from my fieldwork, this storytelling tradition is now on the verge of extinction due to recent reformist activity.

4. In many Muharram narratives in Telugu, 'Ali, the son-in-law of the Prophet, and Fatima are described as leading a normal peasant life, working day and night in their fields. 'Ali is imagined as a warrior in many stories, always there to rescue victims and low-caste poor people.

5. "Public Islam" refers to the diverse range of invocations of Islam as a series of ideas and practices, which are made by self-ascribed religious scholars, religious authorities, secular intellectuals, Sufi orders, mothers, students, workers, engineers, and many others in civic debate and public life. In this "public" capacity, "Islam" makes a difference in configuring the politics and social life of large parts of the globe, and not just for self-ascribed religious authorities. It does so not only as a template for ideas and practices but also as a way of envisioning alternative political realities and, increasingly, in acting on both global and local stages, thus reconfiguring established boundaries of civil and social life. Salvotore and Eickelman, 2004, xii.

6. For more on *jataras*, see Joyce Flueckiger, "Wandering from 'Hills and Valleys' with the Goddess," in Pintchman, ed., *Women's Lives: Women's Rituals in the Hindu Tradition*, (New York: Oxford University Press, 2007), 36.

7. For more on this aspect of redemption, see Ayoub, *Redemptive Suffering*, 1978.

8. This aspect of "merriment," which includes heavy alcohol consumption, and performances of regional folk games and art forms, remain a source of contention between reformist Islamic groups and local Muharram devotees.

9. A book entitled *Hadeesu Velugu* (*The Light of Hadith*) was published in 2000 in Telugu. Originally written by Maulana Jaleel Ahsan Nadvi in Arabic, the Telugu

translation has a detailed preface that explains the importance of its Telugu translation. Focusing specifically on "true practice" (*sahi amal*), this preface emphasizes the centrality of the Quran in personal and social life. Nadvi, *Hadeesu Velugu* (Hyderabad: Telugu Islamic Publications, 2000).

10. Well-known Islamic scholar Maulana Sayyid Abul A'la Maududi's *The Meaning of the Qur'an*, translated under the title *Divya Quran* in Telugu by Shaik Hameedullah Sharrif, ran into several editions. First published in 1995, the translation has a brief preface written by the Telugu publishers, along with a detailed preface by the original commentator. The Telugu preface explains the objective of this translation as an effort to introduce the idea of Islamic reform in Telugu.

11. Maududi's other text *Risala*-e-*Diniyat's* first translation into Telugu was published in 1982 and came out in eight editions. The most popular Islamic text in Telugu, this text focuses on the importance of the Islamic Revival. The preface written particularly for the Telugu edition highlights the localization of the Revival.

Contemporary times are crucial for many revolutionary ideas. Many theories that we have constructed for our survival and many ideological castles that we built upon them are now collapsed. On one hand, the ideology of the communism has suffered setbacks in its birthplace and became less significant, clearly on the countdown. Due to several of its inborn diseases, the idea of capitalism is now turning toward the East for a direction. Against this background, everywhere there is an Islamic renaissance that has been generating new awareness among the humankind. To introduce this new shift in a local idiom is not an easy task. For more on this aspect, see Malik, trans., *idiye Islam* (Hyderabad: Telugu Islamic Publications).

12. For a literary portrayal of the impact of these reformist activities on young Muslims, see Afsar, *Telangee patthaa*, kathaa vedika, 2005. For a recent study on Islamic revivalism, see Megan Adamson Sijapati, *Islamic Revival in Nepal: Religion and a New Nation* (London and New York: Routledge, 2011).

13. "In 1910, the 'categorizing activities' of British administration reached a new peak when the following proposal was made for the 1911 census. Gait, the Census Commissioner, sent a letter to the Provincial Census Superintendents suggesting that they modify the definition of the word 'Hindus.' Hindus were all those who worshipped the 'great Hindu gods,' were allowed into Hindu (read Brahminical) temples and did not cause ritual pollution. In this way the untouchables and tribal people were excluded." Khan, 2004, 78. However, the actual operation of the census began in 1872. For more on the consequences of this census, see Oberai and van der Veer, 25.

14. For more about the idea of modernity in Gurajada's work, see Velcheru Narayana Rao's afterword to Appa Rao Gurajada, *Girls for Sale* (Kanyasulkam), 159–89.

15. First published in the Telugu monthly *Andhra Bharati* in 1910 and later included in the anthology of Gurajada's works (Vijayawada: Visalandhra Publishing House, 1984). This is considered one of earliest and best stories in Telugu. Recently, a translation has appeared in the anthology of Telugu short stories published by Penguin India.

16. Gurajada, 15.

17. Nisar, "Mulki," in Skybaba, ed., *Vatan, An Anthology of Muslim Stories*, (Hyderabad: Kitab Ghar, 2004), 30–38.

GLOSSARY

aikyaṁ: union with god

ākhri: literally, the last, the tenth day of the month of Muharram

'amal: practice

appa: lord, god, or an elderly person

āṣhurā: the tenth day of Muharram and the day of the battle of Karbala

asli Islam: true or proper Islam

avadhūta: an ecstatic tradition popular in Hindu mystical practice

avatāraṁ: skt. avatara, an incarnation

barkatu: local Sufi term for divine blessing

bhakti: devotion

bid'a: Ar. innovation

Bōya: lower-caste group that lives on hard tasks in a village

brahmōtsavam: literally "great festival"

chakkera fātehā: the recital of the first verse of the Quran at the pīr-house while offering sugar to the pīr

citrannam: rice mixed with tamarind juice

daṇḍakāraṇyaṁ: a mythical forest as described in a local place legend

dargāh: Sufi shrine

darśanam: sacred visit

dēhāti: pejorative word for rustic and rural people

dhvaja sthaṁbhaṁ: a flag pillar that usually appears across the entrance of a Hindu temple

dīn: local term for Islamic knowledge

dīni mālumāt: religious knowledge, specifically Islamic related

Dudēkula: Muslim subcasteof cotton carders

fana: self-annihilation

fazar: morning prayer according to Islamic practice

fātehā: the first verse of the Quran, usually recited at local Muslim shrines

fātehā puja: a local term that blends Muslim prayer and the Hindu mode of worship

hadith: the sayings and traditions of the prophet Muhammad

huṇḍī: gift boxes at the temples

hussēniyat: the legacy of Hussein

ibādat: worship

imam: the head of a local mosque

imān: faith

iṣṭa daivaṁ: chosen deity

jāgaraṇa: night vigil ritual

jaladhi: the ritual of immersing idols in water

jannat kā darvāja: literally the door of heaven. Both Muslims and Hindus believe that the pīr-houses are the doors that lead to heaven.

jātara: village fare during public religious events

kaḍu bhakti: intense devotion

kāla jñānaṁ: the knowledge of the time, a local version of the prophecies popularly attributed to a seventeenth-century saint named Potuluri Veera Brahmam

kandūri: a food ritual during the month of Muharram fulfilled as a return of a vow by the devotees

Kāpu: an agrarian caste group

karāmatu: miracle

khurānu mantram: local term for the Quranic verses

khutba: Islamic sermon or speech on special days

kula daivam: family deity

lānatu: Ur, destruction

Mādiga: untouchable caste group that lives on leather work

majlis: Islamic religious gatherings

maṇṭapam: canopy

mātam: ritual of self-flagellation

meravaṇi: temple deity procession

mūḍhamati: illiterate and foolish person

muzāvar: custodian of a local pīr-house who is responsible for everyday rituals in and around the house

naḍi boḍḍu: literally, navel; the center of a village

nēki: acts of faith

nija rūpam: real form

nitya puja: daily worship rituals in temples

niyyatu: localization of an Arabic Islamic term niyya "personal intention."

niyyatu niṭṭu: a hybrid term that blends the Islamic "niyyat," which means "personal intention" and the Hindu term "nishta," which means "pure intention"

panjā: a hand-shaped image used as memorial of the family of the Prophet and local saints

pīrla cāviḍi: the pīr-house

pīrla katha ceppē vāḷḷu: the folk groups that narrate the story of the martyrdom and local pīrs

pīrla paṇḍaga: The festival of pīrs

pīr-makānam: the pīr-house where the icons of the martyrs are installed during the month of Muharram

porlu daṇḍālu: usually a temple practice performed by devotees by rolling their wet bodies around the temple in return of their vows

pradakṣiṇa: a ritual walk around the idol

prapatti: total surrender

prasādaṁ: sacred food

puja: worship

punarjanma: rebirth

raccabaṇḍa: village-level informal roundtables or village squares

rasūl: messenger

sama: music

sarigettu: (*shahar gastī* in Urdu), "cordoning off the city"; Muharram processions

sātāni vaiṣṇava: A caste group of lower castes who converted to Vaishnava

satāve ke rōje: fasting on the seventh day of Muharram

shahādat: literally "witnessing"; rituals that signify the martyrdom in Shi'i Islam and the tenth day rituals during the public event of Muharram

shirk: forbidden ritual or practice or un-Islamic practice

silsilah: Sufi orders

Sri Rama Navami: The Wedding Ceremony of Rama

sthala purāṇaṁ: place legend

śuddhi: the ritual of cleaning

swami: lord or god

tapas: austerity

tārīkh: history

tārīkhu katha: historical story

tawhīd: Islamic notion of unity

tīrtha: ford or pilgrim center

turaka dēvuḍu: Muslim god

ukku dēvuḍu: literally metal god, a local name given to the icons of the martyrs

ummah: community

ūru: village

Vaddera: stonemasons caste group

vaikuṇṭhaṁ: heaven

vali: friend of the god

vatan: motherland

vazū: ablution before an Islamic prayer

viśva rūpam: cosmic form

vokka poddu: fasting

zikr: the rememberance of God. In local Muslim context, this term is also about the rememberance of the martyrs of Karbala and local Sufi saints.

ziyāratu darśanam: a local hybrid term to denote the idea of a blended pilgrimage. Ziyarat is an Islamic term for a sacred visit and *darśanam* is a Hindu term for visit. However, this blended term is used only in the context of a visit to a pīr-house.

BIBLIOGRAPHY

Telugu

Anwar, Mohammad. *Muharram Urdu śōka Gītikalu* (The Muharram Songs of Mourning in Urdu). Anantapuram: Sweeya Mudrana, 1993.

Apparao, Gurajada, ed. *Anantapuram Charitra*. (The History of Anantapuram). Budaraju Radhakrishna, trans. Madras: V. Ramaswamy *Sastrulu*. Anantapuram: Andhra Pradesh Rythu Sangham, 2003.

Donappa, Thoomati. *Jānapada Kaḷā Sampada* (The Heritage of Folklore). Hyderabad: Visalandhra Prachuranalu, 1987.

Ekkirala, Bharadwaja. *Śrī Hazarat Tājuddīn Bābā Divya Caritra* (The Holy History of Hazarat Tajuddin Baba). Ongole: Sree Guru Paadukaa Publications, 2003.

Eswara Rao Setti, ed. *Gurajāḍa Racanalu – Kathānikalu* (The Works of Gurajada: Short-Stories). Vijayawada: Visalandhra Book House, 1984.

Gangadhar, K. *Nizāmābād Muharram Pāṭalu* (Muharram Songs of Nizamabad). Armuru: Jaateeya Saahitya Parishat, 1998.

Hameedullah Sheriff Shaik, trans. *Divya Qur'an* (The Holy Qur'an) Hyderabad: Telugu Islamic Publications, 2004.

Husain, Maulana. *Islām Prabōdhini* (Islam: Reader). Abbadullah, trans. Hyderabad: Telugu Islamic Publications, 2000.

Imam, Shaik, ed. *Kadalika*, Anantapur: Kadalika Prachuranalu, 2005.

Malik. S. M. *Idiyē Islām* (This is Islam). Hyderabad: Telugu Islamic Publications, 1998.

——. *Qur'an: Abhyamtarālu-Vāstavikata*. (The Qur'an: Objections and Reality). Hyderabad: Telugu Islamic Publications, 2005.

Nadvi, *Hadīsu Velugu* (The Light of Hadis). Hyderabad: Telugu Islamic Publications, 2000.

Ramaraju, Biruduraju. *Andhra yōgulu* (The Saints of Andhra). Hyderabad: Navodaya Book House, 1998.

Ruknoddin Ahmed Hussaini. *Hazarat Sayyad Bābā Fakruddīn Hussēni vāri Jīvita Caritra* (A Biography of Hazarat Sayyad Baba Fakruddin Husain). Dargah Publications: Penukonda, 2006.

Vasireddy, Naveen, and Papineni Sivasankar, eds. *Katha 2002* (Story: An Anthology of the Best Stories, 2002). Hyderabad: Kathaa Sahiti, 2003.

Yusuf Baba, Shaik, and Panduranga Reddy, eds. *Zalzalah: Muslim Telugu Kavitwam* (An Earthquake: Anthology of Muslim Telugu Poetry). Nalgonda: Nasl Ghar Prachuranalu, 2002.

——, eds. *Vatan: Muslim Telugu Kathalu*. (The Home: An Anthology of Muslim Short Stories). Nalgonda: Nasl Ghar Prachuranalu, 2004.

English

Abdullah, Zain. "Sufis on Parade: The Performance of Black, African, and Muslim Identities," in *Journal of the American Academy of Religion*, 77 (2009): 199–237.

Aghaie, Kamran Scot. *The Martyrs of Karbala : Shii symbols and Rituals* in Modern Iran. Seattle and London: University of Washington Press, 2004.

Ahmad, Aziz. *Islamic Modernism in India and Pakistan*. London: Oxford University Press, 1967.

Ahmad, Imtiaz, and Helmut Reifeld. *Lived Islam in South Asia: Adaptation, Accommodation, and Conflict*. Delhi: Social Science Press, 2004.

Ahmad, Imtiaz, ed. *Ritual and Religion Among Muslims in India*. New Delhi: Manohar, 1981.

Aneesuddin, Mir. *Elements of Namaz for Students*. Hyderabad: Islamic Academy of Sciences, 2001.

Antoun, Richard T. *Muslim Preacher in the Modern World: A Jordanian Case Study in Comparative Perspective*. Princeton: Princeton University Press, 1989.

Assayag, Jackie. *At the Confluence of Two Rivers*. New Delhi: Manohar Publications, 2004.

Ayoub, Mahmoud. *Redemptive Suffering in Islam: A Study of the Devotional Aspects of 'Ashura in Twelver Shi'ism*. New York: Mouton, 1978.

Babb, Lawrence A. *The Divine Hierarchy: Popular Hinduism in Central India*. New York: Columbia University Press, 1975.

Bard, Amy C. "Desolate Victory: Shi'i Women and Marsiyah Texts of Lucknow." PhD Dissertation. Columbia University, 2002.

Bastin, Rohan. *The Domain of Constant Excess: Plural Worship at the Munneswaram Temples in Sri Lanka*. New York: Berghahn Books, 2002.

Bayly, Susan. *Saints, Goddesses, and Kings: Muslims and Christians in South Indian Society, 1700–1900*. New York: Cambridge University Press, 1989.

Bigelow, Anna. "Sharing Saints, Shrines, and Stories: Practicing Pluralism in North India." PhD Dissertation. University of North Carolina, 2004.

Blackburn, Stuart. *South Asian Folklore: An Encyclopedia*. New York: Routledge, 2003.

Chelkowski, Peter J., ed. *Tazi'yeh—Ritual and Drama in Iran*. New York: New York University, 1979.

Clark-Deces, Isabelle. *The Encounter Never Ends: A Return to the Field of Tamil Rituals*. Albany: State University of New York Press, 2007.

Cohen, Robin. "Creolization and Cultural Globalization: The Soft Sounds of Fugitive Power," *Globalizations*, vol. 4, no. 3: 369–73.

Cole, Juan. *The Roots of North Indian Shi'ism in Iran and Iraq: Religion and State in Awadh, 1722–1859*. Berkeley: University of California Press, 1988.

Cornell, Vincent. *The Realm of the Saint: Power and Authority in Moroccan Sufism*. Austin: The University of Texas Press, 1998.

Currie, P. M. *The Shrine and Cult of Mu'īn al-Dīn Chishtī of Ajmer*, Delhi: Oxford University Press, 2006.

D'Souza, Diane. "In the Presence of the Martyrs: The 'Alam in Popular Shii Piety." *The Muslim World* 88, 1998: 67–80.

Daniel, E. Valentine. *Fluid Signs: Being a Person the Tamil Way*. Berkeley: University of California Press, 1984.

de Tassy, Garcin. *Muslim Festivals in India and Other Essays*. Delhi: Oxford University Press, 1995.

Denny, Frederick Matthewson. *Introduction to Islam*. New York: Macmillan, 1994.

Dumont, Louis. *Homo Hierarchicus*. Chicago: University of Chicago Press, 1980.

Eaton, Richard M. *Sufis of Bijapur 1300–1700: Social Roles of Sufis in Medieval India*. Princeton, NJ: Princeton University Press, 1978.

——. *The Rise of Islam and the Bengal Frontier, 1204–1760*. Berkeley: University of California Press, 1993.

Eck, Diana L. *Darsan: Seeing the Divine Image in India*. Chambersburg: Anima Books, 1985.

Eickelman, D. F. *Moroccan Islam: Tradition and Society in a Pilgrimage Center*. Austin: The University of Texas Press, 1976.

——. "The Study of Islam in Local Contexts," *Contributions to Asian Studies*. 17 (1982): 1–16.

Ernst, Carl W., and Bruce B. Lawrence. *Sufi Martyrs of Love: The Chishti Order in South Asia and Beyond*. New York: Palgrave Macmillan, 2002.

Ewing, Katherine P. *Arguing Sainthood: Modernity, Psychoanalysis, and Islam*. Durham: Duke University Press, 1997.

Fischer, M. J. *Iran: From Religious Dispute to Revolution*. Cambridge: Harvard University Press, 1980.

Fischer, and Mehdi Abedi. *Debating Muslims: Cultural Dialogues in Postmodernity and Tradition*. Madison: University of Wisconsin Press, 1990.

Flueckiger, Joyce, Burkhalter. *In Amma's Healing Room: Gender and Vernacular Islam in South India*. Bloomington: Indiana University Press, 2008.

Francis, W. *Madras District Gazetteers: Anantapur*. Madras: Addison and Co., 1905.

Fuller, Chris J. *Servants of the Goddess: The Priests of a South Indian Temple*. Cambridge: Cambridge University Press, 1984.

——. *The Renewal of the Priesthood: Modernity and Traditionalism in a South Indian Temple*. Princeton, NJ: Princeton University Press, 2003.

——. *The Camphor Flame: Popular Hinduism* and *Society in India*. Princeton, NJ: Princeton University Press, 2004.

Furuqui, Munis. "At Empire's End: The Nizam, Hyderabad, and Eighteenth Century India," *Modern Asian Studies* 43 (2009): 5–43.

Gilmartin, David, and Bruce Lawrence, eds. *Beyond Turk and Hindu*. Gainesville, FL: University Press of Florida, 2000.

Goldman, Robert P. trans. *The Ramayana of Valmiki: An Epic of Ancient India*. Princeton, NJ: Princeton University Press, 1990.

Gottschalk, Peter. *Beyond Hindu and Muslim: Multiple Identity Narratives from Village India*. New York: Oxford University Press, 2000.

Green, Nile. *Indian Sufism Since the Seventeenth Century: Dervishes, Devotees, and Emperors*. London, New York: Routledge, 2006.

Hardy, Friedhelm. *The Religious Culture of India: Power, Love and Wisdom*. New York: Cambridge University Press, 1994.

Hirschkind, Charles. *The Ethical Soundscape: Cassette Sermons and Islamic Counter-publics*. New York: Columbia University Press, 2006.

Ho, Engseng, *The Graves of Tarim: Genealogy and Mobility Across the Indian Ocean*. Berkeley: University of California Press, 2006.

Howarth, Toby M. *Twelver Shia as a Minority in India: The Pulpit of Tears*. London: RoutledgeCurzon, 2005.

Hyder, Syed Akbar. *Reliving Karbala: Martyrdom in South Asian Memory*. New York: Oxford University Press, 2006.

Imperial Gazetteer of India: Madras. Calcutta: Superintendent of Government Printing, 1908.

Jacobson, Knut A., ed. *South Asian Religions on Display: Religious Processions in South Asia and in the Diaspora*. London: Routledge. 2008.

Kamrava, Mehran, ed. *Innovation in Islam: Traditions and Contributions*. Berkeley: University of California Press, 2011.

Khan, Dominique-Sila. *Conversions and Shifting Identities: Ramdev Pir and the Ismailis in Rajasthan*. New Delhi: Manohar Publications, 1997.

Kishan, Rao V., and A. Satyanarayana, eds. *A Thousand Laurels: Dr. Sadiq Naqvi*. Hyderabad: Osmania University, 2005.

Knudsen, Are. "Islam in Local Contexts: Localised Islam in Northern Pakistan," in Gerald Jackson, ed. *NIASnytt: Asia Insights*, December 3, 2008.

Korom, Frank J. *Hosay Trinidad: Muharram Performances in an Indo-Caribbean Diaspora*. Philadelphia: University of Pennsylvania Press, 2003.

Langer, Robert, *et al.*, eds. "Transfer of Ritual." *Journal of Ritual Studies* 20 (2006): 1–10.

Lawrence, Bruce. *Notes from a Distant Flute: The Extant Literature of Pre-Mughal Indian Sufism*. Tehran : Imperial Iranian Academy of Philosophy, 1978.

Ludden, David, ed. *Making India Hindu: Religion, Community, and the Politics of Democracy in India*. New Delhi: Oxford University Press, 2005.

Madan, T. N., ed. *Muslim Communities of South Asia*: *Culture*, *Society and Power*. New Delhi: Manohar, 2001.

Mahmood, Sabah. *Politics of Piety: the Islamic Revival and the Feminist Subject*. Princeton, NJ: Princeton University Press, 2005.

Marsden, M. *Living Islam: Muslim Religious Experience in Pakistan's North-West Frontier*. Cambridge: Cambridge University Press, 2005.

Masselos, Jim. "Change and Continuity in the Format of the Bombay Mohurrum During the Nineteenth and Twentieth Centuries." *South Asia: Journal of South Asian Studies* 5 (1982): 46–67.

McGilvray, Dennis B. *Crucible of Conflict: Tamil and Muslim Society on the East Coast of Sri Lanka*. Durham, NC: Duke University Press, 2008.

Metcalf, Barbara D. *Islamic Revival in British India: Deoband 1860–1900*. New Delhi: Oxford University Press, 1982.

——, ed. *Moral Conduct and Authority: The Place of Adab in South Asian Islam*. Berkeley: University of California Press, 1984.

——. *Islamic Contestations: Essays on Muslims in India and Pakistan*. New Delhi: Oxford University Press, 2004.

Mines, Diane. *Fierce Gods: Inequality, Ritual, and the Politics of Dignity in a South Indian Village*. Bloomington: Indiana University Press, 2005.

Mines, Diane, and Mary Lamb, eds. *Everyday Life in South Asia*. Bloomington: Indiana University Press, 2002.

Momen, Moojan. *An Introduction to Shi'i Islam*. New Haven: Yale University Press. 1985.

Monsutti, Alessandro, Silvia Naef and Farian Sabahi, eds. *The Other Shiites: From the Mediterranean to Central Asia*. Berlin: Peter Lang, 2007.

Naqvi, Sadiq, and Kishan Rao, eds. *The Muharram Ceremonies among the non-Muslims of Andhra Pradesh*. Hyderabad: Bab-ul-ilm Society, 2004.

Narasimhacharya, Madabhushi. *History of the Cult of Narasimha in Telangana*. Hyderabad, 1989.

Narayana Rao, Velcheru, trans. and ed. *Twentieth Century Telugu Poetry*. New Delhi: Oxford University Press, 2002.

——, David Shulman, and Sanjay Subrahmanyam. *Textures of Time: Writing History in South India 1600–1800*. New York: Other Press, 2003.

Nasr, Seyyed Vali Reja. *The Shia Revival: How Conflicts Within Islam Shape the Future*. New York: Norton, 2006.

Nasr, Seyyed Hossein. *Sufi Essays*. London: George Allen and Unwin, 1972.

Nasr, Seyyed Hossein, *et al. Shi'ism: Doctrines, Thought, and Spirituality*. Albany: State University of New York Press, 1988.

Newby, Gordon D. *A Concise Encyclopedia of Islam*. Oxford: One World, 2002.

Oberoi, Harjot. *The Construction of Religious Boundaries: Culture, Identity, and Diversity in the Sikh Tradition*. New Delhi: Oxford University Press, 1994.

Obyeysekere, Gananath. "The Fire-walkers of Kataragama: The Rise of Bhakti Religiosity in Buddhist Sri Lanka." *The Journal of Asian Studies* 37 (1978): 466–67.

Olivelle, Patrick. *Rules and Regulations of Brahmanical Asceticism: Yatidharmasamuccaya of Yadava Prakasa*. Albany: State University of New York Press, 1995.

Pinault, David. *The Shiites: Rituals and Popular Piety in a Muslim Community*. New York: Palgrave, 2001.

——. *Notes from the Fortune-telling Parrot: Islam and the Struggle for Religious Pluralism in Pakistan*. London: Equinox Publishing, 2008.

Pintchman, Tracy, ed. *Women's Lives, Women's Rituals in the Hindu Tradition*. New York: Oxford University Press, 2007.

Pinto, Desiderio. *Pir-Muridi Relationship: A Study of the Nizamuddin Dargah*. New Delhi: Manohar Publications, 1995.

Prasad, Dharmendra. *Saints of Telangana*. Hyderabad: Abul Kalam Azad Oriental Research Institute, 1969.

Prasad, Leela. *Poetics of Conduct: Oral Narrative and Moral Being in a South Indian Town*. New York: Columbia University Press, 2007.

Rahman, Fazlur. *Major Approaches to the Quran*. Chicago: Bibliotheca Islamica, 1980.

Raman, Srilata. *Self-surrender (Prapatti) to God in Srivaishnavishnavism: Tamil Cats or Sanskrit Monkeys?* Hoboken: Taylor and Francis, 2006.

Ramaraju, Biruduraju. *Muharram Folk-songs in Telugu*. Hyderabad: The Institute of Indo-Middle East Cultural Studies, 1964.

Ranga Rao, V., ed. *That Man on the Road: Contemporary Telugu Short Fiction*. New Delhi: Penguin Books, 2006.

Renard, John. *Seven Doors to Islam: Spirituality and the Religious Life of Muslims*. Berkeley: University of California Press, 1996.

——. *Friends of God: Islamic Images of Piety, Commitment, and Servanthood*. Berkeley: University of California Press, 2008.

Richman, Paula, ed. *Many Ramayanas: The Diversity of a Narrative Tradition in South Asia*, Berkeley: University of California Press, 1991.

——, ed. *Questioning Ramayanas: a South Asian Tradition*. Berkeley: University of California Press, 2001.

Roy, A. *The Islamic Syncretistic Tradition in Bengal*. Princeton, NJ: Princeton University Press, 1983.

Rozehnal, Robert. *Islamic Sufism Unbound: Politics and Piety in Twenty-first Century Pakistan*. New York: Palgrave Macmillan, 2007.

Ruffle, Karen G. "A Bride of One Night, a Widow Forever: Gender and Vernacularization in the Construction of South Asian Sh'i Hagiography." PhD Dissertation. University of North Carolina, 2007.

Safi, Omid, ed. *Progressive Muslims: On Justice, Gender, and Pluralism*. Oxford: One World, 2003.

Saheb, S. A. A. "Dudekula Muslims of Andhra Pradesh," *Economic and Political Weekly*, vol. 38 (2003): 4908–12.

Saikia, Yasmin. *Women, War, and the Making of Bangladesh: Remembering 1971*. Durham, NC: Duke University Press, 2011.

Sainath, Palagummi. *Everybody Loves a Good Drought: Stories from India's Poorest Districts*. New York: Penguin Books, 1996.

Saiyed, A. R. *Religion and Ethnicity among Muslims*. Jaipur and New Delhi: Rawat Publications, 1995.

Salvatore, Armando, and Dale F. Eickelman., eds. *Public Islam and the Common Good*. Leiden and Boston : Brill, 2004.

Schimmel, Annemarie. *Mystical Dimensions of Islam*, Chapel Hill: University of North Carolina Press, 1992.

Schomburg, Susan Elizabeth. "Reviving religion: the Qadiri Sufi Order, Popular Devotion to Sufi Saint Muhyiuddin `Abdul Qadir al-Gilani, and Processes of 'Islamization' in Tamil Nadu and Sri Lanka." PhD dissertation. Harvard University, 2003.

Schubel, Vernon. *Religious Performance in Contemporary Islam: Shi'i Devotional Rituals in South Asia*. Columbia: University of South Carolina Press, 1993.

Sells, Michael. *Approaching the Qur'an: The Early Revelations*. Ashland, OR: White Cloud Press, 1999.

Senapati, Fakir Mohan. *My Times and I*. John Boulton, trans. Bhubaneswar, Orissa, India : Orissa Sahitya Akademi, 1985.

Sharif, Ja'far. *Islam in India or the Qanun-i- Islam*. G. A. Herklots, trans. Oxford University Press, 1921; reprint ed., London: Curzon, 1975.

Sherwani, H. K. and P. M. Joshi, eds. *A History of Medieval Deccan (1295–1724)*. Hyderabad: Government of Andhra Pradesh, 1974.

Shulman, David, ed. *Syllables of Sky*. Delhi: Oxford University Press, 1995.

Sikand, Yoginder. *Sacred Spaces: Exploring Tradition of Shared Faith in India*. New Delhi: Penguin Books, 2003.

Simpson, Edward. "The Changing Perspectives of Three Muslim Men on the Question of Saint Worship over a 10-year Period in Gujarat, Western India." *Modern Asian Studies* 42 (2008): 391.

Soifer, Deborah A. *The Myths of Narasimha and Vamana: Two Avatars in Cosmological Perspective*. Albany: State University of New York Press, 1991.

Srinivas, M. N. *Religion and Society Among the Coorgs of South India*. Oxford: Clarendon Press, 1952.

———. "A Note on Sanskritization and Westernization." *Far Eastern Quarterly* 15 (1956): 481–96.

———. *The Cohesive Role of Sanskritization and Other Essays*. Delhi: Oxford University Press, 1989.

Stewart, Charles. "Creolization: history, ethnography, theory." In Charles Stewart. *Creolization: History, Ethnography*. Walnut Creek, CA: Left Coast Press, 2007. 1–25.

Stewart, Tony K. *Fabulous Females and Peerless Pirs: Tales of mad adventure in Old Bengal*. New York: Oxford University Press, 2004.

Surorova, Anna. *Muslim Saints of South Asia, the Eleventh to Fifteenth Centuries*, M. Osama Faruqi, trans. London and New York: RoutledgeCurzon, 2004.

Takim, Liakat Ali. *The Heirs of the Prophet*. Albany: State University of New York Press, 2006.

Thurfjell, David. *Living Shi ism: Instances of Ritualisation Among Islamist Men in Contemporary Iran*. Leiden and Boston: Brill, 2006.

Tirumali, Inukonda. *Against Dora and Nizam: People's Movement in Telangana, 1939–1948*. New Delhi: Kanishka Publishers, 2003.

Turner, Victor. *The Ritual Process: Structure and Anti-structure*. Chicago: Aldine Publications, 1969.

van der Veer, Peter. *Religious Nationalism: Hindus and Muslims in India*. Berkeley: University of California Press, 1994.

Varghese, Anila. "Court Attire of Vijayanagara Empire (from a Study of Monuments)." *Quarterly Journal of the Mythic Society* vol. 82 (1991): 43–61.

Vedantam, T. and Khaja Moinuddin. *A Monograph of Muharram in Hyderabad City*. Delhi: Controller of Publications, 1977.

Wagoner, Philip B. "Sultan Among Hindu Kings." *Journal of Asian Studies* vol 55, no. 996: 851–80.

Werbner, Pnina. *Pilgrims of Love: The Anthropology of a Global Sufi Cult*. Bloomington: Indiana University Press, 2003.

Werbner, Pnina, and Helene Basu, eds. *Embodying Charisma: Modernity, Locality and Performance of Emotion in Sufi Cults*. London, New York: Routledge, 1998.

Young, Robert. *Colonial Desire: Hybridity in Theory, Culture, and Race*, Routledge, 1995.

INDEX

16130664R00126

Printed in Great Britain
by Amazon